Mad for Speed

D1478397

Mad for Speed

The Racing Life of Joan Newton Cuneo

ELSA A. NYSTROM

Foreword by Dick Newton

McFarland & Company, Inc., Publishers
Jefferson, North Carolina, and London

LIBRARY OF CONGRESS CATALOG ONLINE DATA

Nystrom, Elsa A.
Mad for speed : the racing life of Joan Newton
Cuneo / Elsa A. Nystrom ; foreword by Dick Newton.
p.   cm.
Includes bibliographical references and index.

ISBN 978-0-7864-7093-8

softcover : acid free paper ∞

1. Cuneo, Joan Newton, 1876–1934.   2. Women automobile
racing drivers — United States — Biography.   I. Title.
GV1032.C84N97 2013   796.72092 — dc23   [B]   2013016947

BRITISH LIBRARY CATALOGUING DATA ARE AVAILABLE

Front cover image: Joan Newton Cuneo at the wheel of a 1905
White steam car (photograph courtesy of the National Automotive
History Collection, Detroit Public Library)

Manufactured in the United States of America

*McFarland & Company, Inc., Publishers
Box 611, Jefferson, North Carolina 28640
www.mcfarlandpub.com*

To my husband, Chuck:
I would never have finished this book
without your help and support.

Table of Contents

Acknowledgments

Piecing together the story of Joan Cuneo's life would not have been possible without the help of dozens of people in many areas of the United States during a three-year period. The interlibrary loan staff at Kennesaw State, especially Amy Thompson and Chris Sharpe, helped me get my research started by finding me dozens of obscure books and articles about Joan and related auto-racing topics like the Glidden Tour. I then discussed my findings at length with our administrative assistants, Nancy Hill, Megan MacDonald and Gayle Wheeler. Then I branched out a little, as I began to write the first chapters and my colleagues Howard Shealy and Jane McKinzey kindly read them and made some excellent suggestions while Rita Impey-Imes' encouragement encouraged me to work harder.

At this time, I contacted the Richmond Hill, Long Island Historical Society, which led me to Carl Ballenas, historian extraordinaire for Richmond Hill, who has since provided encouragement, valuable information and photos about the Cuneos' life in Richmond Hill and also became my source for questions about New York City and Long Island. Carl had long hoped that someone would write about Joan Newton Cuneo and was eager to help make this book happen. Mark Dill, the creator of the excellent First Super Speedway website, an authority on the early years of racing and the Indianapolis Motor Speedway, encouraged me to continue my research on Joan, answered questions I had about race cars and racing and introduced me to Donald Davidson, the archivist of the Indianapolis Motor Speedway Museum. Thanks so much, Mark. Mr. Davidson was able to answer two very important questions, though unfortunately in the negative. I learned that Joan Cuneo never raced at Indy and the AAA minutes that were in the museum archives made no mention of why women had been banned from racing. Thanks, Donald, for convincing me to stop trying to find something that probably didn't exist. Mark also put me in touch with Howard Kroplick, who has written several books about the Long Island Motor Parkway. Not only did Howard send me an article written by Joan that I had never seen, but he also sent another news item about Joan. Thanks, Howard.

By now I had gathered enough information to present a paper about Joan Cuneo's life at the Night at the Athenaeum series hosted by the Kennesaw State Archives. Shortly afterwards, my research got an unexpected jump start. An Internet announcement of the program caught the attention of Richard Newton, one of Joan's many relatives on the Newton side, who routinely searched the Internet for any information about his cousin. He e-mailed me immediately and over the past two years he and his wife, Marge, have been invaluable helps in my research. Living on the East Coast, closer to Holyoke, Massachusetts, where Joan was born, and other archival sites, they graciously became my eyes and ears in New England. Their first visit was to the Holyoke Community College, where the Holyoke Library Archives are located. I had already e-mailed Jim Massery, the archivist, and when they got there he had already set out materials he thought might be useful. Thanks so much, Jim, for your help and especially the wonderful newspaper article about Joan's wedding. Forestdale Cemetery, where Joan was buried, was another stop. There they photographed Joan's grave in the John C. Newton family plot. Thanks also to the Forestdale staff for sending me a Xerox of that same family plot. Their next stop was Historic Holyoke State Park, a source of the history of the Holyoke mills and canals, many of which were built by the Newton family. They visited John Y. Hess, the president of the Knox Motor Car Club, who has written extensively about Knox automobiles. John generously allowed them to examine his extensive collection of photographs and documents relating to Knox automobiles and Joan Newton Cuneo. Many thanks, John, for allowing me to use some of your photos in my book. Most important, Dick and Marge also contacted other members of the extensive Newton family whom they had lost touch with, asking if they had some family stories about Joan they might share. Through their efforts, I was able to contact Susan Neighbors, another member of the Newton family who has been incredibly helpful. Not only did she help clarify the early history of the Newton family who came to the colonies in 1638, but Susan has also shared a number of family pictures of Joan and her family that have never before been published. In addition, Susan's skills as a graphic artist and editor were invaluable (to me).

That Internet listing of my first talk on Joan brought me in contact with yet another scholar willing to share information about Joan Cuneo. One day, Michael Britt called me out of the blue and when he asked if I was working on Joan Cuneo my heart sank. I thought, Oh no, someone else is working on a biography of Joan. However, although Joan does figure in his research, his focus has been on the Glidden and Good Roads Tours, especially the 1909–11 Tours that either ended in or circled Georgia. Michael is a videographer rather than a writer, and we have since enjoyed discussing many aspects of Joan's activities in Georgia and on the road. Since Michael had been working on his project for years, he graciously shared both information and documents as well as photographs he had already collected that dealt with Joan. He also had contacted Joan's family in the Upper Peninsula of Michigan and gave me their e-mail addresses. Thanks to Michael, I was able to contact Joanie Zbacnik, Joan's granddaughter, and Kathy Cuneo, her great-granddaughter, both of whom have provided me with valuable information on family history and also, from Kathy, a photo of one of Joan's trophies. Paige Plant, archivist at the Skillman Branch of the Detroit Public Library, was a great help in locating the best photographs for the book, as was Jack Deo at Superior View photos. Julie Moore of the Wilmington, Vermont, Historical Society and especially Mike Eldred, the editor of the *Deerfield Valley News*, provided me with some wonderful photos of Joan during the summers she spent at Wilmington, Vermont. Bob Lawrence, "the sprint guy," confirmed that Elfrieda Mais had some kind of IMCA license but never got to race, while Ann Kramer, my British expert on Dorothy Levitt, kept me on the right track in writing about Joan's British rival. Patricia L. Yongue helped me track down pictures as we engaged in a lengthy e-mail discussion of Joan and other female racers. Linda Rock and Mike Aft of Elgin, Illinois, sent me great articles and wonderful photos of Alyce Byrd Potter, the eccentric young woman who challenged Joan to race in 1909. Finally there were a number of helpful and interested people whom I met via the Internet, including Pete Vack of Veloce Today, Richard J. Ring, Head Curator and Librarian of the Watkinson Library, Trinity College, and Emma Peterson, Reference Librarian at the Springfield City Library. If I have inadvertently left out someone, *mea culpa*.

Foreword: In Search
of Cousin Joan
(by Dick Newton)

On a cold afternoon in January 2011, I sat down at my computer and did a search under "Joan Newton Cuneo"; I had done this often, but that day, in addition to the usual sites with information about Joan, a new site popped up. It referred to a lecture given by Dr. Elsa Nystrom, at Kennesaw University. The lecture covered the role Joan Newton Cuneo had played in women's sports, particularly in motor sports at the turn of the twentieth century. I was excited to find this information and immediately sent a message to Dr. Nystrom. I told her I was surprised and excited to learn about her lecture, as Joan was my cousin, and her father and my great-grandfather, James Hale Newton, were brothers. Dr. Nystrom's research was even more exciting to me because I had formerly been a nationally licensed road-racing car designer, builder, and driver and one of my "bucket list" goals after retiring was to research and write about my cousin and fellow race car driver. Within minutes I had a reply from Dr. Nystrom. She was even more excited to hear from a member of Joan's family, especially one who also raced, although several generations later. Thus began a fantastic voyage of discovery, additional research and documentation, related to the writing of this book.

From my earliest years, I have been fascinated by anything with wheels. The opportunity to visit Newtons, Merricks, or Fays (the latter two families were on my mother's side) living close by in Holyoke, Massachusetts, was an excuse to ride my first tricycle and later a bicycle. My earliest summers were spent on a one-hundred-acre farm that we owned in the Berkshires. In the barn was a Model A Ford truck that I would sit in for hours and pretend to "drive." I worked the hand controls, shifting and thoroughly flooding the engine so it probably would not start when needed. After we moved from Holyoke over the mountain to Easthampton and its more rural environment, friends and I built "coaster buggies" using carriage wheels and scraps of wood. We spent afternoons and weekends searching for the biggest hills we could find to race down. By the time I was 12, I was thoroughly captivated by cars and, especially, any form of auto racing; I read every book and magazine I could find on the subject, and had already memorized every Indy 500 winner since 1911.

As family members became aware of my intense interest in cars and racing, they told me about a somewhat mysterious and bigger-than-life cousin who had raced in the early 1900s. I always sensed that information was being held back, and that this cousin was considered somewhat of a "black sheep" within the family. After Joan Newton married Andrew Cuneo and moved to New York, my branch of the family had very little contact with her. However, there were rumors that the Cuneos had connections with the New York underworld and that her husband's family had urged or persuaded her to get rid of her trophies, probably by melting them down for the silver content.[1] No one ever talked about the reasons for her marriage to an Italian banker from New York, her divorce, more than 15 years later, or her remarriage to a man from Holyoke. Occasionally someone gave me a picture or article about her when their old family homes were sold or cleaned out after the death of a family member.

As I entered my teenage years, my passion for cars and racing grew, and by the age of 14 I had saved for and purchased my first car. I spent the next two years modifying it so it would be ready to drive when I turned 16 and got my license. Before he let me drive it, my father took it for a trial run and was shocked by the power of its modified engine. He made me sell it, as he thought it was too fast for a 16-year-old to drive. However, I continued to work on a series of cars with less radical performance modifications, and almost every weekend my friends and I attended drag races or stock-car races at local tracks.

Dick Newton in his model XK 120 S 1953 Jaguar race car, following the trail blazed by his cousin, Joan Newton Cuneo (courtesy of Dick Newton).

As I grew older, I became increasingly captivated by another form of racing — road racing on tracks designed to simulate actual road conditions, with right- and left-hand corners, hills, and fast and slow corners. This type of racing had a long history in Europe, as Formula 1 Grand Prix racing went back to the earliest days of racing on the public roads of the Continent. Ironically, although Joan Newton Cuneo longed to compete in a road race and entered several, she was always turned away by the organizers of the races.

My passion and enthusiasm for sports cars and open-wheel racing grew through my high school years. I joined the Sports Car Club of America (SCCA) as soon as I was eligible for membership, at 21, and built and raced sports and formula (open-wheel Grand Prix–type cars) as a nationally licensed driver. My own racing career lasted from 1963 through 1967 while I was a student at American International College in Springfield, Massachusetts. Ironically, the college was not far from the 1909 location of the Knox Factory, which had built the two fastest cars Joan owned and raced. I worked multiple part-time jobs while in college to fund my own racing, and loved every minute of it.

I graduated from college at the height of the military buildup for the Vietnam War and, not waiting to be drafted, joined the air force. I served in Southeast Asia, and returned to marry and raise a family while working in the Massachusetts high-tech industry. As a result, there was little time for racing after my military service and I knew I could not

Dick Newton in his Formula Vee race car (courtesy of Dick Newton).

go back to racing with a lower level of commitment, as I would not be competitive. I am now retired and live on one of Rhode Island's tidal saltwater ponds. Racing is still in my blood, however. I now compete throughout the summer not in a car, but in a Beetle Cat, a classic wooden sailboat, racing weekly on the pond and throughout southern New England at our yearly Nationals. Already our grandchildren are learning to sail and are eager to crew and race with Grandpa ... the racing tradition has obviously been passed down in the Newton genes through several generations.

It was because of my family history of racing and my own personal interest and deep involvement in racing that I wanted to learn more about Cousin Joan and eventually write a book about her. I wanted to find out what kind of person she was and whether she loved racing as much as I had, and even if the rumors I had heard were true.

Finding that Dr. Nystrom had already begun research on a book about Joan gave me an opportunity to have a role in seeing my dream realized. I was able to bring to the book both the Newton family perspective as well as input from someone who also loved to race. We began exchanging e-mails on a regular basis as we discussed ideas and areas to research, and held conference calls to review progress. We were also able to meet in Georgia while on winter vacation, and instead of the expected brief meeting, our first visit turned into an all-day session. Marge, my wife and a strong supporter of my involvement in the project, became deeply involved herself, as a sounding board for my ideas and by sharing the perspective of a woman who was married to a race-car driver.

Marge and I went back to Holyoke and visited many sites in the surrounding area in search of information about Cousin Joan and her legacy that would fill holes in her story. First, we located my childhood home where my interest in racing began. We then found the Newton family cemetery plots in Forestdale Cemetery. We visited the graves of my branch of the Newton family and Joan's, and took pictures of her simple granite headstone. We were able to visit my cousin Alice Newton Childs Smith and met "Rosa Belle," the doll that Cousin Joan had given her as a child many years ago. We went to the church that had been under construction in 1886, when Joan walked across its ridge beam at the age of ten. We then traveled to the Holyoke Heritage Museum built on land donated to the city by the Newton family. It stands in an area where many of the Newton paper mills were located.

Traveling to East Longmeadow, Massachusetts, we then spent many hours with John Hess, president of the Knox Motor Car Club, combing through his huge collection of Knox car history and memorabilia. John was an invaluable asset as he shared many pictures and articles about Joan and her exploits in Knox cars. However, one of our most important discoveries occurred when we visited the History Room at Holyoke Community College.

Jim Massery, the Holyoke Public Library archivist, had prepared a collection of articles and pictures of the various Newton family members, the mills, and history about Joan's era for us to look through. As I quickly scanned articles about individuals and mills, Marge suddenly read aloud from an 1898 article in the *Holyoke Transcript*. The article provided long-forgotten information about the wedding of Joan Newton and

Andrew Cuneo, as well as the perfect introduction to the following book on Joan Newton Cuneo's life.

Special thanks are due to the many people who provided help, information, additional leads, and support for what we hoped to accomplish, including Alice Newton Childs Smith and her daughters Katharine Jones and Eliza Melton; both provided leads to additional family members I never knew. Jim Massery at Holyoke Community College, the staff at Holyoke's Forestdale Cemetery, and especially John Hess also provided much help and information.

Many thanks also to John Howe and Roger Barr. They were my mentors when I started racing. I teamed with John during the building of the Jaguar XK 120 S that he and I raced, and then developed the Formula Vee under Roger's guidance. Special thanks go to Elsa Nystrom, who helped me realize my own dream by including me in her project. Finally, my greatest appreciation goes to Marge, my wife and closest friend since childhood, who has lived with my unending passion to race and has embraced and encouraged the writing of this book.

Dick Newton, a Sports Car Club of America regional/national driver from 1964 to 1967, lives in Charlestown, Rhode Island. Joan Newton Cuneo was his great-grandfather's brother's daughter.

Preface

The following is the result of a four-year search for more information about Joan Newton Cuneo, who is remembered today mainly as the woman who got women banned from racing. When we moved to Georgia, 25 years ago, I revived my latent interest in auto racing. Although I had already established a reputation as a scholar in the field of newspaper comics, newspapers had declined in number and with them the comic strips they carried. Since my main area of interest had always been social and cultural history I decided to focus my research on auto racing instead. Switching from comic strips to auto racing was not that difficult a move.

My first step was to attend as many races as I could. This was not a difficult task in Georgia, as a host of races are held in the Southeast every year. Depending on one's interest and pocketbook, a fan can watch open-wheel races, road races, NASCAR races at many levels, dirt track demolition derbies and drag races. My next move was to read as much about auto racing as I could, from its earliest days to the present. Initially I presented a few papers on NASCAR at history and popular culture conferences. I even considered writing a book about Bill Elliott, who lived not far from Atlanta, in the North Georgia mountains. However, when not one but two books about Bill Elliott came out a few years ago, plus several others about racing and moonshiners, I quickly tabled that idea.

I then realized that while I enjoyed going to modern-day races, my real interest lay in the early days of racing and the men who drove the noisy, fire-breathing cars of the so-called brass age. My husband and I then visited as many automobile museums as we could find, including Harrah's in Reno, Nevada, and Henry Ford's collection at Greenfield Village in Dearborn, Michigan. Although he didn't always enjoy going to museums with me, he loved this task, as he is a real "car guy," a talented driver and mechanic who has been my technical advisor on this book from the start. At the same time, I continued to read as much as I could find about this period, and wrote several articles about early racetracks and the people who drove on them. Initially I had decided to write a synthesis of primary and secondary sources that would answer the question "Why do Americans love to race?" However, several chapters into my initial racing history project, I read about Joan Newton Cuneo for the first time. I was intrigued by this woman, and wanted to learn more. I found very little, just a paragraph here and a page or two there in a dozen or so books. Frustrated, I looked up the full texts of articles that had been cited in the books I had read, and learned a little more. It didn't take me long to realize why more hadn't been written about the elusive Mrs. Cuneo to make a book. There were no easy ways to learn about Joan's life, no cache of letters, diaries or manuscripts. If I wanted to write about Joan, it would be a long slog. I would have to search through dozens of newspapers and periodicals from a 25-year period extending from 1895 to 1920. However, I was used to working with old newspapers and periodicals from working on comic strips, and made a quick decision to see if I could uncover enough about Joan's life for a book-length biography, tabling my first project for now. Actually, I wouldn't have been able to find enough information to make a book five years ago, but the growing number of digitized periodicals and newspapers available to scholars and researchers online has increased exponentially in the last five years. It is hard to imagine what else might be available in the future, but researchers will undoubtedly get more hits when they type in "Joan Newton Cuneo" and hit the search button.

Much of the original scholarship in this book was actually gleaned from hundreds of newspaper articles I found on the Web, starting with the historical *New York Times* and the *Atlanta Constitution*, which were available on Proquest at Kennesaw State University, and then branching out to many other newspapers and other archival records and interviews. At the end of the major portion of my research I found that besides being the woman who was said to have single-handedly gotten women banned from racing, which is not true, Joan Newton Cuneo was a cultured but feisty lady who reigned as a national celebrity for a decade. She first made the news as a contestant in the 1905 Glidden Tour, started racing the same year, and gradually became a spokeswoman and advocate for women drivers and the Good Roads Movement. It wasn't until the exclusion of women from sanctioned racing was accepted by most of the population around 1915 that she faded from the public eye. Although Joan Cuneo always appeared as feminine, not a feminist, dressed as a lady should and was a devoted mother, she was not afraid to challenge the male establishment when she felt it was necessary. She was at home with celebrities such as Enrico Caruso and Mrs. Woodrow Wilson, as well as with tough race car drivers and mechanics. She did love fast driving and everything about the automobiles of the day and got many speeding tickets. Her life history is not just about racing but is also the story of the development of the automobile and auto racing in America as well as the changes that occurred in family and social life at the time.

Perhaps because she had moved to an obscure small town in the Upper Peninsula of Michigan, remarried, and changed her last name, her death in 1934 went almost unnoticed by the *New York Times*. Hopefully, this book will go some way towards restoring her to her rightful place in the history of automobile touring and racing in the first two decades of the twentieth century.

Introduction

"Rising to the call of adventure, they took risks in order to reach the top. Few succeeded.... And yet exceptional women are often superior to 'exceptional' men!"—Annie Soisbault, the Marquise de Montaigu[1]

Mad for Speed is the life story of Joan Newton Cuneo, who held center stage as the premier woman racer in America from 1905 to 1915. She truly was an exceptional woman who proved herself, if not always superior, at least the equal of the best male drivers of her day. Unfortunately, today her achievements have been largely forgotten and she is only mentioned in books about auto racing's early days as the pushy female who got women banned from racing. This book follows her amazing life, detailing her accomplishments not only in the field of auto racing but also as an activist for better roads, a supporter of children's charities and a role model for women of her day. She was truly "mad for speed," as she often admitted. Her love of fast driving and competition pushed her to test her mettle against the best male racers of her time whenever possible until women were excluded from sanctioned racing in 1909. But there was more to Joan Newton Cuneo's life than racing, even though at times it resembled a melodrama with a bittersweet ending.

Joan was a national celebrity for more than a decade. She was looked up to as an experienced motorist who supported the cause of outdoor exercise for women, especially at the wheel of an automobile. At the same time, she was a cultured, well-educated woman with a well-developed sense of humor and the devoted mother of two children who believed that engaging in motoring and other outdoor activates did not make a woman lose her femininity. Between 1905 and 1909, she would enter a number of competitive automobile events, not always winning but determined to do her best against all comers.

Joan Newton was born in Holyoke, Massachusetts, in 1876 to John Carter Newton and Lela Vulte Newton; she was the youngest of four daughters. Her father was one of six Newton brothers, who traced their heritage back to the 1630s. All made fortunes in the development of Holyoke. She admitted to being a tomboy, and enjoyed outdoor activities such as horseback riding, driving a team, and riding a bicycle. She was treated like a boy by her doting father; he even let her drive a steam engine on his short-line railroad. Family lore says that she walked across the roof beam of a church under construction on a dare at the age of ten. She also spent several summers on the family's California ranch, where she enjoyed considerable freedom, unusual for a girl of good family in the 1890s.

Despite her tomboy activities and enjoyment of the outdoor life, Joan Newton benefited from the conventional education common to young ladies of her class. She dressed conventionally, wearing dresses with long sleeves and full skirts with her luxuriant dark hair pinned up in a Gibson Girl style. In later interviews she was always described as a soft-spoken, cultured and refined lady, not a hearty Amazon or a mannish female.

It is unclear how Joan Newton met Andrew Cuneo, her future husband; it is likely the marriage was arranged. In 1898 at the age of 22, she married the 25-year-old Cuneo, a wealthy Italian-American who would provide her with all the niceties of life.[2] At first the young couple lived in Queens, New York, with Andrew Cuneo's aunt Maddelena, the widow of Antonio Cuneo.[3] Andrew's uncle Antonio had come to the United States a penniless immigrant and amassed a fortune through a variety of enterprises. Called the "Banana King" because he had made his first fortune in the produce business, he was known and respected as a banker in New York's Little Italy before his death in 1895. Andrew Cuneo inherited most of his uncle's fortune, as Antonio Cuneo had no direct heirs, and Andrew was already a wealthy banker at 23. The union of Joan Newton and Andrew Cuneo was an exchange of wealth and social standing, but initially a happy one. The young Cuneos mixed with New York society after their marriage and they seem to have been well accepted despite Andrew Cuneo's ties to the immigrant community. Two children were soon born to the young couple, Antonio Newton (A. Newton) Cuneo, in 1899, and Maddalena (Dolly) Cuneo, in 1901. They moved to a beautiful home at Richmond Hill, Long Island, in 1905. Joan's marriage brought her to New York City just as automobiles became popular, and her husband's wealth afforded the means for her to both compete in the Glidden Tours and race a series of increasingly powerful autos.

When Joan Cuneo chose a fairly inexpensive used steam Locomobile in 1902 as her first vehicle she had never sat in an auto. However, after one driving lesson that lasted one and a half hours, the 25-year-old wife and mother was captivated by the freedom and exhilaration provided by her automobile. Later that day, she took her young son and baby daughter and their nurse for a ride around Central Park in New York.[4] That was the beginning of what would become a passionate love affair with driving, especially fast driving, that lasted almost two decades.[5] In the next ten years, Joan would be nationally recognized as the pre-eminent female motorist in the United States. She was celebrated not only for her success in racing but also for her skill in cross-country driving. Her success as a racer did not find favor with many Victorian males, who believed that women were weak creatures needing protection, rather than daring racers. Unfortunately, Joan's successes behind the wheel would draw her into the heart of the struggle for the control of racing between the American Automobile Association, the Automobile Club of America and the American Automobile Manufacturers Association.

The book provides a detailed picture of family life at the turn of the century, while looking at the varied experiences of women automobilists after 1900. It provides eyewitness accounts of the problems of cross-country driving as well as the very real dangers in racing in the bulky, noisy hard-steering machines of the day. Above all, it is the story of how a small but determined woman pitted her skills against the male drivers of the day while facing growing discrimination. In 1905, when she was not allowed to compete in the Climb to the Clouds on Mount Washington, New Hampshire, she fumed, "If some of the cars went up the course in the time accredited them, I can put my car up in faster time. I believe I could back it, run it sideways, or any old way, and land there in better time than some of the men drivers did."

After her experience in the 1905 Glidden Tour, she was asked to race at the Pough-keepsie County Fair. This was her first attempt at driving on a race track and as she said later, "I had my first experience at track racing ... it was a case of love at first sight and my love for track racing grew each time I drove around one."[6] In the next three years, Joan Cuneo continued to gain racing experience at various tracks, mainly flat dirt ovals designed for horse and bicycle racing. She showed her extraordinary courage and determination while driving in a gymkhana for autos at the Danbury Fair in October 1906. While going at full speed carrying two women passengers, her car caught on fire. Although her passengers threw themselves over the back of the car, Joan Cuneo calmly shut off the engine and turned off the gasoline before she jumped out. Although her burns were painful, she shrugged the incident off as nothing unusual.[7] In spring of 1907, she came in third in a hundred-mile race with a time of 2 hours and 23 minutes, no mean feat for a small woman in a car with no power steering, no windshield and minimal brakes.[8] Many who interviewed or met her seemed quite startled by her appearance; the female daredevil who had beaten some of the best male drivers in the country was not an Amazon but a compactly built woman of less than medium height with a steady gaze and low voice.[9]

During this period, she became even more involved in the care and maintenance of her cars. She learned to change a flat tire and do small repairs and was not afraid to get dirty working in her garage. At the New Orleans Mardi Gras auto races in February 1909, she defeated several well-known male racers, including George Robertson and Bob Burman, and finished second to Ralph De Palma in a 50-mile race. Unfortunately, the Automobile Manufacturers Association had already petitioned the Contest Board of the American Automobile Association to ban women from competition. Midway through 1909, they got their wish as competition in sanctioned races was limited to men 18 years and older by the AAA Contest Board. Even the Glidden Tours now excluded women because they came under the umbrella of AAA Contest Board Sanctions. Joan Cuneo was effectively barred from top-level competition. Never a vocal proponent of women's rights, she felt strongly that women should have the opportunity to compete if they had the ability and desire. As she had already demonstrated many times, she had more than her share of both.

The rest of this book covers her unsuccessful attempts to continue racing, the breakup of her marriage and her eventual move to the Upper Peninsula of Michigan. There she married for the second time, to James Francis Sickman, and threw herself wholeheartedly into improving life in her new hometown. The last chapter of the book looks at the other female automobilists of her day and concludes that while many were skilled drivers, none had mastered as many aspects of the automobile as Joan.

When Joan died in 1935, the Ontonagon newspaper made no mention of her career as a race car driver but focused on her charitable and civic activities. Her death rated only a brief paragraph in the New York newspapers. Hopefully this book will restore Joan Newton Cuneo to her proper place in racing history and successfully explain why the AAA banned women from competition in 1909. Was it because of lingering Victorian attitudes that regarded women as weak and emotional? Was it part of a backlash against track racing, which had resulted in so many deaths in the prior ten years? Was it, as many historians currently believe, because men feared competition from exceptional women like Joan Newton Cuneo, to save the sport of auto racing, or, did the AAA cave in to the demands of the Manufacturers Association?

1

From Holyoke to New York

At six o'clock in the evening of February 17, 1898, Joan Newton, the youngest daughter of wealthy entrepreneur John Carter Newton, married Andrew Cuneo of New York, a millionaire banker, at the Newton home in Holyoke, Massachusetts.[1] According to the *Holyoke Daily Transcript*, the wedding date had been moved up several months to accommodate Andrew Cuneo's business concerns in Europe. Rescheduling the date of her wedding was no problem for his bride, as she was eager to set out on her first trip to Europe.

It was an Episcopal service in deference to the Roman Catholic groom and was held not in the Second Congregational Church, which the Newtons attended, but in their home.[2] The Reverend E. A. Reed, longtime rector of the church, presided over the ceremony. Sadly, Joan's mother, Lela V. Newton, did not live long enough to see her youngest daughter marry, having died two years earlier at age 58. Although Joan had three older sisters, her only attendant was Miss Eveleen V. Newton, the sister closest to her in age, who served as maid of honor. Andrew Cuneo's best man was Louis Campora, a business associate, from New York. The slight, dark-haired bride wore a gown of heavy cream satin embroidered with pearls ending in a demi-train, showing off her 19-inch waist, while the slim young banker was dapper in his dress suit. The newspaper commented that her traveling gown was "tailor made" of heavy dark brown cloth.[3]

Holyoke friends and family were present at the wedding, along with a number of guests from Vermont, where the Newtons owned property. Curiously, there were no guests attending from the groom's side. This seems to indicate that Andrew Cuneo's relatives who lived in New York City and San Francisco either chose not to attend or were not invited to the Holyoke wedding.

A few days after the ceremony, the young couple were to sail on the *Normadie* [sic] for Paris. Their ship was actually *La Normadie*, owned by the *Compagnie Générale Transatlantique* (the French Line) and the first of four fast new ocean liners that sailed on a regular basis between Le Havre and New York at the end of the nineteenth century. Chillingly, a few months later *La Bourgogne*, next in the French Line's rotation, sank with great loss of life.[4] The Cuneos' timely departure on *La Normadie* was, perhaps, an early instance of the famous "luck" Joan Cuneo enjoyed during her life. How ironic that *La Normadie* could carry up to one thousand poor Italian immigrants in steerage while high above wealthy Italian-American Andrew Cuneo and his bride crossed the Atlantic in a first-class cabin.

Paris was an exciting place in 1898, not only the European center of art, literature and fashion but also the site of series of industrial expositions that drew visitors from all over the world. Joan Cuneo, who had an interest in mechanics inherited from her father, was fascinated by the hundreds of innovative machines she saw there, including the new automobile. After a month in the City of Lights, Andrew and Joan Cuneo sailed to Sicily, which Joan would find to be in stark contrast to the refinement and culture of Paris. There they would live for six months with Andrew Cuneo's relatives while he further developed his import business, amidst the poverty and class divisions common to southern Italy. In September 1898, the young couple returned to New York, settling at Port Richmond, Staten Island, where they would live with Andrew Cuneo's aunt Maddalena Cuneo.[5]

Marriage to Andrew Cuneo would change Joan Newton's life in many ways. She left the comfortable haven of family and friends in western Massachusetts forever for a new life in New York. Although she and her husband began their married life in New York living with his aunt at Port Richmond, his wealth and Joan's social standing allowed them access to the lower echelons of high society in New York City. Quickly adjusting to a series of different environments, she showed an amazing adaptability for a gently reared Victorian young woman from a wealthy family.

The Newton-Cuneo wedding raises several questions to even a casual reader. Why were there no attendants besides Joan Cuneo's sister as maid of honor and Louis Campora, a fellow banker, as best man? Why were no guests from the groom's family present at the reception? Where and how had Joan Newton met Andrew Cuneo? Was this an arranged marriage, or was there something darker behind this union that would cause some members of the extensive Newton family to consider the Cuneos as "black sheep"? If Joan Newton had not married Andrew Cuneo, she would never have had the opportunity to become the first American female to gain international fame as an auto racer. Her marriage allowed her to travel to the epicenter of the new sport of auto racing, Paris, and then to New York, where interest in auto racing was also growing rapidly. Most important, her husband's wealth provided funding for race cars, transportation, entry fees, a full-time mechanic and many other luxuries.[6]

To understand as much as we can about Joan Newton Cuneo and the significance of her life and the society that formed her character, it is crucial to study her family history, examine her formative years in Holyoke, and learn something of her husband's background as well. Finally, it is also vital to understand what western Massachusetts and Holyoke in particular were like in the decades after the Civil War.

Today, Holyoke is one of the poorest communities in the state of Massachusetts, with many derelict factories; almost half of its population of forty thousand are immigrants and nearly a third live below the poverty level. Although it is situated near important transportation corridors and sources of hydroelectric energy, experts believe that it will take massive investments to turn Holyoke around.[7] This was not the case in 1898, when it was a bustling manufacturing center, with a sizeable percentage of self-made millionaires like John Carter Newton and his brothers in residence.

The Newton family can trace its history back to the early days of the Massachusetts

Colony. Richard Newton was the first of his family to leave England for America. He and his wife, Ann Loker Newton, arrived in 1638, 18 years after the arrival of the *Mayflower*.[8] Richard and Ann Newton were not content to settle in an established town and moved on to the wilderness territory of Sudbury, Massachusetts. They joined with a group of like-minded settlers to form a frontier plantation and town. Around 1656, the couple and their nine children secured land for a farm in nearby Marlborough, an agricultural haven and thoroughfare from Boston to the Connecticut River. It was there that Richard Newton lived until 1701, nearly reaching one hundred. His descendants continued to occupy the Marlborough farm for seven generations. "A rare instance in the history of families in this ever-changing world," the town minister noted years later. As the Newtons were Puritans in both theory and practice, allegiance to God and family, self-reliance and industriousness were core values for them. These traits were inherited by the Newton generations that followed them.

Family lore recounts that this Richard Newton was Isaac Newton's great-uncle. The family claims kinship with the famous mathematician, who didn't marry or have children of his own. Family lore also mentions a Church of England minister who wrote a famous hymn (John Newton, the author of "Amazing Grace").[9]

Certainly these "can do" attributes led the Newton brothers of Holyoke to achieve monetary fortune and regional recognition in the nearby areas of New England. However, the only member of the Newton family to achieve nationwide fame was Joan Newton Cuneo. Between 1905 and 1915, she would accomplish this feat by being the first American woman to drive a variety of fast cars in a number of races and speed trials. In later years, the press would refer to her as "the driver of large racing cars." During and after her racing career she would also become a well-known advocate for women drivers and road improvement in the United States.

Joan Newton's grandmother Esther Hale came from a somewhat different background. James Newton had always lived at home on the family farm in Hubbardstown, located in western Massachusetts. The 155-acre property was considered to be one of the best farms in the area. However, Esther Hale left her family's home at age 11 to work as a servant for several families. She then worked in a factory and briefly taught school. James Newton married Esther Hale in February 1824 and brought her home to live on the family farm. Although an unequal marriage, it was a good one, as eight children — Laura, Sarah, Daniel Howe, Joseph Drury, Susan, James Hale, Moses and Ebenezer — were born in the next ten years. All but Sarah survived, unusual for the time.

In April 1835, James and Esther Newton, Joan Newton's grandparents, traveled by oxcart with their seven children, ages 10 months to 12 years, into western Massachusetts. This area, near the Berkshire Mountains, was frontier territory at the time. They settled on a small farm where two more children were born: Esther and John Carter Newton, Joan's father. Their property was heavily wooded and included a stream to provide water-power. James Newton, Sr., realized the potential to set up a water-powered sawmill and gradually was able to employ six of his sons in the lumber business. Not only did their sawmill provide lumber to sell, but there was plenty left to construct their own farm buildings.[10] In later years, when they were grown men, four of the Newton sons would use their knowledge of the area's lush woodlands to great advantage.

Eventually the Newtons had eleven children, four daughters and seven sons. Although six of the seven boys worked with James in the sawmill business, sons Daniel Howe, James Hale, Moses and John Carter Newton were unusually successful, becoming millionaire capitalists who consistently worked to develop the economy of the area.[11] Although they grew up in Greenfield, Massachusetts, as young men they roamed the wilderness of western Massachusetts and southern Vermont, noting its potential for later development. The Newtons were an unusually close and caring family and practiced the golden rule that others only talked about.[12] Holyoke was the paper-manufacturing center of the eastern United States during the 1860s and '70s and provided many opportunities for the civic-minded brothers to develop the economy and infrastructure of the area.[13]

The oldest, Daniel Howe Newton, was born in 1827. After attending Williston Seminary, he helped manage his father's business. In 1862 Daniel moved to Holyoke to partner with his younger brother John Carter, in the construction business. They built four paper mills that maintained the status of Holyoke as the premier paper-making center of the area. They also built mills that produced a variety of products from silk to blankets. When the Newton brothers began the development of the pulp and paper industry in Vermont, Daniel Newton served as president of the Hoosac Tunnel and Wilmington Railroad, which supported the new industry. He was active in local and state politics and served for a time in the state legislature.[14]

James Hale Newton, born in 1832, was a studious child who graduated from Dartmouth College with Phi Beta Kappa honors in 1859. He then served as the principal of Thomas Grammar School in Worcester, Massachusetts for five years. However, he couldn't resist the opportunities in Holyoke and joined his brothers in the construction business. James H. Newton was the most accomplished of the brothers, and eventually left the family firm for the baking business, where he was hugely successful.

Moses Newton, born in 1833, was the last of the four brothers to move to Holyoke, in 1868. After graduating from Deerfield Academy, he worked in the family lumber business before developing a successful career as an entrepreneur in Holyoke.[15] He would eventually found several of the largest paper mills in the country.

John Carter Newton, Joan's father, was the tenth and next-to-last child of James and Esther Hale Newton. He was born April 21, 1838, in Greenfield, Massachusetts, and would die unexpectedly in 1899, a year after his youngest daughter's wedding and shortly after moving to Wilmington, Vermont.[16] John C. Newton grew up at his family home and initially struggled at school in Greenfield; although he was a self-taught mechanical genius, many regarded him as a *peculiar* boy.[17] His father sent him to a private school in Westminster, Vermont, where he finally began to flourish as a student. He eventually attended the Normal School in Westfield, Massachusetts, for a year.[18] Graduating in 1858, he taught school for a time in Massachusetts and Vermont. Neither John C., who was 22 at the start of the war, nor his older brothers Daniel, Moses and James served in the Union army. Instead, the Newton brothers developed a number of business ventures to meet the demands of the Holyoke community on the way to becoming millionaires. By the 1880s, the Newton brothers were well known throughout western Massachusetts and southern Vermont for their entrepreneurial skills.

In 1860, John C. Newton started his own construction business, building gasworks at Westfield and Greenfield, Massachusetts, and an addition to the Normal School at Westfield. He moved to Holyoke in 1862. There he took on larger and even more lucrative construction jobs while still in his twenties, including the construction of a woolen mill, a machine company, a brass foundry and a sewing machine factory. The Newton brothers were among those who prospered during the industrial boom that was created by the Civil War and continued into the last years of the nineteenth century. John seems to have had an innate knowledge of engineering that made his construction projects — which included bridges, dams and eventually a tunnel and railroad — so successful. Often described as a whirlwind of energy, John C. Newton soon was counted among the wealthy entrepreneurs of the city.[19]

In 1865, he married Lela Frederica Vulte of New York City at Trinity Chapel in New York; Miss Vulte was the daughter of a well-to-do New York sheriff whose family was descended from the Dutch settlers of New Amsterdam. She had attended finishing school, where she gained a modest education. The Newtons eventually had five daughters: Pamela,

Left: John Carter Newton, circa 1889, at 51. He would die at 61. *Right:* Lela Frederica Vulte Newton, circa 1889, at age 51. Joan's mother, would die at age 57 (courtesy of Harriet Newton Draper).

who died at birth in 1866; Harriet Ensign, born in 1868; Mary Elizabeth, 1870; Eveleen Vulte, 1873; and Joanna, 1876. Although her name is listed as Joanna on her birth certificate she was always listed as Joan Newton Cuneo in the newspapers, so I have used this spelling in the book.

Only Harriet had married before Joan (Joanna) in 1895 when Joan was 19. Mary Elizabeth married at 29 and Eveleen at 28. While Joan married at the age of 22, her sisters would all have been considered "old maids" at the time of their marriages. It is hard to say why they married so late, as they were attractive and well dowered; perhaps they were not ready to settle down. During the 1890s, the Newton girls played an important role in Holyoke society, as they were considered lively and fun loving. However, all of them would leave Holyoke for good when their father died.[20] In 1896 John C. Newton's first wife died, and he married Eva Nash Wheeler in 1897, in New York. About this time, he sold his Holyoke properties to his brothers and moved to Wilmington, Vermont, where he died two years later of peritonitis from a burst appendix.[21]

As John C. Newton's family grew, he and his brothers continued to prosper, building more paper mills, canals and even a railroad, the extension of the Hoosac Tunnel and the Wilmington Railroad. This narrow-gauge line allowed the development of Wilmington, Vermont, as a vacation destination, and several of the Newton brothers, including John C., bought property in the area. In the 1870 census, 32-year-old John C. Newton was listed as being a manufacturer and agent of paper mills, with real estate worth $3,500 and personal property worth $14,000. He employed a live-in maid and a nurse for his young daughters. His 36-year-old brother, Moses Newton, who lived close by, was also a paper manufacturer, had real estate worth $4,000 and personal property worth $6,000 and employed only one domestic.[22]

Why were the Newton brothers so successful? Besides being in the right place at the right time, they grew up in a family that valued discipline and hard work. The closeness of the family no doubt helped with funding their projects, as did their sterling reputations. Holyoke is a ghost of its former self today; in 1860 there was an insatiable demand for the products of its mills, which would continue for decades. Ever visionary, the brothers had certain advantages not available to any other group of capitalists. They had complete trust in one another, had worked together since their youth and continued to support one another as adults. Following the death of John Carter Newton in 1899, their direction of industrial expansion in Holyoke and Wilmington gradually ceased. John C., the youngest brother at age 61, had been the engine that pushed them along. The remaining brothers, all in their seventies, did not have the heart to continue.

Years of hard work had taken its toll on John C. Newton by the time he reached his forties. He spent the greater part of 1875 in Southern California with his family to restore his health. During the 20 years that followed, the Newtons traveled to California on a regular basis. The girls no doubt accompanied their parents on these trips. Joan later recounted some of her girlhood experiences in the wild ranch country out west. In 1908 she said, "I was a good horsewoman around my New England Home, spent two seasons on a far western ranch and have driven the six-horse team on the Mail and Express out of Los Angeles many times, sixty miles into the wild."[23]

Joan Newton's childhood in Holyoke and California must have been both pleasant and happy. The Newtons were well-respected members of the community and enjoyed a lively social life. John C. Newton seemed to allow his daughters, or at least Joan, an amount of freedom unusual for the time. Perhaps because he had no sons and his youngest was a bit of a scamp — and by her own admission a" tomboy" — he allowed her do things that would have ordinarily been reserved for boys. Newton family legend relates that in 1886, when she was ten, Joan walked across the ridge beam of the Second Congregational Church then under construction, on a dare. Making her way along a narrow timber high in the air would have taken an extraordinary amount of coolness, daring and concentration. Even climbing up to the beam itself was something few girls of her era would have contemplated. Joan would never lose these traits and they would serve her well throughout her adult life. Her father was secretly delighted with his free-spirited youngest daughter and he made concessions for behavior that most Victorian parents would consider unladylike, at best.

To counter this wild streak in Joan, the Newtons sent her to three different boarding schools: Mrs. Piatt's School in Utica, New York, the Catherine Aiken School in Stamford, Connecticut, and Temple Grove Seminary in Saratoga New York.[24] All three were ladies seminaries (often known as finishing schools), which were often affiliated with a Protestant religious group. Their curricula provided both an education and social skills a wealthy young woman would need to find a husband, entertain guests and run a large home and staff. A young ladies seminary was almost always a boarding school, although some took day students. Joan Newton would have boarded at the three schools she attended.

Joan Newton at age 11 (courtesy of Harriet Newton Draper).

Mrs. Piatt's School in Utica, New York, had a checkered history. Starting as the Utica Free Academy in the 1840s, the school had a series of name changes after the original building burned and was rebuilt in 1865. It became the Utica Female Seminary, then Mrs. Piatt's School, and finally the Balliol School until it ceased operation in 1907. The building was then used to house the Utica YMCA.[25] Mrs. Piatt's School was also the farthest from Holyoke, a distance of 176 miles. It would have been a difficult trip by carriage, but Joan and her sisters, who also attended Mrs. Piatt's, traveled there by train. Joan's parents may have initially chosen Mrs. Piatt's for her because of its loose affiliation with the Presbyterian Church and because several of her sisters had also attended the school.[26] However, its uneven reputation may have caused her parents to move Joan to the much more prestigious and strict Catherine Aiken School. In addition, Utica, although a bustling mill town, similar to Holyoke was also the home of the state Lunatic Asylum![27]

The Catherine Aiken School in Stamford, Connecticut, was the closet to Holyoke at 108 miles, not far by today's standards, but it would have taken two days in a carriage in 1890. Joan probably traveled there by train, accompanied by a chaperone. Stamford was also fairly close to New York City, where her mother's family lived and she may have visited them while boarding. The school was strongly influenced by its first principal and later owner, Catherine Aiken. She was a Quaker intellectual who gained a far-ranging reputation as the author of books and articles on a mind-training system based on intense concentration. Aiken came to Stamford in 1855 at the age of 27 and ran her school for 41 years. During her tenure, she tried to provide an education for her female pupils similar to that offered at the best boys schools in New England. The course of study included "mathematics, science, history philosophy, English, classical and foreign languages and literature as well as music, art and physical training."[28] Higher education was strictly segregated by sex. Only young women could attend the Catherine Aiken School, while young men took similar classes at Betts Academy. The Aiken school was so well known that teachers were willing to travel from New York to work there and students came from as far away as South Carolina and Wisconsin.[29] Of the three schools Joan Newton attended, the Catherine Aiken School may have been the best fit. Her later interest in science and mechanics may have been sparked by her courses, and mind training would certainly prove to be handy for a racecar driver.

Temple Grove Seminary, however, was a cut above the others. More a college than a finishing school, it would eventually be incorporated into Skidmore College in 1909. The founder of Temple Grove was Charles A. Dowd. He and his wife, Harriet M. Dowd, served as coprincipals. Dowd gained fame as the first person to propose multiple time zones for the United States (or any other country). Time zones would become very important for cross-country railroad schedules, although the system of time zones adopted by the railroad industry in the 1880s was actually designed by William F. Allen.[30] Perhaps the most famous student who attended Temple Grove School was Louis Howe, the close friend and campaign manager of Franklin Delano Roosevelt. Howe was so sickly and delicate as a youth that his parents sent him to Temple Grove, a girls school, instead of a boys prep school. After Dowd's death in 1904 (ironically, he was crushed by a locomotive) his wife was unable to maintain the school and it was taken over by Skidmore College. Joan Newton probably enjoyed attending school in the pleasant resort town of Saratoga Springs; she would visit the town several times during her career as an automobilist.

When she wasn't away at school Joan Newton enjoyed the company of her mother and sisters in Holyoke and at their summer home in Vermont. A family portrait of Joan with her sisters Harriet and Eveleen taken in 1891 shows a slight girl wearing a dress covered in ruffles, abundant hair piled on top of her head in the Gibson Girl style of the time, with a wistful look on her face. Joan must have spent quite a bit of time with her father, as she later mentioned that she got to drive a steam engine on the narrow-gauge railroad built by her father; the Hoosac Tunnel and Wilmington Railroad. According to Joan, "My father ... built a little twenty-five mile railroad from the Hoosac Tunnel up into Vermont — the Deerfield Valley road — and I often sat on the engineer's seat and held the throttle and ran the locomotive engine. There I learned the rudiments of steam propulsion and steam engines."[31] She and her sisters enjoyed a busy social life until they married. None would remain in Holyoke, but Joan's life would change the most.

Available sources provide little information on the early history of the Cuneo family. According to the *New York Times*, Andrew Cuneo's uncle, Antonio Cuneo, arrived in the

The Newton sisters are enjoying summer vacation at Readsboro, Vermont, in 1884. Harriet is seated at the left front, Elizabeth is in the center strumming her banjo and Joan is standing at the far right. Joan, eight when the photograph was taken, is a tanned and grubby urchin wearing a fancy straw hat. The other two girls were local friends Mattie Carpenter and Elizabeth Dix (courtesy of Harriet Newton Draper).

United States from poverty-stricken southern Italy sometime before 1860, with no possessions except a pack on his back.[32] He probably came to the United States in 1855 with his wife, Maddalena De Martini Cuneo.[33] In 1861, the *Times* reported that Cuneo's grocery, which occupied the first floor of a tenement on 31 Baxter Street, burned in a devastating fire that dispossessed 18 families living in the upper stories. The uninsured building was a total loss. However, Cuneo who "lost all his stock and fixtures, which were valued at $1,500," had cannily insured his business for $2,000.[34] The fire supposedly started in the basement, which housed an Italian dance hall.

In the Census of 1870, Cuneo stated his occupation as a grocer. The census indicated that both Antonio and Maddalena Cuneo were literate English speakers, which was an unusual accomplishment for poor Italians who immigrated to the United States at that time.[35] Cuneo became a naturalized citizen in 1876. However, the naturalization card lists neither his date of birth nor the date of his arrival in the United States and his place of birth only as Italy.[36]

Joan Newton (center) and two of her sisters, Harriet Ensign Newton (left), born in 1868, and Eveleen Vulte Newton, born in 1873. Mary Elizabeth Newton, born in 1870, is not shown (courtesy of Harriet Newton Draper).

It appears that Antonio Cuneo was one of the first slumlords in what is believed to have been the first slum in the United States, Mulberry Bend. Before the Civil War, the area around Mulberry Street had been a middle-class neighborhood. However the "Bend on Mulberry Street" was plagued by an underground spring that caused many water problems for the area. Gradually, the urban poor, mostly immigrants, replaced the middle class and the first slum in New York City was born. By the 1880s the area held thirty-seven thousand tenements with more than a million occupants, mainly Italian. Most of the five- to six-story buildings were divided into one- or two-room apartments with no running water and few windows. The buildings were crowded so closely together that people could hand things to each other across the alleys. In December 1884, Cuneo was cited by the Fire Commissioners of New York City for not having fire escapes on the tenement houses he owned at Number 59½, 61, 63 and 65 Mulberry Street.[37] According to an inspector from the Bureau of Buildings, these buildings were crowded with occupants, as they were "in the center of the Italian colony in Mulberry Street."[38] In April 1885, Cuneo was summoned to Police Court for failing to build the fire escapes and he was ordered to pay a fine of $250 for each offense or suffer imprisonment of six months. Cuneo paid the fines.

The tenements owned by Cuneo in Mulberry Bend, which were later sold to the city, were considered to be among some of the worst slum housing in New York. They were demolished in 1896 and replaced by Columbus Park, much to the delight of Jacob Riis, who had crusaded against these slums in the newspapers. Many of the photographs in his book *How the Other Half Lives* were taken in the Mulberry Street area.[39] Today Mulberry Street is in the heart of New York's Chinatown. (Ironically, when Andrew and Joan Cuneo moved to Richmond Hill in 1905 one of their neighbors was Jacob Riis.) Of course, Antonio Cuneo was not the only person to profit from owning tenement buildings. Many were owned by holding companies to effectively conceal the names of their socially prominent owners.

In 1894, Cuneo again was summoned to court to explain the financial difficulties incurred by a Roman Catholic church in the Italian community. Evidently Cuneo held a $53,000 mortgage on the church property and payments were in arrears. Cuneo and several other creditors sued to take over the church building, while the church trustees wanted the property to go to its parishioners.[40] The suit was settled out of court, and its outcome didn't seem to hurt Antonio Cuneo's standing in the Italian community.

Remarkably, by the time of his death in 1896 Antonio Cuneo controlled the shipping of nearly all the bananas to the United States and was known in the city of New York as the *Banana King*.[41] Cuneo was a savvy businessman who poured his profits into real estate, targeting property that was in or near Little Italy. When the idea of Mulberry Park was first conceived in 1887, it was discovered that Cuneo owned six large tenement houses that the city wanted to raze. Eventually Cuneo received more than $200,000 from the city for the property. He then opened a bank on 28 Mulberry Street. Over the years, Antonio Cuneo's reputation grew within the New York banking community. He dealt mainly with the Italian community, but the Wall Street bankers were well aware of the Cuneo Bank, "although [Cuneo was] by no means a Wall Street man himself."[42] At that time, an obvious social gulf existed between the WASP bankers of Wall Street and most Roman Catholic Italian immigrants, no matter how wealthy. However, the fact that the Wall Street men *knew* him tells us that Antonio Cuneo's influence in the Italian community could not be ignored. A study of the New York City Directories reveals his rising status; in 1882 he lived in Little Italy near his bank on 28 Mulberry, in 1888 the Cuneos had moved to 203 Grand Avenue and in 1891 their address was listed as 101 Park Avenue.[43] Antonio Cuneo must been born with a keen intelligence, amazing energy and excellent judgment to have achieved such success in the United States after arriving as a penniless young immigrant.[44]

Unlike the prolific Newton family, Antonio Cuneo and Maddalena Cuneo had no children. However, her brother, Louis De Martini, had a son, Andrew De Martini, born in 1875. It was common at the time for working-class boys to quit school for a job by the age of 12 or earlier. After a basic public school education in New York City, young Andrew probably went to work for his uncle Antonio. Andrew's father, Louis De Martini, was also a partner in the Cuneo business, but it was Antonio who had amassed a small fortune by this time. Andrew learned from him the business of produce importation, real estate management and banking. Under Antonio's tutelage, Andrew learned quickly and was soon a trusted member of the family business. Antonio Cuneo adopted his nephew Andrew some years before his death and Andrew De Martini changed his last name to Cuneo. Young De Martini/Cuneo would work closely with his uncle until unforeseen events changed the course of their lives.

In 1894, Louis De Martini and Andrew Cuneo organized the Cuneo Banana Company, a prosperous venture that brought Antonio more than $100,000 and the title of Banana King. Unfortunately, by 1890 Antonio Cuneo had serious health problems. According to his lawyer, R. Ellery Anderson, about four years earlier, Cuneo had become very ill. The New York physicians who attended him thought he had paresis. "Paresis" was a nineteenth-century euphemism for syphilis. At that time there was no cure and Antonio Cuneo's prognosis was grim. However, he made a temporary recovery and continued growing his fortune with the help of his brother-in-law and nephew until he was found wandering the streets of San Francisco in June of 1896.[45]

By 1896 Louis De Martini had immigrated to San Francisco, and Antonio Cuneo traveled to Northern California in the spring of 1896 to rest and recover his health. Unfortunately, Antonio suffered a recurrence of the symptoms of paresis two weeks after his arrival.[46] De Martini had him committed to the Home for the Cure of Inebriates. Somehow, Cuneo escaped from the Home and wandered the streets of San Francisco for two days and nights in a demented state until he was found by a friend, E. M. Batto. De Martini knew that drink was not the problem and said in an interview that he would move to declare Antonio Cuneo insane. Under the circumstances, given Cuneo's medical condition, De Martini probably had no other choice. Antonio Cuneo was examined by the

Commissioners of Insanity at the Receiving Hospital in San Francisco, but the article made no mention of their decision.[47] The *San Francisco Chronicle* reported that on June 28 "the millionaire Banana King was shipped out of town in a comatose condition accompanied by attendants."[48] Whether insane or dying from an advanced case of syphilis, Antonio Cuneo never recovered his health and died during the first week of September 1896.

Back in New York City, Cuneo's funeral was a major event in Italian community, as he had been, according to the *Times*, one of their most popular and best-known leaders. The Roman Catholic Church of St. Joachim was filled to overflowing with friends, acquaintances and employees of Cuneo. There were not enough places for half of those who wanted to attend, especially when more than one hundred of Cuneo's employees were assigned seats for the service. No expense was spared by his family. His coffin was covered with black velvet and heavily ornamented with silver.[49] There were more floral tributes than the church could hold, so they were placed in three open carriages that waited along the sidewalk in front. So many people were milling around outside the church attempting to gain a glimpse of the funeral party that police were required to keep order. When the Solemn Funeral Mass ended, more than one hundred carriages followed the hearse to Calvary Cemetery for the interment.[50]

Because Antonio and Maddalena Cuneo were childless, it had been necessary for Antonio to designate a member of his family as his heir. Maddalena Cuneo inherited some of her husband's business property after his death. In 1897 she even appeared as a plaintiff before the City of New York in a property condemnation hearing.[51] However, a woman of her class and ethnicity would never have been considered qualified to run the family business and administer her husband's fortune. Maddalena also inherited a large house on Staten Island where she seemed content to stay. Although her brother, Louis De Martini, remained a presence in the business, his son, Andrew De Martini Cuneo, inherited the majority of Antonio's fortune. By the time Antonio died, Andrew had probably been working with him more than ten years. Antonio recognized Andrew's real talent for business and was comfortable in naming him as his heir. The Cuneo fortune was now Andrew's to grow or squander; initially he would be even more successful than his uncle in amassing wealth. Great wealth however would not have been enough for Andrew Cuneo to have been considered as an acceptable bridegroom for the charming and well-dowered Joan Carter Newton.

A decade after his uncle's death, Andrew Cuneo would be referred to as a "progressive New York Italian banker" by the *New Orleans Picayune* when he visited the city in September 1906. Cuneo spoke about investments that could be made in New Orleans, while expressing his confidence in the expansion of the New Orleans economy.[52] Branching out from his New York businesses and reaching out to fellow Italians in New Orleans, Andrew Cuneo formed the Southern States Alcohol Company. He invested $150,000 of his own money in the construction of a distillery on the levee in New Orleans. According to Cuneo, the plant would utilize the latest machinery to turn the blackstrap molasses produced by Louisiana sugar plantations into alcohol, as well as utilizing molasses brought by ship from Cuba to the port of New Orleans. In addition, the *Picayune* reported, Cuneo was the proprietor of the Atlantic Macaroni Company, which was the largest macaroni company in the United States. It was capable of producing five thousand cases of macaroni a week. Andrew Cuneo wanted to market his macaroni to New Orleans' sizeable Italian community and was at this time looking for a suitable distributor.[53] In 1908, Cuneo was appointed to the Oyster Commission of Louisiana and bought two lots in New Orleans's French Quarter.[54]

In 1898, only two years after his uncle's death, at the time of his marriage to Joan Newton, Andrew had already applied the Cuneo business model to grow his business interests. Perhaps not surprisingly, John Carter Newton had employed many of these same strategies in establishing and building his own business. Although their backgrounds were worlds apart, Andrew Cuneo and John Carter Newton shared a common approach to

A clam seller in front of Andrew Cuneo's bank on Mulberry Street, in the heart of the Italian ghetto in Mulberry Bend, taken in 1902 (Library of Congress Print and Photographs Division, Washington, D.C.).

creating great wealth. Bring products and resources to the people with whom you share roots and religion and they will become the bedrock from which your fortune and your standing in the community will grow.

For the highly respected John C. Newton to have welcomed into his Holyoke home such an usual bridegroom indicates that he appreciated Andrew's drive to succeed in business. The young man's impressive achievements and social polish must have convinced John C. that his favorite daughter would continue to enjoy the privileged lifestyle in which she had been raised after her marriage.

Nevertheless, at the turn of the twentieth century the Newton-Cuneo marriage was a rare union. It was uncommon for the educated and well-dowered daughter of a wealthy and respected Protestant family with ancestors who arrived in 1638 to marry a first-generation Catholic immigrant. It is difficult to envision what factors brought these two young people together or even where they met. Did they fall in love? Was the marriage of Joan and Andrew arranged by John C. Newton? If her father had heard rumors about Andrew's possible connection to the Mafia, he must have chosen to turn a deaf ear, as the marriage would take place in his family's home. Unfortunately, he would not live to see if he made a wise choice, as he died unexpectedly a year later.

Mystery and questions would continue to be a part of Joan's relationships, not only with her husband, Andrew, but also with a young man who entered their lives shortly after their move to Richmond Hill, Long Island.

2

Joan Newton Cuneo
Learns to Drive

Upon their return from Europe, Andrew and Joan Cuneo were "at home" after September 1, 1898. This meant they were ready to receive callers at the residence of Andrew's aunt, Maddalena Cuneo, at Port Richmond, Staten Island, where they would live until 1905.[1] Maddalena was close to her nephew, who now bore her family's name, and she seems to have regarded him as her son. Living in a house with many unused rooms, the senior Mrs. Cuneo was lonely after her husband's death. Victorian homes were made for extended families, and it was common for young couples to move in with a family member until they decided where they wanted to live.[2] During the years Joan Cuneo lived at Port Richmond she became very fond of her aunt by marriage. Joan's mother had died in 1895, and Joan began to regard Maddalena as a second mother, even taking the elderly woman along on several automobile trips.

At the turn of the century, Port Richmond retained a small-town atmosphere that was steeped in history dating back to the days of Dutch settlement. Staten Island, separated from the mainland by Kill Van Kull and surrounded by the Newark River and the Upper Bay, quickly became a transportation hub that served numerous ferries between New York and New Jersey until the Bayonne Bridge was built in 1931. Port Richmond, set along the Kill Van Kull waterfront, provided landings for numerous ferries. In 1883, it was described as a model village, having "dwellings [that] range from pretentious mansions to quiet cottage [sic]."[3] In 1902 a Carnegie library was built in Port Richmond, and the little town soon attracted substantial numbers of Italian, Polish, Norwegian and Swedish immigrants. It is easy to see why Antonio Cuneo might have been drawn there, as his increasing wealth and prominence allowed him to maintain not only an apartment in Manhattan but also a house outside the city. Because Port Richmond was linked to the mainland only by ferry, it is easy to understand why Andrew and Joan Cuneo would move to their Richmond Hill home on Staten Island in 1905.

In 1901, Joan Cuneo appeared to be a typical Victorian stay-at-home mother, as were most married women of her class. She was responsible for the management of her family, home, and staff, which included a nursemaid who cared for Joan's two small children. Given their wealth, and the size of Maddalena Cuneo's home, they probably had several more servants, including a cook and gardener, who came when needed but lived elsewhere.

On February 17, 1899, a son was born to Joan and Andrew. He was named after Andrew's uncle and benefactor, Antonio Newton Cuneo. The year 1899 had to have been very traumatic for Joan Cuneo, as the joy over the birth of her son was overshadowed by the unexpected death of her father, John Carter Newton, in September. Nevertheless, on January 13, 1901, Antonio was joined by a baby sister, Maddalena (Madeleine) De Martini Cuneo, named after Andrew's aunt. When she was two, Maddalena caught a childhood disease (probably mumps), which left her totally deaf. She needed special attention and education as she grew older, eventually learning both sign language and lip reading.[4] One of the Cuneos' two live-in servants was a nursemaid who cared for the little girl.[5]

Their daughter's disability must have been a shock to the young parents who had, up until then enjoyed a comfortable and carefree life at a level well above that of the average American family. Whether or not Maddalena's disability put a strain on their marriage is impossible to determine, but they would have no more children. Although she didn't have a large family of her own, Joan loved children. Improving the lives of orphaned children was a cause that she embraced. She began with supporting Orphan's Day in New York and for the rest of her life she worked for charities that tried to better the lives of children With servants to run the household and care for her children, Joan still had time on her hands despite a busy social life and the charitable work expected of a woman of her class and standing. Joan drove her aunt's carriage in Port Richmond, often taking her husband to the ferry landing in the morning. When they moved to Richmond Hill, Andrew Cuneo took public transportation; the train station was only a block from their home However, they also kept a carriage of some kind, as Joan enjoyed driving a team. Without one, Joan would have had to hire a carriage if she wanted to go somewhere outside walking range. She must have been intrigued by the occasional auto she saw on the streets of Richmond Hill, recalling those she had seen in Paris. Bored and restless, she thought an automobile might provide a distraction while providing more freedom of movement. Never did she imagine that learning to drive an automobile would change her life beyond her wildest dreams. However, less than a year after Maddalena's birth Joan Cuneo took up the automobile, and a few years later driving had become the consuming passion of her life.

Joan Cuneo never explained why she decided to buy a used Locomobile Steam Car in 1902, saying that it was "just a notion she had" in a later interview.[6] However, there were a number of reasons for her decision. She admitted she had been a tomboy and couldn't resist a challenge. Young Miss Newton had enjoyed horseback riding and driving a carriage as well as a variety of outdoor activities. She never lost her skill at driving a carriage and was for a time a member of a coaching club in New York. In addition, she had a keen interest in all things mechanical. The automobile allowed her to enjoy the outdoors, traveling the countryside near her home, and tinkering with the machine provided an outlet for her mechanical interests. In 1908 she told a reporter, "I was always fond of outdoor sports. Yes, I will answer the question you want to ask but will not, I was a tomboy, I am afraid. I was a good horsewoman around my New England home."[7]

After her brief stay in Paris, Joan Cuneo's interest had been piqued by the automobile. American magazines and newspapers began to feature articles and advertisement about automobiles, which Joan could not have missed. By 1902, readers were bombarded with an increasing number of stories about new automobile models and their innovative features. Readers could learn about the adventures of intrepid automobile travelers either in the newspaper or in one of the new periodicals that specialized in automobile news such as *The Horseless Age*. William Kissam Vanderbilt was one New Yorker who had already made headlines about his automobile-related exploits in Paris.

In November 1900, little Mrs. Cuneo may well have read with interest, and not a little envy, the exploits of a certain Miss Mudge at the Long island Automobile Club (not too far from the Cuneo home on Staten Island). Evidently the promoters of an automobile show on Long Island had tried to entice people into taking trial drives on a board track they built for the show. According to the *Brooklyn Eagle*, "a number of women were out driving the machines themselves and the cleverness with which they handled their charges was an object lesson of the adaptability of the auto for women."[8] Miss Genevra Delphine Mudge (Eva), the most noticeable and skillful of the women drivers, was quoted as saying, "I have driven horses, handled yachts and managed an auto, and the easiest of them all is the auto."[9] The challenge inherent in Miss Mudge's statement certainly intrigued the woman who had once walked across the roof beam of the Second Congregational Church in Holyoke.

In 1902, the streets of Jamaica, New York, were crowded with automobiles, causing the first traffic jam in the area. According to the *New York Times*, "never before have so many machines propelled by gasoline, steam and electricity been seen together."[10] Automobilists had assembled there for a one-hundred-mile endurance run sponsored by the Long Island Automobile Club. Although she was still living on Staten Island, Joan Cuneo may well have come to witness the start of this exciting event. She certainly was familiar with the area.

The women of Joan's social set already had taken an interest in the auto. Despite the prevailing male attitude that automobiles were not for women, a substantial number of New York socialites, as well as comfortable middle-class housewives, were already driving or being driven in their own autos. A few proclaimed their feminist leanings; many enjoyed the speed and comfort of automobiles; while others considered the auto a new kind of fashion accessory. Although many women preferred the sedate electric cars, initially very popular, some chose steam-powered or gasoline engine cars. In the days before the electric starter, few women chose to drive gasoline engine cars, as cranking not only was hard work but also could be dangerous. Of all the autos built in 1902, electrics were most directly marketed to women. Most were at least partly enclosed. They were quiet and simple to operate, and some even provided a bud vase on the dashboard. The silent electric was especially popular with city women because it started with the turn of a key and was easy to steer with a boat-like tiller. When traveling short distances, they didn't have to worry about having their battery run down. However, for women who wanted to tour the countryside, steam or gas engine cars were necessary because the electric had a range

One-hundred-mile endurance run, Jamaica, Long Island, New York, 1902. This was one of the earliest endurance runs held on Long Island. Note the large mix of gasoline, electric and steam cars parked helter-skelter on the street. All the cars are open, despite the cold weather (courtesy of Carl Ballenas, Richmond Hill historian).

of only 30 to 40 miles, at best. Faced with the choice of steam or gas power, Joan Cuneo first asked her husband to buy her a steamer, as did many of her peers. Several articles state that her first car was an electric Victoria, but this seems unlikely because she would soon buy a more powerful White Steamer.

In a 1908 interview, Joan Cuneo recommended an electric as the perfect starter car for a woman:

> To gain the best results and to learn the first rudiments of good driving [according to Mrs. Cuneo], an electric is the best to begin with. In it, she may learn how to steer, to give the proper power as it may be needed and to become familiar with the rules of the road and the many city traffic laws; she must learn not to drive all over the road, making everyone else turn out for her. After having mastered the elementals she should try a small gasoline runabout."[11]

Her advice is interesting because by 1908 the gasoline engine car had overtaken the steamer and electric in popularity. Because of their costly batteries, electric cars were also more expensive.

As early as 1900, stories about auto races, held mainly on the Continent, began to creep into the sports pages of newspapers across the country. Because Paris was still the center of the automotive world, Parisian racing events got the lion's share of the news. It was in Paris that the glamorous intercity road races started. Gossip about the dashing Mademoiselle Camille du Gast who dared to race with men had reached New York, carried by wealthy sportsmen such as Foxhall Keene and William Kissam Vanderbilt.[12] Du Gast, a dashing, statuesque beauty, certainly knew Long Islander William Kissam Vanderbilt (Willie K), who shared her fascination with speed and competed in French races at this time. In 1890, at the age of 22, du Gast married Jean Crespin, although she used her maiden name when racing. Crespin, a wealthy stockholder and the manager of Dufayel, one of the largest department stores in Paris, was considerably older than his wife. Amused by his beautiful wife's adventurous nature, he encouraged her sporting activities, which included fencing, shooting and ballooning. Du Gast was fearless to a fault, even jumping from a balloon to test a primitive parachute in 1895.[13] In the summer of 1901, she drove in the Paris to Berlin race, using her husband's 20 hp Panhard-Levassor, which had not been prepared for racing. She completed the course faster than a number of the male entrants.[14] The statuesque du Gast drove sitting bolt upright because she insisted on wearing the tight corset that was fashionable at the time. She would later compete in the 1903 Paris-Madrid race (still wearing her corset) with a much more powerful car, a massive De Dietrich, which could reach speeds of 80 mph. Tragically, the much-awaited race was abruptly halted in Bordeaux due to the horrific number of deaths, injuries and crashes that had occurred even before the cars reached the French border. Later in the year, the Automobile Club de France banned women from racing, basing its decision on a perception of feminine nervousness behind the wheel and the fear that a woman might be seriously injured or killed in an automobile race.

Thwarted from racing her car in France, du Gast turned to motorboat racing and narrowly escaped with her life in a 1905 race when a storm capsized the boats of all the competitors. In an interview before the Paris-Madrid race, du Gast said that whatever happened (in the race) she would go to America, where "the great auto races will be held." She went on to say that she "would challenge Vanderbilt or Winton or any of your great racers." Finally, she concluded with the following provocative statement: "I am surprised that no American woman has yet made a record at automobile racing. American women usually lead in everything. Perhaps I shall be the occasion of getting them to develop their talents in this direction."[15] Although du Gast never came to America to challenge the best American (male) racers, Joan Cuneo would pick up her gauntlet only two years later.

Although we don't know for sure what influenced her purchase, Joan Cuneo acquired a small used Locomobile steamer in the summer of 1902. She noted that until then she had never sat in a car.[16] The fact that she had never before been in a car probably meant that neither her aunt-in-law nor her husband owned a car at that time, as few people did. Andrew Cuneo never developed any interest in driving, much less racing, and would always let his wife drive. Growing up in Little Italy, he probably had not learned to drive a horse and team, either. As his wife mastered a succession of autos, he was often seen as a passenger but never behind the wheel, content to let her take charge.

The 1902 Locomobile the Cuneos bought resembled a horse-drawn carriage more than an auto. It had a single bench seat, high bicycle-style wire wheels and a tiller instead of a steering wheel. The selection of a used Locomobile as her first auto leaves room for speculation. The wealthy Cuneos could have afforded a much more expensive model. It is likely her husband didn't want her to take on anything too powerful at first and Joan, possibly unsure she would enjoy automobiling, didn't want a vehicle that was too big. Her steam model Locomobile, which sold for $900 new, was not, even for 1902, one of the better-built cars on the road. It was notorious for boiler problems.[17] Locomobile also built bicycles and they used some bicycle parts in the construction of the steam car, especially for its wheels. Although this was not unusual, steam-powered Locomobiles were considered somewhat flimsy.[18] However the vehicle she chose was lightweight and easy to steer and resembled a carriage, which she knew how to drive well. Steam vehicles had a complex mechanism and were tricky to maintain. However, Joan already had some knowledge of steam-powered vehicles, although the only one she had actually driven was her father's narrow-gauge steam engine. After her first driving lesson, it was love at first sight! She was smitten first with driving and touring the countryside, which would soon expand to driving competitively and racing.[19]

According to several accounts, in July 1902 a "demonstrator" gave Mrs. Cuneo a driving lesson in Central Park that lasted about one and a half hours in her new/used Locomobile.[20] Flushed with excitement, she drove the vehicle home from her lesson, gathered up her two children and their nursemaid and took them back to Central Park for a ride.[21] Although Joan Cuneo made her drive home appear to be both fast and easy, such would not have been the case (unless the family was visiting friends in New York City or staying at a hotel). Port Richmond was accessible only by ferry, which would have made her trip home and return to Central Park fairly time consuming. Nor did she mention how the nursemaid enjoyed the trip; the Locomobile had only one bench seat, and the nanny had to manage a three-year-old and an infant while Joan handled the driving. The next day, instead of using a carriage to make her social rounds, Mrs. Cuneo drove the Locomobile by herself down the length of Fifth Avenue to call on an acquaintance, as was the custom of the time. Unfortunately, despite or perhaps because of her knowledge of steam propulsion she didn't shut off the Locomobile during her visit. On her return Joan found that all the water had boiled out of the tank and burned up the boiler.[22] The boiler problem did not mean that a steam car had been a poor choice for her first auto. The steam cars of 1902 had one huge advantage over gasoline-powered cars: the engine did not have to be cranked to start. Cranking required both strength and dexterity to start a gas engine without seriously bruising or breaking an arm. In addition, a steamer was quiet and responsive, although it couldn't go anywhere until steam had built up in its boiler.

Joan Cuneo said absolutely nothing about the ignominy of having her new vehicle pulled to a garage by a team of horses before the end of her second outing. Now she realized that she needed to know more about the Locomobile than how to start and drive

Style No. 2, $750, F.O.B., Bridgeport, Conn.

Locomobile steam car ad from *McClure's Magazine*, January 1901. This is the car in which Joan Cuneo began her career as an automobilist. It is a fairly flimsy vehicle with a chain drive like that of a bicycle and boat-like tiller steering.

it. Although steam cars didn't lose their charge like the electrics, their water tanks had to be refilled on a regular basis; thus operators of steam vehicles usually took a jug of water along. What Joan's instructor probably didn't tell her was that her particular model ran out of water after running about 20 miles. Its water supply would not have provided enough steam to get her to Fifth Avenue and back.

The Locomobile wasn't an ideal choice for Joan's first car. It was noisy and the drive chain had a tendency to slip off the sprocket. Instead of the driveshaft common to today's cars, many early autos were propelled by a drive chain similar to that on a modern bicycle. Since many early automakers had first built bicycles, it's not too surprising that they used the same mechanism to propel their four-wheeled vehicles. The chain's location close to the middle of the Locomobile's underside made it tricky to replace at the best of times. Nevertheless, Joan Cuneo kept the Locomobile for about a year before switching to a better model.[23]

After she became a celebrity, Joan Cuneo consistently told the reporters who interviewed her that after having a garage built at their home she did all the maintenance on her cars. However, there is a mystery here. Where did this wealthy young matron gain her automotive knowledge and when did she have the garage built? Joan Cuneo may have had some experience with steam engines, but even the relatively simple Locomobile had the same complicated steam-generating mechanism of its bigger brothers, with little resemblance to a locomotive engine. She definitely needed someone to teach her about steam-powered cars. The local blacksmith was no doubt pressed into service to repair the burst boiler. In 1902, a smithy or carriage maker was where an auto in need of repair was usually towed behind a team of horses. By then there were even a few auto repair shops; forward-looking blacksmiths and carriage builders had already realized auto repair might be a profitable business.

After the Locomobile's breakdown, Andrew Cuneo made a fateful decision that would bring many changes to Joan and Andrew's married life. In 1909 Cuneo, who was by then well known in New Orleans, gave a rare interview to a reporter for the *New Orleans Picayune*. Cuneo said that, at first, he was worried that his wife might not be able to handle driving a car. She was a petite woman and he didn't think she was particularly strong, although he would be proved wrong about that. Since they were trading the Locomobile in for a more powerful White Steamer, he decided to hire a chauffeur-mechanic who could keep Joan's car running and be ready to help her if she couldn't manage her car. He selected Louis A. Disbrow, a wild young man from a wealthy and respected Long Island family who had narrowly escaped being convicted of murder in January 1903, for the job. Although Louis Disbrow was a partner along with two of his brothers in an electrical business and later a car dealership, his main talents at this time seemed to be playing pool, excelling at sports and charming young women. In 1902, he was accused of murdering a young female acquaintance but acquitted in the trial that followed six months later. The incident created a huge scandal and was very embarrassing to his upstanding family and known to the Cuneos.

A look at the Disbrow family history and more information about the murder and trial itself is needed to understand why Andrew Cuneo selected such an unlikely candidate to work closely with his young wife. In the 1900 Census, the Disbrows were recorded as living on Church Street, Richmond Hill, Long Island, in a large home. It held parents Thomas A. Disbrow and his wife, Lucy, and their seven children: Joseph P., age 26, Harriet L., age 24, Louis A., 23, Grace L., 21, Thomas A., 19, Douglas A., 17, and Charles C., 11.[24] The Disbrows employed two maids and a butler who lived in the servants' quarters upstairs. Disbrow Sr., according to the *New York Times*, had made a fortune in the meat business at Jamaica, Long Island, and increased his wealth through investments in a fertilizer plant.[25] Like the Newtons, the Disbrows could trace their family back to the early days of the Massachusetts Bay Colony. They were related to the Tilly family, which included a signer of the Mayflower Compact. They also claimed kinship with the famous nineteenth-century writer Robert Louis Stevenson.[26] The oldest son, Joseph Pell Disbrow, was a solid citizen who had gone into the automobile business for himself in 1898 on St. Anne's Avenue in Richmond Hill. He handled White steam cars and later Rainer and Cadillac autos, He also served in the 106th Infantry Regiment during World War I.

The family was well thought of in Richmond Hill society, and the small suburban community was startled to learn that Louis A. Disbrow, the second of their five sons, might be involved in the death of two young people: Clarence Foster, a local playboy, and Sarah "Dimp" Lawrence, the daughter of another prominent local family. A *New York Times* headline dated June 15, 1902, declared: "Drowned During Trip in a Boat at Night: Bodies of Clarence Foster and Miss Lawrence Found; LOUIS A. DISBROW MISSING."[27] The paper stated that the recently divorced Disbrow and the still-married Foster were both interested in Miss Lawrence and while some expected Foster to elope with Lawrence, others considered Disbrow her fiancé. Sarah, "Dimples" or "Dimp," Lawrence's mother had not wanted her to go out with Disbrow, as he was a divorced man. However, Sarah, according to the *Times*, had spoken up for him earlier that morning and her mother finally consented as long as her daughter was chaperoned. Disbrow assured Mrs. Lawrence that he would bring along the Pearsalls, a respectable father and daughter boarding at his hotel, as chaperones. Mrs. Lawrence agreed to this arrangement, but when Disbrow arrived that evening he had no chaperones and was driving a two-seat buggy. This was the last time Mrs. Lawrence saw her daughter alive. Disbrow and Dimples Lawrence must have picked up Foster along the way, as there were three occupants in the buggy according to Rogers, the club steward, when they arrived at the Hampton Pine Club. The threesome ate dinner there and according to Rogers were "in good spirits although *no intoxicants* had been served to them ... before they left together at 11 P.M."[28] Other witnesses said the threesome had been drinking all evening. At this point, there is conflicting evidence as to what might have happened to cause the deaths of Dimp Lawrence and Clarence Foster sometime before daybreak.

Mrs. Lawrence, regretting giving her 17-year-old daughter permission to go off with 25-year-old Louis Disbrow, was worried when she was not home by midnight. Her mother had reason to worry, because Sarah Lawrence, just out of a convent school, was a wild child. She had already spent time unchaperoned with both Foster and Disbrow during her summer vacation, at the Ocean View Hotel. Waiting outside the hotel in the shadows at 2:00 A.M., Mrs. Lawrence saw a buggy carrying two men and a woman heading towards the hotel at a good clip. She was sure the woman was her daughter and called out to her to come home, but the buggy did not stop.[29] Horrified that Sarah's reputation would be ruined by this escapade, Mrs. Lawrence soon feared that something bad had happened and spent a sleepless night. Later it was learned that Foster, not Disbrow, had ordered the carriage for the trip to the Hampton Pines Inn Monday night. He also made a reservation for three to dine that evening at the private club, about five miles from the Ocean View Hotel on Shinnecock Bay.[30]

Early Tuesday morning, Mrs. Lawrence went to the local authorities to report her daughter missing. The lifeguard service then dragged the bay between the Ternall and

Ocean View Hotels, but the searchers found nothing. Some believed that Dimp Lawrence had eloped with Clarence Foster, although Foster's young wife tearfully claimed her husband would come back, as they were happy together. Later in the day, the searchers found an upturned skiff that belonged to the Ternall Hotel floating about a mile and a half from the landing. Mrs. Lawrence immediately cried out that her daughter had been drowned while sailing.[31]

The morning of June 15 a lifeguard noticed the body of a man floating about three hundred yards from where the abandoned boat had been found. Towing the body ashore, the lifeguard recognized the corpse as that of Clarence Foster; the body was somewhat discolored but in good shape except for an abrasion about the eye. When coroner Dr. John Nugent arrived, he gave Foster's body a cursory examination and stated the cause of death was drowning. Dr. Nugent then released the body for burial. Later that evening Foster was buried in a local Methodist cemetery after a brief service. Dimp Lawrence's body was found at ten o'clock that same evening, floating close to the spot where Foster's body had been recovered, and the now hysterical Mrs. Lawrence had her worst fears confirmed.[32] The body was totally unmarked, but her mother refused to look at it.

Dimp Lawrence's body was taken to the local undertaker's, where it was also examined by Dr. Nugent. At this point, Louis Disbrow became a "person of interest" in the investigation. The coroner, now unsure about the cause of Foster's death, began to collect information on the missing young man and stated he would place his findings in the hands of the district attorney.[33] New evidence showed Disbrow had been involved with Miss Lawrence. She had disappeared three weeks ago for a few days and he had met up with her at Coney Island, where they spent time together. Foster had one of the tintypes the couple had taken at the beach in his pocket when they found his body.[34]

Miss Annie Pearsall, the woman Louis Disbrow had suggested as a chaperone, was staying in the room next to his at Ternall's Hotel. She had met Dimp Lawrence and Clarence Foster the day before when the girl came into the hotel after sailing in the bay with Foster. Miss Pearsall again heard their voices Monday night, as Disbrow said goodbye to Foster. However, about 15 minutes later Foster returned and he and Disbrow began to argue. Then Foster said, "Well, Lou, we might as well settle this matter here and now," and Miss Pearsall heard sounds of a scuffle and breaking china until one man left, slamming the door behind him.[35] A few minutes later, she heard Lawrence and Foster talking outside her window. A boat was mentioned and finally the girl said, "I'll go if Lou goes too."[36] Creeping over to the window, Miss Pearsall observed the trio walking amicably towards the bayside. The next morning Disbrow had breakfast with Miss Pearsall, but neither spoke of the previous night's events, although she thought he seemed nervous.[37]

Other witnesses stated that Disbrow had checked out of the hotel and boarded a train for Eastport after trying to pay his bills with checks written on a nonexistent Richmond Hill bank account. Although he didn't call upon Mrs. Lawrence before leaving Good Ground, Disbrow later sent her a telegram stating: "I am sure that Dimp and Clarence are together and I will not rest until I find them."[38] Despite his brave words,

Disbrow's actions seemed suspicious to the local residents, and more witnesses came forward. Despite the coroner's insistence that the deaths were accidental, the District Attorney would soon investigate the deaths of Foster and Lawrence.

When a *Times* reporter interviewed Thomas Disbrow at his home on Richmond Hill on June 15, Disbrow Sr. said he had no idea where his son might be, but he was not at home and even if he was he wouldn't say so, but added:

> "Louis called here yesterday. He called on Monday. I was out driving and Louis made no mention to his younger brother about any trouble. If my son had listened to my advice since and immediately before he became of age he would know enough to appear now and explain. He has been rarely at the house of late, but told me three weeks ago that he expected to go to Europe about this time. He may have gone. I know that he is, if he knows of it as shocked at the tragedy as I am. He was never an obedient boy but he was always honest and decent."[39]

The residents of Richmond Hill had believed that Louis Disbrow would settle down after his marriage to Jessie Everett, the daughter of a stableman, in October 1897.[40] He was only 20 at the time and his bride 16. His father was not pleased that his son had married beneath him, and the marriage did not last. Marriage had not reformed Louis

Newspaper headline prominently featuring Louis Disbrow's arrest for murder, *New York World*, January 19, 1903.

Disbrow; he was still as wild as ever. He soon began a competition with Clarence Foster for the favors of vivacious, fun-loving, and out-of-control Dimp Lawrence, which would end badly.

On September 26, 1902, Louis Disbrow was formally charged with murder in the first degree for killing Clarence Foster by the Suffolk County Grand Jury.[41] The slight, handsome Disbrow faced the Court and pled "not guilty."[42] His trial was then set for January 12, 1903. The prosecution had decided to charge Disbrow only with the killing of Clarence Foster, although they tried but failed to show that Miss Lawrence had been strangled.[43] Of course the evidence was all circumstantial. The prosecution developed a scenario that had Disbrow hitting Foster with an oar in the rowboat, knocking him out of the boat, and fending him off with the oar as Foster tried to climb back in. Only the three people involved knew what had happened, and two of them were now dead. However, Foster had only a small abrasion on his face and Miss Lawrence none. Without modern evidence-gathering techniques, the police were forced to depend on witnesses and physical evidence, of which they had little, after the trial began. One of their key witnesses, Miss Annie Pearsall, who allegedly heard the fight between Foster and Disbrow, left the area before testifying.[44] The judge then disallowed any mention of Miss Lawrence's death or that Disbrow had written several bad checks the day after the murder.[45]

On the fourth day, the trial went to the jury and Disbrow was acquitted in forty-five minutes. Most of the spectators had expected this verdict since the prosecution presented no new evidence and had no witnesses to the supposed meeting at sea of Disbrow, Foster and Lawrence. Looking at the evidence that was presented more than one hundred years earlier, it is difficult to determine what Louis Disbrow's role, if any, had been in the deaths of Foster and Lawrence. Disbrow and Foster could have fought, but Disbrow was much the slighter of the two men and Foster was reported to be strong and athletic. The drunken couple could have taken the boat, capsized it and drowned, despite being good swimmers. Dimple Lawrence's father, John Smith Lawrence, a direct descendant of Commodore Lawrence of "Don't give up the ship" fame, died two months after the trial. He was said to be distraught after his daughter's death.[46] Louis Foster, Clarence Foster's brother, drowned near the same spot his brother's body was found less than a month after Disbrow's trial.[47]

Acquitted by a jury of his peers, Louis Disbrow was a free man and he seems to have made the most of this second chance. Despite the huge scandal, his family stood by him and his eldest brother, Joseph, continued to employ him in his garage and auto dealership. Joseph P. Disbrow had been the first member of his family to get involved with automobiles, setting up an automobile garage at 117–01 St. Anne's Avenue in Richmond Hill by himself in 1898. In 1901, he added Louis and his younger brother Douglas as partners, changing the name of his business to Disbrow Brothers. In 1903 he relocated the dealership to Hillside Avenue in Jamaica, New York, where they added Ford and White automobiles, and from 1905 to 1909 their agency sold Rainier and Chalmers autos, eventually carrying Cadillac and Cleveland brands.[48]

Despite his checkered past, sometime between 1903 and 1905 Louis Disbrow was hired by Andrew Cuneo to help his wife, Joan, hone her driving skills and maintain her cars.[49] In 1905, the Cuneos moved to a new home on Church Street in Richmond Hill, Long Island. They were now near neighbors of the Disbrows, who also lived on Church Street a few blocks away. The Cuneos knew of the family when Louis Disbrow was tried for murder in 1902: they were certainly of the same social class. In addition, there were few automobile dealers on Long Island and they bought Joan's 1903 White from the Disbrow agency even before their move.

Louis Disbrow's knowledge and skill in working on and driving automobiles was obviously more important to Andrew Cuneo than his scandalous reputation. Because he was a handsome and personable young man from a well-respected family, as well as a skilled mechanic and driver, Andrew Cuneo took a chance on him. Hiring Louis Disbrow as his wife's mechanic would mark the start of a long friendship between Andrew, Joan and Louis.

Her husband's New Orleans comments in 1909 indicate that Joan Cuneo had omitted at least one important fact from all of her interviews: she had learned about cars from a skilled mechanic hired by her husband. She also made no mention of when Louis Disbrow started working for them. However, it is likely that he accepted a position as the Cuneo's chauffeur after Joan got her first White steam car. Since it was not a full-time job, he could continue his work at his brother's auto dealership. It is also likely that the Cuneos did not build a garage and workshop for Joan's automobiles until they moved to their own home in Richmond Hill in 1905.

In 1903, Joan traded the Locomobile for a new White touring car, probably at the Disbrow dealership. No doubt she was tired of the slow, noisy vehicle driven by a bicycle-like chain with only kerosene lanterns for lights. The White was quite a change from the Locomobile. It was one of the most luxurious cars built in 1903, with room for at least four people. However, she was somewhat taken aback by the size of her new vehicle when she got it. More than a decade later, she wrote: "I'll never forget the sensation of driving the White for the first time. It seemed like handling a huge ferry boat."[50] The White Steamer, built by the White Sewing Machine Company, was more than a step up from the Locomobile. Though not as well known today as the Stanley Steamer, it was a strongly built and expensive machine. The Cuneos probably chose the White because it was sold by the nearby Disbrow Brothers dealership at a time when automobile dealers were scarce.

The 1903 White Model C Mrs. Cuneo got was a four-passenger steam touring car with rear entrance, a stationary top, side baskets over its rear mudguards, carbide generators for light, and shaft instead of chain drive.[51] A photo of this White shows a vehicle almost twice the size of the Locomobile; no wonder she felt apprehensive when she first got behind the wheel. Joan Cuneo would drive this White Steamer nearly every day until the summer of 1905, when she decided to buy a new and even more powerful 1905 White model.[52] This was an even larger car with a 93-inch wheelbase, boasting 15 hp, as opposed

Joan Cuneo showing off her 1903 White at the Newton family summer gathering in Wilmington, Vermont, in the summer of 1904. Joan is not at the wheel but is sitting at the left rear with her arm resting on the seat back. Next to her is a young girl who may have been Harriet's daughter. Joan's sister Eveleen is seated beside the girl. Her sister Harriet is sitting next to Irene Fowler, who is pretending to drive. Fowler's sister Iona is standing at left. Others in the picture are Martin Brown, with his arms crossed, and Louis Disbrow at the far right. Joan and Disbrow drove the car up from Staten Island. (courtesy of Julie Moore, president, Wilmington, Vermont, Historical Society).

to the 1904 model, which had only 10 hp and an 80-inch wheelbase.[53] By 1905, Joan Cuneo had gained much experience behind the wheel, following the example of the growing number of women drivers in the United States.

One of the most famous women automobilists of the decade was Mrs. A. (Alvah) Sherman Hitchcock. Mrs. Hitchcock had already earned a reputation as an automobile correspondent of note and would write many articles for magazines such as *Motor* and *Country Life Magazine*; almost all were directed towards encouraging women to take up the sport of motoring. Mrs. Hitchcock was well qualified to write about automobiling for women, as she and a female companion, Miss Rose L. Downes, had made a 100-mile drive on Thursday November 20, 1902, in a little curved-dash Oldsmobile. The Olds was a small carriage-like vehicle without a windshield or a top and was steered with a tiller, not a wheel. They were the first ladies of Providence, Rhode Island, to drive a gasoline machine on a lengthy road trip. Mrs. Hitchcock reported that they had a delightful time with only one stop for lunch.[54] According to Mrs. Hitchcock, "If women in general understood the vast pleasure to be derived from driving their own car I feel confident that the number of woman motorists soon would be vastly increased."[55] Because of the growing interest women had taken in automobiles, *Motor* published an unsigned article in 1902 purportedly showing the latest styles in automobile touring apparel, some quite hideous. As the author quipped, "That the motor girl is willing to make any sacrifice for the sport she so loves is plainly shown in the new automobile face protectors."[56] With thinly veiled sarcasm, the article poked fun at the society women whose latest fad was to wear motoring apparel that matched the color of their vehicles.[57] Although even Joan Cuneo confirmed that she had seen a woman at an auto show trying to match a fabric swatch to a car color, these antics were relegated to a relatively few socialites rather than serious automobilists like Mrs. Hitchcock and Mrs. Cuneo.

As early as 1901, *The Automobile* published an article written by Mrs. F. P. Avery, a woman who had already accompanied her husband on a trip of more than one thousand miles in their "horseless carriage." It is true that Mrs. Avery was a passenger, not the driver, but she had some useful tips for anyone contemplating a lengthy trip in an open automobile. She recommended liberal use of rubberized cloth and storm covers for their suitcases and hampers, gauze underwear that could be easily rinsed out when they stopped for the night, and mending and medicine cases. According to Mrs. Avery, a lady's hat must be well fitting and secured with an elastic in case "her husband wished to go a mile a minute." She hesitated to recommend eye coverings, which were needed because of insects, dust and sand, because everyone had their own preference, although she used a chiffon veil and her husband mica protectors. The Averys traveled through New England for over a month, driving 40 to 75 miles a day, and "enjoyed every minute."[58]

In 1905, the Cuneos settled into their own three-story home on Church Street, Richmond Hill, Long Island, only a short walk from the train station and much more convenient for Andrew Cuneo's commute to work. Although close to the hubbub of New York City, Richmond Hill provided a small-town respite for its well-to-do residents, and Joan and Andrew Cuneo quickly established a daily routine. With the Long Island Railroad station a block from their home, he took the train to the ferry and crossed to the city. There he spent weekdays at his bank on Mulberry Street in the heart of the Italian community in the borough of Manhattan.[59] Besides supervising her servants and playing with her children, Joan Cuneo worked on her cars in the new garage they had built behind their house on Richmond Hill and hours driving her White Steamer in the Long Island countryside and beyond, often with her children at her side.

The young couple had a busy social life as active participants in lower echelons of New York Society. One day a week, Joan Cuneo would be at home to her friends. On other days she would make a series of formal calls herself, always in her White steam automobile. While Andrew Cuneo's ties to the Italian immigrant community were socially unfortunate, he was a millionaire, dressed well, and was cultured and good looking, while Joan Newton Cuneo's family background was above reproach. She also, according to

Andrew and Joan Cuneo's new home, a large Victorian mansion, at #5 Church Street, Richmond Hill, Long Island. The photograph was taken from the train station across the street. From there Andrew took the train to the ferry to get to Manhattan (courtesy of Carl Ballenas, Richmond Hill historian).

many interviewers, was a soft-spoken, refined woman who dressed well.[60] Their circumstances and standard of living in 1905 were typical of a wealthy young couple in the first decade of the twentieth century. Nothing in their lives indicated that Joan Cuneo was on the brink of earning a national reputation as the most accomplished female race car driver in the country.

Given Andrew Cuneo's lack of interest in automobiles and busy schedule, the dandified banker was an unlikely candidate for shade tree mechanic. Thus Louis Disbrow came into his own as Joan Cuneo's mechanic and friend. The Disbrows lived a short distance away at the intersection of Division and Church, and the families quickly became friends. Louis lived at home and was nearby when Joan needed help with her machine.[61] They quickly developed a close friendship that would last more than a decade. When Joan Cuneo began racing, Disbrow went along as her riding mechanic, although Andrew also went along when he was in town. Louis Disbrow and Joan Cuneo were the same age. He had considerable charm and bad-boy good looks, being arguably much better looking than her husband, Andrew. Joan, not quite pretty, had what twentieth-century writers had begun to call personality and amazing force of character. Her notable features were her beautiful, long hair and her piercing light eyes, which had a steely focus found in many automobile racers. She wore her hair up in the style popularized by Charles Dana Gibson and she had the Gibson Girls' willowy figure and athleticism, if not their height. Was her and Disbrow's relationship ever more than friendship? The author has found no evidence either way. It is anyone's guess.[62]

By her own admission, between 1902 and 1905 Joan Cuneo spent considerable time alternately learning how to maintain her auto and driving through busy New York streets filled with a mixture of carriages, horse-drawn drays, equestrians and the occasional automobile. She also ventured out on the bumpy, potholed roads of the surrounding countryside. Although sadly lacking in power, her Locomobile was a good choice for her first attempts at touring, as its high wheels kept the car from bottoming out on the rough roads. In 1903, high wheels and generous ground clearance were characteristics of most American cars so they could navigate the rutted potholed roads found almost everywhere in the United States. The sleeker, lower European cars built for the excellent Continental roads often got stuck or even hung up when touring in the United States. The White with its superior power and comfort made driving even more fun. It also carried four passengers and a driver, had a top, and had room for picnic gear.

Since the turn of the century, various automobile clubs and civic organizations had begun to hold reliability runs to promote automobile travel. Mrs. Cuneo may well have witnessed the endurance run that was held in Jamaica, New York, in 1902, not far from her home. In 1904, Charles Jasper Glidden organized an automobile reliability run that would strongly influence the course of Joan Cuneo's life. Glidden, who had made a fortune in the budding telephone communication industry, retired in early middle age to embark on a series of adventures. After an initial fascination with ballooning, Glidden found his true love, the automobile. In 1901, he decided that the best possible adventure he could have would be to drive an automobile in every country in the world, at a time when few paved roads existed!

He and his wife sailed to London, where Glidden purchased a British Napier, one of the best-built cars in the world at that time. In little more than a year, the Gliddens put 6,775 miles on the Napier, often running on railroad tracks with special flanged wheels when no roads were available.[63] Although risky, this was a common practice at the time in areas where there were literally no roads. After returning to the United States, Glidden surveyed the state of the automobile industry in America and saw that it lagged behind Europe. He decided what was needed to stimulate interest and sales, as well as capture the interest of current owners, was a lengthy reliability run over challenging roads. To this end, he decided to undertake a trial run from July 25 to August 10, 1904, over a route that extended from New York City to St. Louis, Missouri. The route featured only a few paved roads and little signage and was an adventure indeed. This would turn out to be the second longest of the nine Glidden Tours, as it covered a distance of 1,964 miles.[64] The difference between this first informal tour and the eight that followed was that Glidden did not bother to set up rules for the contestants, which was both good and bad. Neither were prizes awarded to the competitors, but 66 out of 67 entrants finished the tour anyway.[65] He had stipulated mandated stops at various cities and the Gliddenites were given 26 days to finish. It was mandatory to travel at least 75 miles a day in order to complete the run on time, but the only reward was getting to the finish. This doesn't sound difficult today, but given the barely passable roads, the chance of bad weather, huge mud holes, and problems with tires and repairs, it was a great challenge for the entrants. Surprisingly, most had a wonderful time. In reality, the run was barely organized mayhem, as competitors ran off the road, took wrong turns, got stuck in the mud and had mechanical breakdowns almost every day.

Buoyed by the success of his informal tour and the enthusiasm of the entrants, Jasper Glidden decided to hold another in 1905. This time, however, there would be detailed rules and regulations as well as a dazzling first prize. Gathering together a committee of interested auto enthusiasts, he approached the American Automobile Association with his proposition and they agreed to sanction the tour. To enhance the event, he had a beautiful silver trophy crafted as an award for the overall winner. In November 1904, he gave the trophy to the AAA to hold. As the American Automobile Association Contest Board was gradually gaining recognition as the official sanctioning body of auto racing in the United States, it would determine the winner and award the trophy.[66] Today there are almost one hundred different auto race sanctioning organizations in the United States alone; in 1905 there were two. The American Automobile Association, with leadership and members largely middle/upper middle class, had a growing number of affiliated clubs throughout the United States. The Automobile Club of America, with an upper-class membership, had its headquarters in New York. For a time, the two groups competed to become the main auto race sanctioning body in the United States. The AAA, or three A's as it would be called by 1909, eventually triumphed and would hold this position until 1955.

Glidden saw his mission as promoting a series of organized tours that would showcase the reliability and practicality of the automobile, thus stimulating its development and production in the United States. At the same time, he added an element of competition to the tour that he hoped would bring prestige to both the driver and the manufacturer of the winning automobile. Finally, the tourists were expected to have fun during the tour and were offered various entertainments along the route.

William Kissam Vanderbilt had the same desire to promote the automobile in America but he believed the way to do it was thorough racing. Instead of reliability tours, Vanderbilt made plans for a series of road races on Long Island — the Vanderbilt Cup races.[67] While the Glidden Tours were not races, some of the competitors did race one another, creating quite a competition to arrive first at the day's destination. Although the tours fulfilled his expectations in regard to promoting automobile use and manufacture, Glidden had no idea that his proposed reliability run would have an unwanted side effect. The first official Glidden Tour in 1905 catapulted to fame its first (and only) female entrant, who would eventually complete her third tour with a perfect score. Jasper Glidden never considered that a mere female might want to enter such a strenuous completion, although his wife had been his constant companion on the trip around the world.[68] However, he didn't anticipate the strength and determination of a small woman from Richmond Hill, Long Island. The first Glidden Tour would provide the first but not the last opportunity for Joan Cuneo to test her driving ability against male drivers on a very public stage — with the reluctant approval of the AAA.

3

Mrs. Cuneo Makes the News!

As soon as she heard about the tour Jasper Glidden had proposed for the summer of 1905, Joan Cuneo knew she had to be part of this great adventure. Each new article promoting the event in the *New York Times* increased her desire to enter the "First Official " Glidden Tour. It also provided another reason for Joan to trade in her well-used 1903 White Steamer for a 1905 model at the end of June.[1] The new White appealed to her because it had been painted a light gray, instead of the usual black, red or yellow, although it came with the customary black leather interior and a folding top. She later said she was "criticized severely for having such a delicate (colored) and impractical car, but I entered and drove it in the Glidden Tour and later raced it on the beach in Atlantic City in the fall of 1905."[2]

Cuneo had recently joined the Long Island branch of the AAA, which was a requirement for all Glidden Tour entrants. However, she left herself little time to learn the quirks of her new and more powerful car, as the 1905 Glidden was to start on July 11. All the automobilists in the New York area already knew about the route of the tour, the entrants and the magnificent trophy Charles Jasper Glidden had designed for the winner from a series of articles in the New York newspapers. The 1905 tour, unlike the practice run in 1904, was to be a round-trip, starting in New York City, with a midpoint stop at Bretton Woods, New Hampshire. The tourists would return to New York City on July 22 after covering at least 870 miles of mostly unpaved roads.

Participation in the Glidden Tour would be expensive. Tourists would have to take at least two weeks off from work and would be responsible for the cost of food and lodging en route as well as any needed car repairs. This was not a problem for Joan Cuneo; she had a nursery maid for her children and Andrew Cuneo could take time off from his flourishing businesses. After discussing the Glidden with her husband and mechanic, Louis Disbrow, and with fellow enthusiasts and other White owners, she decided to send in her entry. The tour route looked to be physically demanding enough to test a strong man, yet Mrs. Cuneo had no doubts about her ability to complete it. She worried just a little that the other (male) drivers might not appreciate her participation. In 1905, there was a quite a sense of camaraderie among automobilists, since they were still relatively few in number, but would it extend to a woman who dared to take on the male role?

Advance publicity for the tour had stirred up considerable interest among those who either loved or feared the automobile, and a number of reporters were expected to cover the event. Photographer Nick Lazarnick would also travel with the tourists to provide a photographic record. Many newspaper and magazine accounts of the Glidden Tours still survive and much has been written about them, but this chapter focuses on Joan Cuneo's experiences for the most part.

Joan Cuneo had already spent nearly three years learning the quirks of steam propulsion, driving almost daily on city streets and country roads. She was quietly confident that she had the skills and the stamina needed to complete a lengthy endurance run. Yet, despite her wealth, social status and AAA membership, Cuneo must have debated whether entering the Glidden Tour was a wise decision.[3] Although change was stirring, it was still customary for women of her class to defer to their husbands and fathers. Joan Newton Cuneo was a determined and fearless young woman who had enjoyed unusual freedom growing up, but she was in no way a suffragist. Throughout her extraordinary career as the premier woman automobilist in the United States, she remained a conventional Victorian wife and mother in all other areas of her life, albeit one with nerves of steel and a lead foot. Deciding to take a chance, she filled out her application form and sent it along with the $50 entry fee to the AAA. Neither Charles J. Glidden nor the AAA ever expected that a woman would enter the tour and expect to do all the driving.

Piloting a primitive (by modern standards) auto without power steering with minimal two-wheel brakes on unpaved roads for hundreds of miles for two weeks was understood to require manly strength and stamina. For example, Lucy Glidden, who loved automobile touring, had accompanied her husband on many lengthy drives but always as a passenger.[4] There were, however, already a few women like Mrs. Hitchcock, who were experienced tourists and encouraged other women to take the wheel.

Because driving was still considered a male prerogative, the brand-new AAA rules issued for the 1905 tour said nothing about age or gender. Article 1 **Concerning Entrants** began: "It will be assumed that every contestant is acquainted with the rules of the contest, and by entering therein agrees to abide by said rules, agrees to accept the official records and authorizes the AAA to publish them in such a manner as it shall determine. Under Article 2, **Qualifications**, a contestant was required to have been a member of a recognized auto club for at least thirty days, and under Article 4, **Touring Conditions...,** that the car should be driven by the owner or a driver approved by the Glidden Committee, the owner being a passenger in his own car. However at the end of Article 1, the Glidden Committee somewhat ominously did reserve the right to alter and amend these rules ... *as they may deem expedient.*[5] Though the rules did not exclude women from driving a car in the Glidden Tour, this was a sin of omission.

While a handful of women and a few children rode along as passengers in 1905, only Joan Newton Cuneo had the nerve to send in an entry listing herself as the driver. When the AAA received her application, they rejected it immediately on the grounds that the Glidden was limited to male drivers. Joan Cuneo, determined to drive in the tour, was not so easily turned away. She pointed out that the regulations did not actually *forbid* women drivers, so there was no reason to exclude her, as she was already an AAA club member. After much debate, the AAA Contest Board finally agreed that although it was the intent of the rules to limit the competition to men, because they did not expressly forbid women they would let her participate. Gifted with an outwardly calm demeanor and reserved by nature, Joan Cuneo did not reveal her inner excitement when she learned that she could drive in the 1905 tour. Although her first attempt to enter a male-only automobile event was successful, it would be followed by a growing number of rejections in the next five years, as male opposition to female competitors increased. Female participation in automobile races, endurance runs and hill climbs was regarded as an interesting novelty in 1905, but by 1908 there was growing resistance to letting women take part in any of these potentially dangerous competitions.

Her application finally accepted, Joan Cuneo began her preparations. She was already familiar with the operation of the White steam engine and its drive train. It was fortunate that she had bought a strongly built vehicle, as this particular White would take quite a beating on the 1905 Glidden Tour.[6] In token compliance with the AAA rules, Andrew Cuneo was listed as the vehicle owner on the rosters of the three Glidden Tours Joan Cuneo entered, but she was listed as the driver. This was probably an attempt by the AAA to make her entry appear more conventional. The rules did state that the owner had to ride as a passenger if another was delegated to drive his car. Andrew Cuneo dutifully accompanied his wife on the three Glidden Tours she entered but never took the wheel. Having a female owner and driver was just too much for the harried officials of the AAA Contest Board, and they began to look for a way to exclude women from future sanctioned events.

It is surprising that the AAA took this attitude towards female drivers in a reliability tour such as the Glidden. It was not a race and took place on ordinary roads. It was no more dangerous than any other drive in the country, and Joan Cuneo was certainly not the first woman to drive in a reliability tour. Photos of an endurance run held in Jamaica, New York, in 1902 show several female participants. In June of 1905, just a few weeks before the start of the Glidden Tour, the Chicago Auto Club sponsored a similar run from Chicago, Illinois, to St. Paul, Minnesota. One of the participants was Miss Anna Andrews, who drove her own car in the event.[7] The Chicago tour was not AAA sanctioned and its organizers didn't seem to have any issues about not including women drivers. It did not receive much publicity, as it was a local competition, and seems to have been completed without any spectacular wrecks or newsworthy incidents. Thus Miss Andrews would not gain the public notoriety that came to Joan Newton Cuneo after her performance in the Glidden Tour.

The 1905 Glidden attracted a number of prominent auto manufacturers and business owners who were frequently mentioned in automobile-related news. They included Walter T. White driving a 15 hp White like Mrs. Cuneo's, Ransom E. Olds driving a 16 hp REO, Percy P. Pierce driving a Pierce Arrow, E. H. Cutler, president of Knox Motors, driving a Knox, and Albert L. Pope driving a Pope-Toledo. Ezra H. Fitch, partner in the famous Abercrombie and Fitch store in New York City, was also an entrant.[8] Although not yet a public figure, Joan Newton Cuneo came from a wealthy and respected Massachusetts family and was married to a well-known millionaire banker from New York City who would accompany her on the tour.

The first official Glidden Tour had some striking differences from Glidden's unofficial attempt in 1904. Charles Jasper Glidden wanted to set his tour apart from dozens of similar events that had been held by auto clubs and manufacturers since 1900. Late in 1904, he presented the AAA with the gigantic sterling silver trophy that would be awarded to the overall winner in 1905.[9] The *New York Times* wrote: "The Glidden trophy is one of the handsomest prizes ever offered for an automobile competition. Its chief feature is a sterling silver globe representing the earth. The globe is supported by two caryatides [*sic*] (female figures) standing back to back."[10] A small auto was placed on top of the globe to signify the triumph of the motorcar in circling the earth.[11] Although taken aback by the size of the silver creation (50 inches tall), the AAA reluctantly accepted it. Realizing its value, the club demanded that the winner post a $3,000 bond "for the privilege of having custody of the trophy for a year."[12]

Unfortunately, Glidden made a serious error in creating such an imposing and prestigious trophy. Although he thought the chance of winning it would attract wealthy, sporting car owners, which it did, it had an even more powerful attraction for the automobile manufacturers of the day. Believing that winning such a trophy would provide excellent publicity for their models after the tour ended, they placed ads detailing their vehicles' performance in newspapers and magazines. In later tours, the privately owned cars were outnumbered by finely tuned factory entries of multiple-car teams and auto-club teams, making it impossible for an individual to win the trophy. (In the 1908 tour, Joan Cuneo, by then nationally famous, would drive for the Chicago Auto Club team.)

One advantage of having the tour sanctioned by the AAA was the travel guide created for the tourists by their Touring Committee expressly for the event. The guide was a very basic example of the now famous TripTiks still issued by the AAA. All entrants received a bundle of tour information, including a map of the route, distance between cities, contest rules and even information regarding the Glidden Trophy deed of gift.[13] Contestants also were given information about hotels and garages available en route, and advance hotel reservations were made for them by the AAA.

On the great day, participating cars complete with drivers and passengers, assembled in New York City along with press cars and baggage trucks. They presented a colorful sight early on Tuesday morning, although most of the cars were painted black, green or red and had black upholstery. Their brass headlights and trim shone in the early morning sun. There were a mixture of expensive models like the Pierce Arrow that sold for $5,000 and Mrs. Cuneo's White, which cost more than a Rolls-Royce at the time, and runabouts like the sporty two-seat Maxwells that cost much less. Almost all were open cars, although some had tops that could be unfolded to provide minimum coverage from rain or sun. The windshields of most 1905 cars were minimal at best; both driver and passengers had to wear some kind of eye protection to keep out dust and insects. When it rained, the occupants either got soaked or swathed themselves in voluminous rubber raincoats. Both women and men wore canvas or linen dusters to keep their clothing relatively clean. Driving gloves were also essential, because they helped the driver grip the wheel. Driving at night was also difficult, although by 1905 most cars sported carbide lamps instead of the kerosene lanterns common in 1900. Another essential accessory for any road trip in 1905, rarely seen today, was at least one set of tire chains. A hundred years ago the roads were so appalling that there were chains for every possible condition: chains for mud, chains for sand and chains for more traction, to name a few.

The Gliddenites started their adventure early on July 11, 1905. They left at brief intervals from the intersection of Fifth Avenue and 58th Street in New York City. It was a hot and dusty morning and only a small crowd had come to watch the event. Oddly enough, this corner housed the headquarters of the Automobile Club of America (ACA), the chief rival of the AAA, although the race was sanctioned by the AAA. The cars all had large numerals painted either on their grills or on both sides, similar to those seen on race cars of the time. Joan Cuneo's number was 22. Numbering the cars was an unfortunate, though no doubt necessary, decision. It encouraged both spectators and participants to think that the Glidden Tour was actually a race.

The first day's drive, a 121-mile run from New York City through Larchmont, Mamaroneck, Port Chester, Greenwich and Stamford to Hartford, Connecticut, would have both positive and negative consequences for Joan Newton Cuneo. At the beginning of the day, she was merely one of a growing number of women who enjoyed automobile touring; at the end of it, she would be something of a celebrity, at least east of the Mississippi.[14]

The first car to leave was the 45 hp Pope-Toledo, one of the most powerful in the tour, entered by auto manufacturers Albert and Arthur Pope. The Pope-Toledo led the way into the company's home city of Hartford, the first night's stop, with a fast run. The first day was expected to be a pleasant drive through a number of sleepy suburban towns on the shore of Long Island Sound, and many residents came out on their porches to watch the parade of 33 cars go by.

Although the drive was an easy one for most of the tourists, two of them had problems that day, and one was Joan Cuneo. Even though her mishap was not the first of the tour, it was the most spectacular. Hugh Thomas was credited with the first accident when he skidded into a horse-drawn wagon with his 8 hp Maxwell runabout and bent the Maxwell's axle. Joan Cuneo's accident came a little later near Greenwich where the Boston Post road the tourists had taken was particularly narrow. It was constricted on the left by a telephone conduit currently under construction. A trolley track ran alongside the road, and the right side bordered a steep embankment.

The event that turned Joan Cuneo into a celebrity made the front page in dozens of newspapers. A representative from *Automobile* traveled with the tourists and wrote an extensive article about the 1905 tour. He reported in the July 20 issue that "Mrs. Cuneo encountered a team near a short bridge over a stream, and in an attempt to avoid it, ran the White's left wheels off the unprotected edge of the (bridge) planking. This caused the car to turn over on its side and drop about six feet down into the creek on its left side, throwing out all the occupants, breaking off the condenser, bending the rear axle and steering knuckle connecting rod, and breaking a spring."[15] He concluded that, fortunately, no one had been injured; the driver and passengers, her husband, Andrew Cuneo, and friends Louis Disbrow and his sister Gwen merely suffered bruises. The car was quickly righted and Mrs. Cuneo drove the car out of the stream to have the necessary repairs made so that they could continue on the tour. Annoyed rather than upset by the accident, Joan Cuneo calmly got back into the car after it had built up steam and drove it up the bank and back onto the road.

Both the *New York Evening Telegram* and the *Boston Globe* gave a strikingly different account of the accident. In articles titled "Woman Automobile Racer Escapes Death" and "Mrs. Cuneo's Car Goes into Ditch," they reported that Harlan W. Whipple (a former president of the AAA) of Andover, Massachusetts, had reached the bridge some distance ahead of Mrs. Cuneo. When workmen at the site told him that they were going to do some blasting, without looking back, Whipple reversed his Peerless, heading straight back towards Mrs. Cuneo on the narrow road. Valiantly trying to avoid Whipple by swerving onto the bridge, she caught the White Steamer's wheels on the edge of the bridge and flipped the car into, or next to, the stream, a drop of eight feet. These papers also reported that Mrs. Cuneo was the only one briefly trapped under the car and that she insisted in turning off the White's boiler fire before being helped up the bank.[16] This part of their account may well have been true; she soon gained a reputation for remaining calm in dangerous situations.

The narrative involving Whipple has been repeated in a number of automotive histories, most authors commenting favorably on her pluck except for one singularly mean-spirited, unsigned article in the *Automobile Quarterly*. Its author said disparagingly "it was also Mrs. Cuneo whose driving during the Tour helped give women drivers the sobriquet of derision. Mrs. Cuneo turned her car over in a creek while trying to avoid hitting another car from behind and later picked up a speeding ticket."[17] Mrs. Cuneo would indeed get a speeding ticket on the tour, as she and a number of other tourists were later caught in a speed trap. Although she accumulated many speeding tickets in the years that followed, she was not guilty this time.

Most of the photos of Joan Cuneo's wreck that accompanied the newspaper articles were taken from the same angle. They featured a dramatic close-up of the driver, passengers and onlookers watching workmen attempt to right the steamer. *The Automobile* printed a distance shot from the opposite side that showed a trolley pulled up at the scene. Their photo supported the magazine's account of the accident, although the Whipple story is so detailed it is hard to imagine someone made it all up. Mrs. Cuneo's accident was reported in newspapers throughout New England and beyond. Her mishap received extensive coverage mainly because she was a woman driver, even though no one was injured and only her car was damaged in the wreck. The *New York Tribune*, unable to locate a picture of the wreck for its front page, used one taken just before the start of the

The accident that made Joan famous — or infamous. Her brand-new 1905 White, which had landed on its side in the stream, is being righted by construction workers on the scene. On the bridge, Joan Cuneo in the long coat waits impatiently, her husband, Andrew, hatless, next to her. Disbrow is standing in left foreground supervising the workers (courtesy of Carl Ballenas, Richmond Hill historian).

tour on July 11, which showed Mrs. J. N. Cuneo at the wheel of her White in a lineup of other tourists driving White Steamers.[18]

Ironically, Harlan Whipple would be also be guilty of reckless driving. On July 14, as his car sped over a bump in the road near Sharon, Connecticut, his wife, who had accompanied him on the tour, was "hurled completely over the front of the car and fell heavily to the road."[19] The bump in question was probably the kind most motorists of the day dreaded. Referred to as a "thank you, ma'am," it caused an up-and-down movement. First the car went up over a bump, and then it plunged down into a dip. Drivers could hang on to the steering wheel as they traversed the bump, but unless the passenger was braced, he or she could easily leave the seat, or the vehicle, depending on the speed they were traveling. Mrs. Whipple was severely bruised, although no bones were broken, and she could not continue on the tour. This accident received only a brief mention in the *New York Times.* Charles J. Edwards also ran off a bridge over a small stream near Conway, New Hampshire, and his car was badly damaged. Edwards, his chauffeur, and his wife were thrown into the water and Mrs. Edwards was bruised.[20] Again, this accident merited only a brief paragraph in the *New York Times*. It is evident from the number of accidents reported in newspapers involving male drivers during the tour that, as a group, they were no more skilled than Joan Cuneo and, in the cases of Harlan Whipple and Charles Edwards, probably not as experienced. However, because she was a woman driver, everything Joan Cuneo did was news.

Forced to limp into Bridgeport for needed repairs, Mrs. Cuneo had the condenser re-attached, the damaged axle and spring replaced, and the steering rod straightened. Then the Cuneo party set out for Hartford, more than 50 miles away. As Joan Cuneo remarked in an interview at Mount Washington, "The fastest driving I ever did in my life was from Bridgeport to Hartford after that accident, with the wheels wabbling [*sic*]." Impressed with her pluck, reporters asked if she had been over the road before because of her skill in taking the turns. She answered, "No never, I have never driven as far as Boston and most of my driving has been done on Long Island."[21] ("Plucky" was an old-fashioned adjective first used in 1840 that would often be used to describe Mrs. Cuneo. It means "brave, courageous or fearless." However, it was only used to describe a woman's actions, and although seemingly complimentary, it had some negative connotations as well.)

The accident did nothing to dampen Joan Cuneo's enthusiasm for the tour. In the following days, many participants and spectators commented on her ability as a driver. "If nerve and skill in driving alone determined the final possession of the trophy ... Mrs. Cuneo certainly ought to get it. She is the only woman driver in the Tour and she handles her car like a veteran, and with more skill than many a strong man in the contest."[22] A few days later, the same reporter remarked: "It was a positive delight to note the way the little woman driver took the hills and ruts and especially the dangerously sharp turns at the foot of steep descents, and her dexterity won the admiration of all who saw the performance. Through it all, she was beaming with glee and clearly was enjoying the run hugely."[23] When Joan Cuneo was behind the wheel, she left the cares of daily life behind and concentrated on driving fast. Not all the tourists were in as much of a hurry as Mrs. Cuneo to reach the night's stop; several stopped for a quick dip in one of the small lakes that bordered their route to wash off some of the road dust they had accumulated during the day.

The automobile enthusiasts of Hartford, a thriving city with close ties to the automobile industry, had planned an elaborate banquet for the Gliddenites on their first night's stop. There has been some discussion about whether Joan Cuneo, the only female driver, was shunted off with the women passengers to another dining room to be entertained by the women of Hartford.[24] According to the *Automobile* account, when the tourists neared Hartford the passengers in every car were handed an invitation to a lavish dinner at the Alleyn House, then the premier hotel in Hartford, by a man stationed on the road.[25] However, this did not preclude a separate location for the women's group. John Bentley wrote in 1957 that "the ladies were entertained separately by a special committee of Hartford ladies in a private dining room ... and included besides Mrs. Cuneo ... Mrs. Whipple of Andover, Massachusetts, Mrs. Scarritt of East Orange, New Jersey, Mrs. Pierce of Buffalo, New York, Miss Desmond of Long Island, New York, Mrs. Olds of Lansing, Michigan, and Mrs. Owen, Mrs. Geary and Mrs. Lamson of New York City."[26] The ladies may well have appreciated having their own room, given the preponderance of alcoholic beverages and cigars and the elaborate menu prepared for the men, especially after a long day on the road. The ladies were also able to escape a series of speeches by auto club officials and Charles Glidden himself.

The remaining days of the first half of the tour went well for the Cuneo party, despite the damage to her White, although the water pump had needed repair on the grade up Mount Washington. Mrs. Cuneo managed to arrive fourth at their midpoint stop, Bretton Woods. Rolling up the long curved driveway of Mount Washington House at 1:30 in the afternoon, she had proved both her skill behind the wheel and her aptitude for fast driving, especially since her White had been damaged on the first day of the tour.[27] However, trouble was brewing for the Mrs. Cuneo, despite her growing reputation as a skilled motorist.

She was again interviewed by reporters at the inn, where it was reported she was "a woman of only about 5′4″ in height and weighing probably 130 pounds, and apparently not unusually strong, though the tan on her face and arms and her willowy figure show that she leads an outdoor life.... Asked how she managed to take the short turns on the last day's run so fast, Mrs. Cuneo inquired ingenuously, with a merry twinkle dancing in her eyes, What turns?"[28] The attention given to the personable lady driver must have pleased Walter T. White, the president of White Motors, who was also a contestant, especially when Joan Cuneo stated she would buy another White in 1906, since the current model had performed so well.[29] As it turned out, she did buy a more powerful 1906 White but would use it only for racing. Joan Cuneo must also have been impressed by the performance of the sporty little Maxwell runabouts, as she also bought one to race in 1906.

During her racing career, many reporters would describe Joan Cuneo. One constant was that they were amazed at how small she was. However, estimates of her height varied from 5′1″ to 5′4″ and her estimated weight ranged from 120 to 135 pounds. She was short, probably closer to 5′2″. Looking at photos taken over a ten-year period, one can see her weight, like that of many women, did tend to fluctuate.

At the Mount Washington hotel, one topic of discussion was their possible arrest for speeding on the return trip. As they had driven through Leicester, Massachusetts, on the way to Mount Washington, they had unknowingly passed through a speed trap set up by the Leicester police, although there had been no evidence of unusual police activity along their route. The common speed limit through town was 20 mph, but the wily coppers had set up their timing station at the base of a hill, as they knew the drivers would have to accelerate in order to get up the incline. Before they left Bretton Woods, the tourists learned that warrants had been sworn out for at least some of the participants. These would be served on the return trip, as they would be driving back the same way.[30] Joan Cuneo was one of the unlucky drivers who faced arrest for speeding. Rumors also began

55

to circulate that other "timing stations," better known today as speed traps, had been set up in other Massachusetts towns. Speed traps have been around since shortly after the first automobiles hit the road, with the dual purpose of controlling speeding and raising revenue for the community.

The sophisticated plan of the Leicester police was a stark contrast to the comic antics of the Dover constables who looked like Keystone Kops as they vainly tried to catch speeding tourists when they approached Dover. Forewarned by local motorists, the tourists drove slowly through the town, some hurling jibes against the police as they helplessly watched the slow-moving cars. News had traveled through the town about the police plan and spectators lined the streets at 6:30 A.M. They didn't want to miss the antics of a dozen or more uniformed, but inept, constables who were unable to nab a single tourist.[31] Certainly the Dover police carried their actions against the motorists a little too far, but the tourists did little to endear themselves to the police. By no means did all citizens, whether rural or urban, like or even accept automobiles in 1905. Many believed they were dangerous devil wagons, unnecessary, noisy machines that scared animals and people. Farmers especially blamed automobilists for the loss of poultry (free-ranging chickens), frightening their livestock, and causing their teams to bolt. Some retaliated by strewing nails, broken glass or pieces of barbed wire on the road; others delighted in giving hapless motorists wrong directions in an era before road signs were common. The tourists had to face a traffic court on their return to Leicester, a town that had proved to be hostile to motorists, so they began to plot their response.

Before the tourists had to stand before the judge, they enjoyed one of the high points of the tour: a four-day stay at the inn at Mount Washington. The inn was then almost brand-new; however, the imposing structure still welcomes guests as a member of the Omni chain. Here the tourists had an opportunity to relax and socialize in luxurious sur-roundings, although some of the more daring drivers decided to enter the "Climb to the Clouds." The year 1905 was the second year of a scheduled hill climb up the road to the summit of Mount Washington, noted for its dangerous curves and changeable and inclement weather. Glidden thought the hill climb would be another way the more daring tourists could prove the reliability of their autos. What he didn't realize was that Mrs. Cuneo would want to enter the event. The hill climb also drew a number of other amateurs and professional racers who weren't part of the tour. In all, over 60 cars assembled at the inn to await the climb. The more intrepid drivers, Joan Cuneo among them, were eager to participate in the upcoming Climb to the Clouds, since there might not be another chance in 1906. The mountaintop had just been purchased by a Boston lumber company that would soon be using the road to haul logs to the mill, preventing another contest.[32]

On July 16, the first cars attempted the climb, but although the weather was good at the bottom, it turned rainy and foggy as the cars sped up the mountain. Mrs. Cuneo, busy stripping her car of its tonneau for the attempt, announced that she would try the climb the next day.[33] It is not entirely clear what the reporter meant by the White's tonneau. In 1905, a tonneau was a tight cover that fit over the rear seats to make the back

Mrs. Cuneo, looking very young, sits in her partially stripped-down 1905 White, getting ready for the Climb to the Clouds during the 1905 Glidden Tour. Her car is parked in front of the inn at Mount Washington. Note the AAA logo on the hood (courtesy of Jack Deo, Superior View Photos).

of the car more aerodynamic. It seems more likely that Joan Cuneo and Louis Disbrow were actually removing the rear seats of the White, which would be quite time consuming.

It was probably a mistake on Joan's part not to attempt the climb on the first day, as it gave the officials and some of the male drivers a chance to close ranks against female participation. Citing the dangers of the drive, the AAA officials present refused to allow her to attempt the climb on the seventeenth. Joan Cuneo was furious. This may actually have been the first time in her life that she was unable to attempt something she really wanted to do. She was still fuming a few days later when she was again interviewed by a *New York Times* reporter. Not using the gentle, feminine tone of her earlier interviews, without thinking she blurted out her true feelings, saying angrily, "I have operated a car five years [*sic*] and know my car far better than a lot of men do. If some of the cars went up the course in the time accredited them, I can put my car up in faster time. I believe I could back it, run it sideways, or any old way, and land there in better time than some of the men drivers did." Then reverting to her normal reserved public persona, she concluded mildly, "I can see why the officials bar women from the climb. It is very dangerous and most women are timid ... but [here she fired her parting shot] certainly I have shown them in this Tour that I am far from timid and know how to handle my car."[34] She was also exasperated because she had just spent two days stripping her car for the hill climb and, as a reporter commented, "she was much hurt at being disbarred on account of her sex."[35]

I have no proof that Joan Cuneo ever made the Mount Washington hill climb, but given her character, it is very likely she did. The road is still there and just as dangerous. The hill climb is still held every year in weather that is unreliable and changeable. It is also interesting that *The Automobile* mentioned nothing of Mrs. Cuneo being forbidden to participate in The Climb to the Clouds despite its favorable reports of her driving. For the *New York Times*, however, Joan Newton Cuneo's actions were now major news and the story was featured prominently in the paper.[36]

After their pleasant sojourn at Bretton Woods, the tourists started back to New York on the morning of July 19, knowing that some of their number would have to face a judge when they got to the district court at Worcester, Massachusetts. Upon their arrival that afternoon, the six who had been singled out had to post a bond to guarantee their appearance in court at the Worcester State House the next morning. The list of "convicts" included Carl Page, W. C. Temple, E. H. Fitch, R. E. Olds, R. L. Morrell and *Mrs. J. N. Cuneo.*

As a placatory gesture, the Worcester Automobile Club presented the tourists with tickets to a play at the Franklin Square Theater that evening. Jasper Glidden used this opportunity to speak to the audience, presenting the tourists' point of view to the crowd. Glidden maintained that the people arrested for speeding were law-abiding citizens, promoting automobile touring as safe and healthy outdoor recreation for both men and women. He believed that they should be treated as valued guests, not drawn into a police trap and branded as criminals.[37]

The culprits were sworn in at the District Court at nine o'clock the next morning and were accompanied by several dozen additional tourists who provided moral support. Although they had hired a local lawyer to plead their case, the verdict was never in doubt. The judge's comments from the bench were quite revealing:

> "I don't recognize any difference between these people and anybody else. They are not my guests..." Judge Utley said... "They come here, knowing the law and they must obey it. They come through here flaunting their wealth and defying the honest citizen of the town that makes the complaint.... If they want to come to Massachusetts they must behave themselves and obey the law. Unless they do the legislature will restore the jail sentence for speeding on the streets, which it unwisely, in my opinion, recently removed. Some of these people here ought to be in jail, I think; Fifteen dollars each!"[38]

The judge's verdict simply underscored the beliefs of many at the time that automobiles were the playthings of wealthy owners who used their fancy cars to flaunt their wealth. Unfortunately, some automobilists did just that, thinking nothing of scaring chickens or livestock, picnicking on private property or trespassing to pick a farmer's fruit in season. After the tour had concluded, the *Manchester* (NH) *Union*, a well-respected New England newspaper, was harshly critical of its impact. According to the *Union*, "The lives and property of perfectly harmless people have been seriously menaced; the laws willfully disregarded; and for no earthly reason rather than to afford amusement to a lot of strangers." The editorial went on to complain that most automobile owners were irresponsible, causing accidents and property damage without concern for reimbursement, and drove much too fast. However, it concluded that automobiles could be a positive benefit to the state if used reasonably, not driven by "a lot of crazy mountebanks."[39]

The convicts meekly paid their fines, as they were anxious to get started on the day's drive, The rest of the tourists prepared a rousing welcome for them when they reached the procession of cars lined up before the Bay State hotel. They had draped their auto lamps with black crepe paper, and all honked their auto horns and blew paper noisemakers as the six appeared. The Gliddenites had also hired a band to serenade their departure with funereal tunes. The band dutifully marched through Worcester with the tourist cars following three abreast at a walking pace, stopping briefly to serenade the shop where Constable Quinn, who had set the trap, worked. Although Quinn didn't appear, the band played "Auld Lang Syne," as the tourists and passengers sang along. Hundreds of townspeople witnessed the antics of the tourists, and although some laughed, it is not hard to imagine that many were outraged by the mocking actions of these wealthy folks in their expensive cars. As the tourists quitted Worcester, they dismissed the band and ripped the crepe from their autos, scattering it contemptuously on the road as a souvenir.[40]

Even Joan Cuneo joked about feathers in the grill when she was interviewed after the 1907 Glidden Tour. "Well, maybe now and then we did run over a few chickens," she smilingly admitted when reminded of telegraphed stories of angry farmers, "but I don't think they should mind losing a few fowls when we were making such good records."[41] Needless to say, the Glidden Tour would take a different route in 1906. Unfortunately, the actions of the Gliddenites had done nothing to endear themselves to the local population or improve the Worcester citizens' regard of auto owners in general. The *New York Times* agreed with the *Hartford Courant* as to what might be an appropriate punishment for heedless motorists: "No one wants to see severe punishment inflicted on motorists who break the law unintentionally; half-a-dozen jail sentences for owners who break the law with intention and insolence would have an immediate and more wholesome effect.... The sooner the better!"[42]

As the tour wound to a close, Mrs. Cuneo's White literally ran out of steam. Her much-abused car developed serious mechanical problems on the leg from Worcester to Lenox, Massachusetts. Joan and even Andrew Cuneo worked on the car alongside Louis Disbrow for six hours before they could get it running. Finally, they were forced to replace second gear with reverse gear in order to get it to go forward, possible in 1905 but not today. Nursing along the barely drivable White, the grimy and dust-covered party finally reached the Aspinwall Hotel in Lenox at two o'clock Saturday morning.[43] Although they did reach Lenox, the White was in no condition to take part in the triumphal parade scheduled to finish at their starting point at the Plaza circle in front of the Hotel Savoy. Joan Cuneo's White was one of only two cars that didn't complete the tour due to mechanical failure, although two others didn't finish for other reasons.[44]

The chairman of the Touring Committee, Augustus Post, rode in the first car of the triumphal parade as it headed towards New York City along with Charles J. Glidden, who had donated the trophy.[45] Post was one of the first New Yorkers to own an auto as well as the first to open an automobile garage.[46] However, before they reached their destination the occupants of the 28 cars that completed the tour had to deal with one last potentially dangerous incident. Someone had left a scarecrow resembling a body in the road. Since the scarecrow lay just beyond a sharp bend in the road, the small group of cars in the lead came to a screeching stop when they saw it, their hearts pounding, until they realized it was an effigy.[47] Although one of the drivers threw the scarecrow contemptuously into a ditch, this was not just a harmless prank. It showed that many harbored bad feelings towards the tourists.

At the awards ceremony, Percy P. Pierce, who had entered a 28–32 hp Pierce-Arrow, received the Glidden Trophy.[48] Twenty-two tourists received first-class certificates of completion and Joan Newton Cuneo along with C. J. Edwards, C. W. Kelsey and G. H. Tyrrell received second-class certificates, as they didn't complete the tour. Despite negative criticism in the New England newspapers, the tourists themselves believed the tour had been extremely successful and most looked forward to the 1906 competition. Several months later, the automotive press still spoke favorably about auto-touring events. The consensus was that while the Glidden would be the most important tour in the United States, a number of others would likely be held both in the States and abroad. Some might even offer opportunities for female participation.[49]

Although she couldn't take part in the triumphant procession into New York City, Joan Cuneo's participation in the tour had made her a celebrity overnight, although the Cuneos didn't realize it yet. Glad to be home with her children, Mrs. Cuneo wondered what else she might accomplish with her automobile; she would soon find out. One thing was sure: she was determined to enter the next Glidden Tour and complete it with a perfect score.

4

"A case of love at first sight"

Joan Cuneo had barely recovered from her strenuous drive on the Glidden Tour when she heard that another woman driver had made the news. On August 26, 1905, Mrs. Clarence C. Fitler won two races against male amateur drivers at Cape May, New Jersey, and made headlines in the *New York Times* for her efforts. Driving a 28 hp Packard, she won two two-mile races for gasoline engine touring cars driven by owners from a rolling start, at the very respectable times of 1:15⅗ and 1:13. Mrs. Fitler, a noted horse-woman who had won many equestrian events, set two new women's records as well.

Auto enthusiasts had set up a half-mile oval track on the beach called Cape May Courthouse that opened in September 1905. The *Times* reported that she made her runs on the beach, although it is unclear whether she drove on the half-mile track or on a straightaway. Her times, if correctly reported, would have been quite good for a half-mile beach oval.[1] Despite the acclaim she received for her exploits at Cape May, this was Mrs. Fitler's only recorded attempt at auto racing. On the twenty-sixth, however, she was hailed by a large crowd on the boardwalk and the more knowledgeable fans commented favorably on her driving.[2] It is surprising that Mrs. Fitler never raced her auto again, as she was so proud of her victories that afterwards she drove her car along Beach Avenue and shouted, "Hurrah!" at the cheering spectators who lined the road.[3]

A month after her widely publicized exploits, Mrs. Cuneo received a challenge through the area newspapers "to," as she said, " show what I could do handling a car at speed on the beach," at Atlantic City, New Jersey, on Labor Day weekend.[4] Mrs. Fitler's exploits at Cape May were enough to make Joan accept the challenge. Mrs. Cuneo, who had thoroughly enjoyed her experiences on the Glidden Tour, immediately committed to a different kind of automobile event. Because the races were only a few days away, she reported: "My car was in the shop being overhauled and painted, but out she came and was shipped by express (train) to Atlantic City."[5] In 1905, the interurban roads were generally so bad that drivers nearly always shipped their cars by train or boat to the location of the next race. Mrs. Fitler was also expected to race in Atlantic City.

Mrs. Fitler, described as a society woman from Riverton, New Jersey, was believed to have issued a challenge to Joan Newton Cuneo. A Hawaii newspaper commented: "...just when men who drive racing automobiles have reached the conclusion that this sport is too dangerous to be followed continuously, a woman comes forward with a challenge to meet another woman."[6] According to the *Oahu* (HA) *Evening Bulletin*, Mrs. Fitler was "anxious to meet the reckless Mrs. Cuneo who burned up the roads during the

61

White Mountain Tour, and who wanted to take part in the "Climb to the Clouds" contest up the White Mountains."[7] Despite the challenge she issued to the "reckless Mrs. Cuneo," Mrs. Fitler did not show up at Atlantic City ready to race on Labor Day. Although she would compete in equestrian events for many years afterwards, Fitler retired from auto racing after proving her skill and nerve behind the wheel at Cape May. The *Bulletin* reported that a Mrs. Rogers who had also driven in the Cape May races might enter the Atlantic Beach competition, but she did not appear, either.

The publicity department for the Atlantic City hotels, already popular with vacationers, had heavily promoted a series of automobile events to attract more people to the resort. The speed trials and races were to be held on the beach over the Labor Day weekend in 1905. The promoters built a one-mile oval track right on the beach, which opened on September 3, 1905, and would hold spring and fall races for two years. They also recruited Henry Ford to made a speed run on the beach, probably driving his "red devil" #999 that had set a speed record the previous year. Walter Christie, whose massive front-wheel-drive "freak," the Christie Blue Flyer, had not run well in the Vanderbilt Cup but was now "much improved," also committed to the event.[8] In 1905, "freak" was a term commonly used to describe any car that had something unusual about its construction or did not resemble a normal automobile of the time.

Unfortunately, on Labor Day weekend Mother Nature was not cooperative. Although an estimated forty thousand people came to see the races, a huge crowd for the day, a heavy downpour caused the cancellation of most of the contests. The most publicized competitors, Henry Ford and Walter Christie, refused to run the scheduled one-mile speed trials in their powerful race cars, objecting to the uncontrolled crowds and the poor weather. The harried Atlantic City officials, new to the organization of racing competitions of any kind, were completely flustered by this turn of events. They never expected that their star attractions would be unwilling to perform. As a result, according to the *New York Times*, as the day went on "the officials lost track of the entrants and the conditions, and even forgot to take the times of the cars which did cover the course."[9]

After accepting the challenge to race and hurrying to Atlantic City from her home at Richmond Hill, Mrs. Cuneo was dismayed at the poor condition of the track when she arrived at the beach. However, it was not in her nature to refuse to compete because of bad weather. The *Times* later reported that "Mrs. Cuneo had participated in one of the races which it [the Atlantic City race organizers] attempted to run and got third place."[10] Because women racers were a novelty, she did get a brief mention in the paper after this first attempt. However, Joan Cuneo was not yet a star attraction at the racetrack, although she had gained regional fame because of her exploits on the 1905 Glidden Tour. At Atlantic City she had participated in an unimportant race on the beach with other local (male) amateurs but did not win. In a later account of her first race, Joan Cuneo wrote that "in competing with four men driving gasoline cars I came in second in the one mile race, being timed one minute 18.25 seconds. I was proud of my first record but not satisfied. I knew if I had a faster car I could do better, so I ordered a 1906 model (18 hp White) ... before the body was put on, being invited to give an exhibition at the Dutchess County Fair at Poughkeepsie, September 29, 1905. I drove my new chassis up there and had my first experience at track racing."[11] She had been pleased by what she had accomplished at Atlantic City and was ready to race again at the end of the month, confident she would set an even faster time with a new car. If Joan Cuneo's memory was correct, the widely duplicated photo of her behind the wheel of a stripped-down White was not the 15 hp 1905 model touring car she had just driven on the Glidden Tour but a brand-new 18 hp 1906 model built specially for racing, minus fenders, headlights and rear seat. When photos of the two cars are compared, it is obvious that the White she raced at Poughkeepsie was a longer, more powerful car.

The Dutchess County Fair auto races were held at the Driving Club in Poughkeepsie, New York. There Joan met Barney Oldfield for the first time. In 1905, Oldfield was the most famous race car driver in America. He was there both to attempt a new speed record and to compete in an AAA-sanctioned race. In 1905 the Poughkeepsie track was a stop on the AAA-sponsored racing circuit, and Oldfield would win the AAA championship later that year. After he met Joan and rode as a passenger in her car, Barney Oldfield took an interest in her career in racing. He learned to respect her as a driver, although she gave him quite a scare the first time they met. She later said with a smile, "I once scared Barney Oldfield into yelling 'Slow down!' when I drove him around the wet track at Poughkeepsie."[12]

In 1905 there were no racetracks specifically constructed for automobile racing, except for a few temporarily marked off on the East Coast beaches, although there was already much discussion about building some in a number of locations. Automobile owners who wanted to show off the speed and agility of their new vehicles, much as they might have done with a fast horse, had to make do with existing facilities. They often raced each other informally on city streets wherever the quality of the roads permitted. A humorous example of an impromptu races was recorded in the *Evening World*. New Yorkers strolling down Broadway were treated to an exciting but spontaneous automobile race in March 1906. Spectators scrambled to get out of the way as two rival chauffeurs raced each other up the avenue from 42nd Street to 55th Street, where the slower of the two was finally nabbed by a bicycle patrolman. Charged with exceeding the speed limit, the losing driver gave a false name, pleading that his mistress was waiting for him to drive her to the opera. However, he was later bailed out of jail by his real boss, a wine agent.[13]

Tracks built for horse racing were another popular location for automobile races from 1900 through the 1950s. After 1850, hundreds of fairgrounds were built across the country and all of them included some kind of dirt track. In the twentieth century, fairground tracks provided a venue for both horse and auto racing. Most fairs held several days of horse racing, followed by a day or two of auto racing and time trials. The auto races were usually held on the last day of the fair because the heavy cars did considerable damage to the dirt surface during a full day of racing.

63

The Hudson River Driving Park was a one-mile dirt oval track that had hosted horse races for many years. On September 30, 1905, it was the setting for a series of "thrilling auto races," as well as a sensational "accident" involving Barney Oldfield that both thrilled and frightened the crowd of ten thousand. Unbeknown to the spectators, Oldfield, a consummate showman, as well as a highly skilled driver, staged a spectacular crash for the benefit of the Vitagraph moving picture company. Oldfield drove his Peerless Green Dragon at speed through a fence and was duly carted off in an ambulance dripping with blood. The spectators soon found that neither Oldfield nor the Green Dragon was injured, as the fence was actually made of cardboard and the blood was black ink. When the fans learned that the Oldfield had crashed to create a film, a rumor spread through the stands that he was going to quit racing to make his fortune in vaudeville. This was not the case.[14] While he would often appear in vaudeville theaters with his current racecar, Oldfield made (and spent) a large fortune during his long career setting speed records at fairgrounds throughout the country and competing in sanctioned and unsanctioned races.

Spectacle has always been a part of auto racing. To encourage attendance, today's race fans are treated to flyovers and rock and country music concerts along with a host of automobile-related exhibits. In 1905, the spectacle involved watching a famous driver like Oldfield set a new "world" speed record. These events, really no more than glorified time trials, drew record crowds to their local tracks. At a time when most people had never ridden faster than 10 to 15 mph, the sight of a speeding car hurtling around a track at 60 miles an hour was breathtaking. As the *Poughkeepsie Unity Eagle* reported,

> The sight of the autos making the circuit at less than a mile a minute blowing out fire and smoke and spitting and chugging like a demon was a weird one. The drivers' eyes and most of their faces were covered with goggles and they looked every bit like the genuine boogey man. Before the start when the machines were on the tape waiting for a pistol shot, they sputtered and cracked until they sounded like a battery of rapid fire guns. At the pistol shot, they got away with a swirl and kick while in their wake came a cloud of dust that swept across the track and covered the spectators on the fences.[15]

The *Eagle* correspondent left behind an excellent description of an early auto race for today's readers. Surprisingly, it is in many ways not much different from what fans experience when they attend a modern-day dirt track race.

In 1905, spectators were drawn to watch a sport they considered both thrilling and dangerous. The thought that a petite, gently reared lady actually wanted to participate in this obviously masculine and risky sport was both shocking and thrilling to the crowd. However, Mrs. Cuneo didn't seem the least bothered by either the danger, the noise or the dirt. At Poughkeepsie, Joan Cuneo had her first experience of dirt track racing and found that she loved it. She had already driven on the beach at Ormond and Atlantic City, but not on a track. As she later said, "I had my first experience at track racing. It was a case of love at first sight and my love for track driving increased each time I drove around one."[16] Evidently the near miss on the track at Poughkeepsie, which might have ended her career as a racer before it started, didn't faze her at all.

On the morning of the race day, the competitors spent some time trying out the track, as a number of auto enthusiasts, or speed bugs, as they were called, lined the rail to watch. The infield had been designated as the pit area, so the drivers had to enter the track from the left heading into the inside lane. The Italian champion, Emanuel Cedrino, was making a mile run at speed, while Mrs. Cuneo was also circling the track in a practice run with Barney Oldfield as her passenger.[17] Just as she began to ease over to the left to drive onto the infield, the horse-drawn water wagon, used to keep down the dust between events, pulled up behind her. The bulky wagon effectively blocked Mrs. Cuneo's view of Cedrino in his Fiat rapidly approaching from behind on her left, with wide-open throttle. Neither Barney Oldfield nor Joan Cuneo noticed the speeding Fiat at first, and according to the *Unity Eagle*, the spectators held their breath as a collision seemed imminent. "Just in time, Mrs. Cuneo's attention was called to her danger and with a quick twist of the steering wheel, she threw her car parallel to Cedrino's course and the Fiat flashed by with the driver's face white as a sheet."[18] Joan Cuneo showed that she could make a quick decision under pressure and provided us with yet another example of her famous luck. She would be amazingly lucky throughout her life, surviving many narrow escapes without serious injury.

Undeterred by her narrow escape, Mrs. Cuneo made a three-mile exhibition run

Joan Cuneo at the wheel, ready to set a speed record at a fairground track. Disbrow, who has his hand on the seat edge, has just climbed into the riding mechanic's spot, prior to the run. A large crowd with several women close to the rail eagerly await the start (courtesy of Jack Deo, Superior View Photos).

later that day. According to the *Eagle*, "She made a good flying start after circling the track once with a man [undoubtedly Louis Disbrow, her riding mechanic] who aided in keeping the balance of the machine on the curves."[19] Mrs. Cuneo was very disappointed with her lap times for the three miles; none was as good as the 1:18.25 she had made in Atlantic City. It is possible, with all the problems the officials had at Atlantic City, that her time had been recorded incorrectly. The best time she registered at Poughkeepsie only was 1:22.5. However, this time Joan Cuneo's performance at Poughkeepsie was mentioned right after that of Oldfield and Cedrino in a *New York Times* account of the event.

Mrs. Cuneo also entered a five-mile race at Poughkeepsie. In 1905, racers were usually given a handicap if their cars were slower or they were amateurs competing against professional drivers. Such was the case in Joan Cuneo's Poughkeepsie event, a five-mile handicap race, featuring a mix of professional and amateur drivers. Cedrino in his Fiat started at scratch; Dan Wurgis (also a professional) and his Reo got a five-second handicap, Mrs. Cuneo's handicap was two minutes, and Charles Fleming driving a Maxwell got a three-minute head start. Fleming, driving his sporty Maxwell, promptly won the race in a slow time of 7:15⅖. His three-minute head start was just too much for the faster Fiat and Reo to overcome. Joan Cuneo did not finish the five-mile race, as she had car trouble, "something to do with the oiling system."[20] "As she wryly commented, 'on our drive home, the cause of the trouble was found and remedied and we were arrested for speeding.'"[21] The race promoters at Poughkeepsie awarded her a gold medal for her efforts. This was her first award for driving at speed.[22]

Joan Cuneo wrote in a 1910 article that she had won a three-mile race on the Point Breeze track at Philadelphia November 1, 1905, beating three others (men) and winning a silver cup with a time of four minutes, eight seconds. Records indicate that she did win a race at Point Breeze against only one other competitor a few days later.[23] Her memory regarding her past racing exploits was usually excellent, but this time she got both the date of the race and how she placed wrong.

In November 1905, the New York Oldsmobile owners gathered at the Empire City horse race track in Yonkers, to celebrate the fifth anniversary of the Oldsmobile make's arrival in the city. Celebrating such an event seems strange today, but it also provides an insight into just how quickly auto owners bonded with their cars. The owners of nearly 75 Oldsmobiles, mostly two-seat runabouts, a dozen or more driven by women, gathered in the track clubhouse for lunch. Afterwards, the organizers scheduled several informal races for the members. The special attraction of the day was Mrs. Joan Newton Cuneo of Richmond Hill, Long Island. She attempted to set a new woman's record or, rather, better her own (said to be of the world) of 1:22 set at Poughkeepsie on the one-mile dirt horse track.[24] Evidently, the 1:18.25 mile time she made at Atlantic City had been discounted. Mrs. Cuneo made two runs on the Empire track. After the first run was timed at 1:20⅗ the plucky woman thought she could do better, and her second attempt was timed at 1:15.[25] The female automobilists in attendance, including several women doctors, were thrilled at her performance.

After taking the winter off from competition, Mrs. Cuneo went car shopping in March 1906. *The Automobile* soon reported that she had purchased a Maxwell Speedster that she would drive for her own enjoyment and in beach and track races. It also affirmed that she would enter this car in the 1906 Glidden Tour.[26] Joan Cuneo then continued her fledgling racing career with a return to Atlantic City in March 1906. Again the Atlantic City track promised a series of races over three days that would attract " many of the best known drivers of famous racing cars." Again the weather was unpleasant; the spectators endured a blustery day with a cold wind described as "raw and biting, blowing down Ventnor Beach."[27] This time Mrs. Cuneo raced against another female, Mrs. H. Ernest Rogers of Brookline, Massachusetts, both driving similar 10 hp Maxwells. As the *New York Daily Tribune* announced, "Beach racing is becoming a fad among women drivers, and two took part in today's races."[28] The ladies competed in the first event of the day on a track that was described as hard and fast. Mrs. Cuneo won easily, driving the mile in 1:25⅔, while her feminine rival finished in 1:31. Both women were trailed by another Maxwell, driven by an anonymous man. Joan. Cuneo than drove her Maxwell in another event for middle-weight gasoline-powered cars. She came in second behind a much more powerful Reo Bird but still set a new women's record of 1:23⅗ in this event.[29] She also drove her White on the beach in a mile exhibition, making a fast time of 1 minute, 15 seconds.[30] Despite the daring exploits of Mrs. Cuneo and Mrs. Rogers at Atlantic Beach,, the newspapers focused on the heroics of male professional drivers or owner/drivers like Walter Christie. These men drove specially built cars featuring much more powerful engines ranging from 50 to 110 hp rather than the "stock cars" that were driven by the two women.

Another well-publicized feature of the Atlantic City races was something of a novelty at this time, "the selling race." The selling race resulted from the way automobile dealers promoted popular models that had been raced by their owners or professional drivers in a stock car event. The slogan "Win on Sunday, sell on Monday" has long been an automobile dealer's mantra. if the prospective buyer wanted a fast car, a sales agent often told the customer that the model on the showroom floor was just as fast as the one they had watched win a race. However, if a spectator tried to purchase the winning "stock car" at the track they were told if they came to the dealership the next day they would get one "just as good." Often this was a flat-out lie. In the selling race at Atlantic City, however, if a dealer entered a stock car in a race and it won, they had to sell it, if someone wanted to buy it. The agents could charge only the dealer's price, or slightly more, if several people were interested. The promoters hoped that this ingenious plan would force the entrants in selling races to race their cars as they came off the dealer's floor, without any hidden improvements to the engine.[31] The selling race was a feature at a number of race meetings and hill climbs for a few years. Eventually, it became less practical. Gradually most amateurs dropped out of racing and the cars driven by professional racers were built specially for racing.[32]

In early May, the New York newspapers began to promote the Labor Day races at

Atlantic City. They also mentioned a repeat of the match race between Mrs. Joan Newton Cuneo of Long Island and Mrs. H. Ernest Rogers of Brookline, Massachusetts. The women would drive identical Maxwell runabouts on Memorial Day, May 30, 1906, as part of the annual meet of the Bay State Automobile Association at the Reedville track.[33] The match race was not held, nor would Mrs. Cuneo or Mrs. Rogers compete again at Atlantic City.[34]

It was reported that Mrs. Cuneo planned to race her 18 HP White Steamer as well as the 10 HP Maxwell runabout she had just bought in the summer of 1906. Cuneo had admired the durability of the Maxwells entered in the 1905 Glidden Tour and planned to drive one in the 1906 event. C. W. (Cadwallader Washburn) Kelsey, the youthful sales manager of the Maxwell-Briscoe Company, was impressed by Mrs. Cuneo's performance in the 1905 Glidden Tour, which he had also entered. He financed the entry of her new Maxwell at Atlantic City in March, and she rewarded him by winning an event in the Maxwell on the beach course[35]

Joan Cuneo would not race from the end of April 1906 until she, her husband and her mechanic, Louis Disbrow, traveled to the Rockland County fair in September 1906. It was unlike Mrs. Cuneo not to honor her commitments; however, that summer her husband had business engagements in Europe. Andrew Cuneo traveled to Italy on a regular basis to oversee his businesses. Joan traveled with him in the summer of 1906, making it impossible for her to participate in either the 1906 Glidden Tour or the Labor Day races.[36] No doubt, the Cuneos took time out to look at the latest-model automobiles on the Continent.

Back from Europe in late September 1906, the Cuneos traveled to Orangeburg, New York in her stripped-down White Steamer from their home in Richmond Hill. As she said later," it was unusual to see a car stripped down for racing, driven by a woman on the bad roads of the day." The lack of body and fender guards caused the passengers to get splattered with a liberal coating of mud before they had traveled very far. The Cuneo party had to cross on a ferry from Tarrytown to Nyack, and according to Joan Cuneo "the people at Nyack seemed unusually interested and very much excited at our appearance as we stopped for some gasolene [sic]. We learned afterward that the post-office at Nyack had been robbed the night before and the newspapers contained the information that 'a peculiar looking automobile' with a woman driving it, had passed through the town the next day!"[37] However, they were not arrested and got to the fair without mishap. There Joan Cuneo drove a mile exhibition on the half-mile fairground track, setting a record for that track in 1 minute, 31 seconds, and received a gold and diamond medal for her efforts.[38]

When she wasn't attempting speed records or participating in races at country fairs, Mrs. Cuneo competed in informal automobile contests that were held on the grounds of (horseback) riding clubs. This was not surprising, since Joan was an accomplished horsewoman. Although many well-to-do people like the Cuneos were making the transition from horses and drawn-vehicles to automobiles, they still enjoyed equestrian sports. On

September 9, 1905, shortly after the first Atlantic City races, the Southampton, Long Island, Horse Association held one of these events. Instead of the usual equestrian events, the club scheduled an informal automobile competition called a gymkhana.

The gymkhana, a series of informal competitions on horseback, originated in India during the days of the British Raj, migrating to Britain and later to the United State. Entry in its novelty and obstacle events was often limited to children and teens of both sexes. A gymkhana using automobiles instead of horses was still a novelty in 1905 and drew a large crowd of socialites from nearby resort cottages, as well as ordinary folks on vacation. All cheered the contestants on enthusiastically. The events were a combination of race/time trials for men only and novelty/obstacle events in which women also participated. At Southampton, although autos replaced ponies, the obstacle races were similar, if not the same. Women did participate in these events, but the article does not clarify whether the women drove the autos or were passengers in vehicles driven by male friends. However, a Miss Havemeyer got the silver cup for doing the best job driving between a set of obstacles against two other young ladies, "which occasioned a lot of merriment."[39]

Joan Cuneo drove in gymkhanas just for fun, because she didn't list them among her accomplishments as an automobilist. In October 1906, through her quick reaction, she again narrowly averted a serious accident at Danbury, Connecticut. Joan was driving in a gymkhana race at the Danbury Fair with two women passengers when the gasoline tank of the big automobile she was driving caught on fire.[40] Her two passengers, Miss Maude Tweedy and Miss Flora Shuldice, local residents, "threw themselves over the back of the car and escaped uninjured."[41] Joan Cuneo, despite the flames that scorched her head and face, remained aboard until she was able to shut off the gasoline flow and the engine. The large crowd cheered her plucky, action but the auto was almost destroyed. She suffered painful burns on her hands and face and scorched her hair but was not seriously injured.[42] From the description of her actions, she may have been driving a steam car, which used gasoline to generate steam for the engine. It may even have been her own car, the 1905 White touring car that had a rear entry, that had been almost destroyed in the fire. It almost certainly was not her gasoline-powered Maxwell, which was a small runabout and could not have been described as a big automobile.

Mrs. Cuneo again took the winter of 1906–07 off from racing. Her name did not appear in the automobile pages of the New York papers after the story of her heroic actions during the gymkhana at Danbury until May. This was not surprising, since there was little racing in the Northeast during the cold weather. However, on Memorial Day weekend in 1907 she again made headlines in the *Washington* (D.C.) *Herald.* On May 30, the *Herald* reported that Mrs. Cuneo had arrived in the city to take part in the one-hundred-mile race that would be held later that day at the Bennings Track outside the city.[43] The Bennings Track was a one-mile dirt oval originally built for horse racing, which first opened in 1890. In 1908 horse racing was banned in the D.C. area, and the track was used intermittently for automobile and motorcycle racing until 1917.[44]

On May 28, the Cuneos had checked into the Arlington Hotel, which was, at that time, the most luxurious hostelry in Washington, D.C., as Joan planned to enter the one-hundred-mile feature race.[45] In early 1907, she had switched from competing in her well-used White steam car to a brand-new Rainier touring model. Although not noted for its high speed, the Rainier was reputed to be a sturdy, durable and good-handling car. Mrs. Cuneo, and her mechanic, Louis Disbrow, planned to tune up the Rainer, which had been shipped to D.C. on the 29th, as she took some practice laps on the track.

The *Washington Post* provided its avid readers with some amazing and likely untrue stories about the famous lady racer who had come to Washington, D.C., in an article published on May 28. According to the *Post,* she "had covered a mile straightaway on Ormond Beach in 43 seconds ... had toured abroad for the past three years, covering some impossible roads in Norway and Sweden ... and while in England in 1906, had won the mile championship for women drivers from Miss Dorothy Revell [*sic*], the niece of Napier, the famous auto builder. [The *Post* undoubtedly meant Dorothy Levitt, the most famous British female racer at the time.]"[46] While not all were necessarily untrue, the accomplishments attributed to Mrs. Cuneo by the *Post* were highly unlikely yet difficult to prove or disprove. It is obvious that by 1907 the press was already well on the way to developing a mythic history for Joan Cuneo.

In a lengthy article, another Washington newspaper, the *Herald,* discussed the track conditions, which were supposed to be good, as well as the male drivers who had entered the race. It concluded with a lengthy interview of Joan Cuneo. She was interviewed many times by reporters during her racing career. These interviews, along with her own articles on automobiles and racing, provide valuable insights regarding her career as an automobilist. However, sometimes the information that appeared in print was contradictory and confusing, to say the least. Joan contradicted herself several times when she told reporters how she became interested in automobiles and racing. In the earliest interviews, published in 1905, Mrs. Cuneo was quoted as saying her first car had been a used Locomobile in which she learned to drive in Central Park and she had never looked back. However, on May 29, 1907, she told the *Herald* reporter, "Just five years ago, my husband purchased an electric runabout for me, and I used it as a convenient mode of transportation to and from the station and our Long Island home."[47] She would indeed say, many times, that she first learned to drive in 1902, but in a little Locomobile steamer, not an electric runabout. Furthermore, in 1902 the Cuneos lived on Staten Island, not at Richmond Hill, Long Island, where they moved in 1905. The Richmond Hill home was a block from the train station, but she definitely could have used an auto to get to the Staten Island station.

The next part of the interview is even more interesting. Joan Cuneo continued:

The following winter [1903] we took our usual trip to the beach, at the time of the Ormond Beach races. One race on the program was for women drivers and a friend of my husband had entered his gasoline car, with his wife as the driver. At the last minute, she decided that the sport was too nerve-wracking, and withdrew. There were but three entries, and to prevent the race from being called off, I consented to drive for my friend. I was fortunate enough to win the event and I guess I was inoculated with the speed germ then and there.[48]

If she and her husband "customarily went to the beach each winter," it was very likely that Joan had many opportunities to race on the beach.

She went on to say that "the little electric was sacrificed as soon as we got home, and I purchased a steam car."[49] This could have been the 1902 Locomobile, which she said was followed by increasingly more powerful steam cars (at least one, the 1903 White), culminating with the 1905 steam touring car that she drove in the 1905 Glidden Tour and the 1906 White, which she raced on the beach and local tracks. The car she was to drive at the Bennings Track was a bright red 45 hp 1907 model Rainer, which had been stripped for racing.

Finally the reporter must have asked her if she wasn't afraid to participate in such a dangerous sport, because she replied:

> If I ever felt I was afraid to take any chance that was presented while skirting around a circular track at a mile-a-minute gait, I would quit the sport then and there. I always use the white fence on the inside of the track as a guide and never notice anything else. I have never experienced so exhilarating a sensation as traveling a mile-a-minute or faster. I am entering automobile

Joan Cuneo at the wheel of her brand-new 1907 Rainier, taken before the start of the 1907 Glidden Tour. The car is set up for touring and to carry at least four people. Her entry number is already stenciled on the radiator (courtesy of Carl Ballenas, Richmond Hill historian).

races from a pure love of the sport, and because I don't care for golf or less strenuous diversions. I hope no one will think that I am a professional driver, or that I am connected in any way with the automobile industry. I simply listened to the call of speed mania, and could not resist its beckoning.

She then thanked those who hoped she would win but said she would be satisfied with "being in at the finish."[50]

The *Herald* reporter, impressed with Mrs. Cuneo after their meeting, wrote on the 30th: "Mrs. Cuneo in appearance looks far from being the nervy and skilful woman she is. She is of delicate build and only a pair of determined eyes give evidence of her ability at the steering wheel. But on a circular track, she cuts the turns at a speed that fairly takes away the breath of a spectator and stamps her as one of the remarkable women of the day."[51]

The field of entrants for the one-hundred-mile race was formidable. It listed a number of experienced professionals and amateurs driving powerful cars, including several 60 hp Thomas Flyers. Ralph Mongini, the "terrible Italian," a professional driver, had been relegated to driving the least powerful machine, a 29 hp Columbia, because his primary car broke down before the race. Joan Cuneo soon found that her brand-new Rainier did not work well on the Bennings oval, because it was too "high geared," and she was behind from the start. To make matters worse, she lost one of the four cylinders on the Rainier engine and was forced to make a number of visits to the pits for repairs before the end of the race. She finished in last place, a good 20 minutes behind the winner, W. C. Hood, in his Thomas Flyer. Hood set a new record of 2 hours, 12 minutes and 43.2 seconds for one hundred miles. All the drivers and their riding mechanics, including Joan Cuneo and Louis Disbrow, were covered with dust and grease by the end of the race.[52] Afterwards, Mrs. Cuneo was praised not only for her driving skill but also for her determination to finish the race, even though she had no chance to win. The victor received a silver cup from the United States Motor Racing Association; this was the first race ever held under the jurisdiction of this brand new auto-race-sanctioning organization.[53] It was not recorded how the Arlington Hotel staff reacted when the grimy lady racer and her mechanic appeared at the hotel doors after the race.

After her adventure at the Bennings Track, Joan Cuneo began her preparation for the Glidden Tour of 1907. The tour was to start at Cleveland, Ohio, instead of New York City, wind its way through Indianapolis, Pittsburgh, Baltimore and Philadelphia and end triumphantly, as usual, in New York City. Entrants would have to drive a distance of 1,570 miles, but even so, it attracted 52 entrants, of whom 30 completed the tour, with only 18 achieving a perfect score.[54] In addition, 14 drivers had entered the tour just for fun and would not be part of the competition.[55]

The rules for the 1907 tour had undergone many changes. One of the major issues in 1906 had been the excessive repairs competitors made to their cars en route. Some participants had replaced radiators or changed an axle during the rest period, after the group stopped for the night. In 1906, the tourists were allowed to repair their damaged vehicles without penalty. This certainly benefited those who had the ability or the funds to make extensive repairs to their vehicles overnight. To the rules committee, this regulation seemed to be unfair to more careful or fortunate drivers, who were able to complete the tour having to make only minor repairs to their vehicles. In 1907, the drivers were forced to carry all spare parts along with them from the start of the tour and these would be inventoried by the rules committee on a regular basis.

The other issue was excessive speeding during the 1906 tour. If Joan Cuneo had entered in 1906, she would have been one of the tourists who passed slower autos and tried to get to the night's destination first. In 1907, the tour officials decided they would employ a pacemaker vehicle to lead the procession of cars every day. Passing the pacemaker would result in instant disqualification of the speeding tourist.

Finally, instead of awarding the Glidden Trophy to an individual entrant, it would be awarded to one of the auto club entries. As a result, the 1907 tour received a number of entries from the New York, Cleveland, Chicago and Pittsburgh Automobile Clubs.[56] Joan Cuneo was not asked to join any of the motor club teams in 1907 and, as a result, had almost no chance to win the Glidden Trophy. She again planned to do all the driving herself. Because the Rainier was a touring model, she was required to carry three passengers and a driver, as that was considered a full load for this model. Undaunted by the many rule changes, Mrs. Cuneo looked forward to another great adventure on her second Glidden Tour.

5

The 1907 Glidden Tour
and Other Challenges

Her daredevil run at the Bennings Track in Washington, D.C., would be Mrs. Cuneo's last formal racing event before she embarked on her second Glidden Tour. However, she said later, she had already driven her 35 hp 1907 Rainier more than four thousand miles by the beginning of July. Obviously she had spent much time behind the wheel on the roads near her Long Island home and was quite comfortable driving her new car. Today a four-thousand-mile car trip may take a week or less, driving on the interstate at 70 mph. However, there were no interstates in 1907 and speeds of 50 mph, or more, were possible only on a very few sections of road in the United States. Clearly she spent many hours each day bouncing and bumping along the Long Island roads and in the New York countryside.

Although Joan Cuneo had not been on the 1906 tour, she had read numerous articles about it, many of them not very complimentary towards the quality of the roads, the food and the accommodations. However, the Cuneos must have believed the positive comments that had already been circulated about the route selected for 1907. Although the contestants would travel almost sixteen hundred miles from start to finish, Joan Cuneo believed that the tour would be a relatively easy drive. Thus she invited Andrew Cuneo's aunt Maddalena to be their fourth passenger. Mrs. M. Cuneo was a woman in her sixties at this time. She must have been in good health to have even contemplated such a trip. However, Joan Cuneo regarded her aunt-in-law almost as a second mother and wanted to include her in their party.

During the winter of 1906–07, the AAA Contest Committee and the automobile manufacturers who supported the Glidden events met to discuss how the next Glidden Tour should be run. Some members of the tour committee and most of the auto manufacturers wanted it to be a severe test of the capabilities of an auto.[1] An outstanding performance in a rigorous tour provided excellent advertising copy and would increase sales. Several makes, especially the Pierce, which had already been awarded the winner's trophy twice, had benefited from positive newspaper reports. However, individual tourists, especially those who enjoyed long-distance automobile travel, wanted a tour that would be less taxing and more fun. Many of the complaints about the 1906 tour, which had extended from New Hampshire across the Canadian border into the province of Quebec as far east as Montreal, focused on the very poor quality of the Canadian roads. A close second were complaints about the poor quality of the food and lodging available along the largely rural roads. The 1907 tour route seems to have been the result of a compromise between these two factions. The tourists would get to travel on a number of good roads at first but would face some challenging mountain driving in the second week of the tour. Of course, even the good roads of 1907 were mostly unpaved, liable to turn into quagmires in a heavy rain, and very dusty in dry weather.

The 1907 tour was scheduled to start in the western city of Cleveland, Ohio, extend even farther west to Chicago, and then turn eastward, finishing in New York City. The contest rules had also been re-written in 1907, to prevent the abuses that had occurred in 1906. The 1907 entrants were strictly forbidden from substituting a variety of spare parts for the full complement of passengers (either 4 or 2, depending on the model) in their vehicles. Every car would be checked at the end of each day's drive, to see that no rules had been broken. The tourists' arrival would also be timed, so that no one got to the day's destination either too early or too late.[2]

The tour, lasting two weeks, would start on July 10 and end on July 24, including three rest days: two in Chicago at the halfway mark and one at Bedford Springs, Pennsylvania, during the return trip. Because of the poor quality of the rooms that had been set aside for last year's tourists, the Contest Committee had engaged the famous travel agency Thomas A. Cook and Sons to take care of reservations. The Cook agency would have full responsibility for providing the food and lodging necessary to feed and house the tourists throughout the tour. However, the travel agents would find they were hard-pressed to provide three meals a day and accommodations for such a large number of people, especially in the smaller western towns that were unused to hosting large numbers of travelers.

The *Times* reporter optimistically promoted the 1907 route: the tourists would drive through beautiful country, over roads "that will gladden the heart of the most critical." However, he then admitted that this would not be the case everywhere.[3] In fact, the drives on July 19 and 20 would be extremely difficult. After they left Columbus, Ohio, the tourists would have to travel through rugged and mountainous terrain that would challenge the most skilled drivers for nearly 150 miles. The most dangerous obstacles the tourists had to face were an endless series of water breaks. A" water break" was a speed bump–like mound, found today only on remote lightly traveled forest roads or in parking lots. However, in 1907 motorists might encounter thousands, while driving a hundred miles on dirt roads, especially in hilly areas that experienced heavy rainfall. Joan Cuneo later mentioned that they often crossed several thousand during a day's drive on the tour.

Water breaks or water breakers, as described in the *New York Times* article, were "from 12 to 16 inches high and are made by digging a ditch across the road and at a slight angle, so slight that the ditch seems to run straight across the highway."[4] Imagine driving a 1907 model car, with minimal springs and only two wheel brakes, over a narrow mountain road having a thousand water breaks. The experience compares to driving a modern car over a speed bump and then immediately plunging its front wheels into a shallow ditch. However, Joan Cuneo was a very determined woman and much stronger than she looked, She was sure she could handle her Rainier under these conditions, which many of the male drivers would find difficult.

A local motorist who had traveled the route several weeks before the tour advised caution, saying that "the engine should be throttled down until there is barely enough power to lift the rear wheels over the obstruction. It will be well for the tourists to look to their brakes under these conditions ... part of the road follows the old Greensburg Pike which is ... no race track. It is carved out of the rock, and on it are several thousand water breaks, which also break the driver's heart.[5]

On July 9, the *New York Times* reported that 81 cars were ready to start the following day, on the fourth annual Glidden Tour. Thirty-five makes of cars, all built in America, were on the entry list.[6] Joan Cuneo had eagerly paid her $100 entry fee, along with the 46 other entrants competing for the Glidden Trophy, who would drive four-passenger touring cars. Although the Rainier had not performed well in the one-hundred-mile race at Washington, D.C., she had every reason to believe it would do well on the tour. The Rainier, a well-built and expensive touring car (with a sales price of $5,000) was noted for the strength of its engine. It was also powerful and could carry four passengers with ease. Riding along with Mrs. Cuneo would be her husband, Andrew, listed as the car owner; his adopted mother (actually his aunt), Maddalena Cuneo; and Louis Disbrow, their friend and Joan's mechanician. The car owner, according to the rules, had to either drive the car himself or ride along as a passenger. Andrew Cuneo, listed as the owner, was happy to let his wife handle the chore of driving. In addition to the 46 entrants for the Glidden Trophy, 12 high-powered runabouts were entered for the Hower Cup. The remaining cars on the *New York Times* list were those of folks who were "just along for the ride," and a ride it would be.

At her home at Richmond Hill after the tour Joan Cuneo wrote a little book, at the request of the Rainier Motor Car Company, about her adventures on the 1907 tour. The book, illustrated with photographs and charming Art Deco motifs, was then published by Rainier. Given her growing fame, it probably provided them with excellent publicity. In the introduction, Joan praised the Rainier engine, which "never missed an explosion from start to finish."[7] She then told her audience that she had bought her car on March 15, 1907, and driven it about four thousand miles and then expressed it to Cleveland for the start of the tour. The story of her adventures on the tour is best told in her own words.

> On July 10th we started on a hundred and twenty-one mile drive to Toledo, over one hundred cars, a minute apart, and each one trying to make time, so as to reach the control at Toledo ahead of time to be in readiness to check out bright and early the next morning. All of this being done within two or three blocks of the checking in station, made the Tour turn into a race from start to finish. Tho' we had tire troubles and the roads were deep with dirt, which caused driving in clouds of dust, almost impossible to see a car's length ahead, still it was nothing in comparison with what was to come.[8]

In 1907, there were no gas stations in the entire country. Thus the tourists had to locate and buy gasoline and other supplies they might need for the next day at the nearest hardware or drugstore they could find. They also had to locate a source of water for their radiators, because once they had checked in they couldn't move their vehicles. All 76 automobiles that actually started the run (six were non-starters) finished before 6:00 P.M. on the 10th. Only two contestants had accidents, and one tourist car was forced off the road by a non-tourist runabout. However, except for this unfortunate incident the tourists were welcomed by large crowds along the way. Women and children waved flags and factories gave their workers a break so they could watch the cavalcade pass by. Very few had ever seen such a large number of vehicles pass through their towns at one time.

Mrs. Cuneo at home with her son, Antonio, age seven. She is dressed to go out for the evening in a ball gown (courtesy of Harriet Newton Draper).

Heavy rains during the night made the run to South Bend one in which there are not words in all the languages of the world, adequate to express. One hundred and sixty-six miles, hub deep — in slippery clay, with ruts and mud holes for mile after mile. Car after car we saw in the ditches along the way. The two accidents to the party here cast a gloom over all in the whole Tour, and still those who were able were only too glad to pull out the next morning, trusting to luck that the same fate was not awaiting them that day. Mrs. M Cuneo now found the tour too hard for her,[9] so she took the train on to Chicago, "and we took in a bag of sand and stone for the necessary 125 pound ballast."[10]

While cars like the Rainier had a tonneau that covered a canvas top that could be set up and side curtains that could be rolled down, they had minimal windshields. Because the driving position was high, motorists wore goggles or some other type of eye protection at all times when driving on the highway. In bad weather, the driver and passengers in a touring car got wet to some extent. For protection from the weather on the tour, they wore full-length canvas or linen dusters in dry weather and oilskins or rubberized garments in the rain. However, they were still very dusty or damp at the end of a long day's drive.

To provide traction for their vehicles when driving through mud, sand or clay, motorists carried numerous sets of chains, which they used to combat road conditions that ranged from poor to awful. Today one can buy tires that provide stability or traction while driving in snow or in wet weather. Sport-utility vehicles often have tires with an aggressive tread for off-road driving. Most tires used in 1907 were fairly smooth, so chains were strapped on to give them grip when needed. Manufacturers, like the Weed Tire Chain Co., marketed a variety of chains for varying road conditions. All the cars that embarked on the 1907 Glidden Tour carried at least one complete set of chains with them. They could be put on two or four wheels when needed.

> The run of 101 miles to Chicago was a pleasure, tho' there were stretches of mud holes, where many of the cars "got a horse" or two. Entering thro' [sic] South Chicago, Jackson Park was soon reached and we were able to check in at the Auditorium Annex. After this, we all had to wait in line, pump out every drop of gasoline, and one lone horse was there to pull each car into the Armory. Even here, no horse was needed on the Rainier, for the gasoline left in the carbureter [sic] enabled us to go in under our own power, which by the way, we used every inch of the whole tour. Spending Sunday in Chicago everyone seemed anxious to pull out and retrace our way to South Bend.

The Chicago Automobile Club, along with the Chicago Motor Club and the local dealers' associations, did their best to entertain the tourists during their two-day stopover in the Windy City. The list of activities included something for everyone: a band concert at the Coliseum, a smoker at the Auto Club's new clubhouse, auto races at the Harlem Track, a park (automobile) run, an orchestra concert with Walter Damrosch conducting, and a military review at Fort Sheridan.[11]

When they reached Chicago, Maddalena Cuneo decided that touring was not for her. After a few days' rest at a local hotel, she boarded a train for her home at Port Richmond, Staten Island. There were only a few women riding along on the tour this year, and another, Mrs. Orrel A. Parker, of New York City, also decided to quit. The Parkers had planned to make the Glidden Tour as part of their bridal trip, in a brand-new Royal Tourist automobile. What were they thinking? At Chicago, Mr. Parker declared that "the pace was too fast and the Tour seems to have resolved itself into a road race, According to Mrs. Cuneo, he later changed his mind, as Parker was still part of the Tour on the mountain drive that ended at Bedford Springs."[12]

Mrs. Cuneo didn't mention the automobile races at the Harlem Track in the account of the 1907 Glidden Tour she wrote for Rainier, even though the race meet officials delayed the start of their program until the tourists' arrival. However, she must have spent some time talking to the race officials. The *Chicago Record Herald* soon reported that she was considering running a five-mile trial against Alyce "Byrdie" Potter. Potter had raced her Haynes car at Harlem the previous day. Joan also entertained thoughts of driving in the 24-hour race that would start later that day, in a Napier with Louis Disbrow as her partner. The *Record Herald* had them as *probable* starters in the entry list.[13] Cooler heads must have prevailed, because Mrs. Cuneo did not compete in the five-mile women's race against Miss Potter, nor did she and Disbrow drive in the 24-hour race in an attempt to set a new world's record. Driving a full day on the Glidden Tour, after spending 24 hours behind the wheel of a 69 hp Napier, would have exhausted Joan despite her strength and determination.

[On the return to South Bend] more rain had made the going even worse than before and so many cars plowing thro' only made the ruts and holes deeper. South Bend to Indianapolis, 147½ miles would have been easier had it not rained so hard. We were out in two cloud bursts and tho' seemingly protected from the ordinary rain storms, we were all soaked thro'. The next day, Indianapolis to Columbus, 174 miles in a drizzling rain was not one to be forgotten very soon. During the last few miles we had our first taste of water-breakers, just a sample to be sure, but enough to put many of the cars out of the run. Columbus to Canton, 152 miles, started the hilly country and more water breakers, but the hearty welcome accorded us by the Mayor and the entertainment by all, made the memory of our stop at Canton a very pleasant one.

Canton to Pittsburg, a hundred miles, will be remembered in a very decidedly different way; the grades were almost impossible, the roads impassable, and water-breakers innumerable. The Pittsburghers certainly turned out to greet us royally and we had the right of way thro' the entire city. From Pittsburg to Bedford Springs, 97 miles across the Alleghany [*sic*] Mountains, Mr. Parker [Orrel A. Parker, a member of the Auto Club of America who drove a Royal Tourist on the tour] counted 1900 water-breakers during the day. Then Bedford Springs to Baltimore [after a rest day] 140 miles, with water-breakers from start to finish. Thirty miles out we

Alyce Byrd Potter earned fame setting a ladies' speed record at the Harlem Track near her home in Elgin, Illinois. Here she is dressed in an elaborate late Victorian costume (courtesy of the White-Rock Collection).

skidded, pulled down forty feet of fence, squeezed in between it and a telegraph pole and went down into a ditch, which caused a bend in one of the front axles and a spring to break. The car was jacked up, axle and spring removed, and taken to a blacksmith's shop where one of the neatest repairs of the Tour was made by Mr. Disbrow. Many of the Tourists who stopped to see if they could be of assistance claimed that it was an utter impossibility to repair the axle.[14]

The *New York Times* reported Joan's accident much more dramatically. According to the *Times*, "Driving down a steep grade at McConnellsburg, Maryland, Mrs. Cuneo had a blowout on her Rainier. The Rainier skidded into at ditch, ran through a fence and crashed into a tree."[15] The fence must have slowed down the car as it crashed down hill through the brush, as neither she nor her husband nor Louis Disbrow was thrown out of the car. This saved them from more serious injuries than the bumps and bruises they received. The Rainier wasn't as lucky, suffering, along with the bent axle Mrs.

The wealthy, eccentric Alyce Byrd Potter often donned workman's garb when working on her automobile (courtesy of the White-Rock Collection).

Cuneo mentioned in her account, two broken springs, which Disbrow was also able to repair.[16] Again Mrs. Cuneo continued to lead a charmed life behind the wheel, as blowouts like the one she had just experienced often resulted in serious injuries.

> At five o'clock we started on the 110 mile trip that meant the severest driving that I have ever done, over the summits of the Alleghany [*sic*] Mountains, pitch dark and strange roads, with only a little kerosene lantern, as our head-lights had gone out of business, getting out frequently to hunt confetti, and wake up the toll-gate keepers.[17]

Since there were no road signs, the pathfinder car sprinkled a constant stream of confetti on the road surface showing which direction to turn to keep on their route. This was not the best way of marking a road in daylight, much less in rainy weather or at night. To complicate matters even further, sometimes pranksters laid a false trail with confetti of their own, after obliterating the pathfinder's trail. As a result, many tourists made wrong turns or were misdirected by locals who thought it was a huge joke to play on the city folks. Headlights as we know them today were nonexistent, and drivers used either kerosene lanterns or Prest-O-Lite headlights powered by acetylene gas carried in canisters. The Prest-O-Lite made a fortune for Indianapolis entrepreneur Carl Fisher, who was most responsible for the construction of the Indianapolis Motor Speedway in 1909. It is hard to believe that in 1907 most cars, like the Rainier, were still right-hand drive, that headlights and windshields were accessories, and that the self-starter had yet to be invented. All gasoline cars, even the most expensive models, still had to be started by hand cranking, a dangerous task in itself. A careless motorist could end up with a broken arm or sprained shoulder as a result of injudicious cranking.

> We pulled into Baltimore at midnight, [the Rainier had to be repaired before they could continue after their encounter with the fence], with the cheers of many who had stayed up and made friendly bets as to whether we would have courage enough to come on. [Anyone who knew her would not have bet against Joan Cuneo.] During the run from Baltimore to Philadelphia, 171 miles, we found it advisable to put in a new spring, as we considered our lives worth more than a few points in the tour. We were two hours late in reaching Philadelphia, but I don't think anyone was more heartily welcomed and cheered than we were as we pulled up in front of the Hotel Walton. The last day seemed to me the easiest, 98 miles, with good roads and good weather, 5 hours were allowed but most of the cars reached Jersey City an hour ahead of time. We had the good fortune to follow close behind the official car and in New York to be given the post of honor, leading that most wonderful array of what was left of cars, drivers and Tourists up Broadway.
>
> When I entered the Tour, I was prepared for a showing of ill-feeling on the part of at least some of the drivers, an attitude of "what is a woman trying to enter and compete with us in this kind of a thing for," or some such spirit. But from beginning to end, there was not only shown me by every driver and Tourist, but by all the thousands of people along the way, the utmost courtesy and hearty consideration any one could wish for. Day after day many of the different men would come to me and say that they had followed me for 10, 20, 30 or 50 miles and all had only the highest praise and wonderment for the Rainier car.[18]

The sanitized version of her experiences on the tour, written for Rainier, differed somewhat from the more candid information she provided for a newspaper after her return home. A *New York Evening World* reporter interviewed her at her large Victorian home on a tree-lined Long Island street. He spoke to her just hours after she had completed the tour, with cracked lips and sunburned, peeling nose. However, she had taken the time to bathe and change her dusty, travel-stained clothing for "an elaborate gown of white lace."[19] According to the *Evening World*, Mrs. Cuneo complained that the Rainier now had a sprung frame, busted springs, leaky tires and a spliced front axle after its rough treatment during the tour, "but it never phased the engine."[20] Commenting that the dust they drove through "could have made another Egyptian Plague ... we had dust and little else for breakfast, dust for lunch and dust for dinner ... and then it rained and there was mud, mud, nothing but mud, all through the Allegheny mountains. I counted 10,000 'thank-you ma'ams' in one day on the road to Bedford Springs, Pennsylvania. You can imagine the effect on our springs."[21] When queried about the scenery, she replied that she had little time to look around. She was forced to concentrate on the "long brown ribbon of road that stretched endlessly ahead and deal with the constant bumping of the car over the dips and water breakers." According to Joan Cuneo, "the men couldn't stand it, and for miles they stood out on the running board," while she drove doggedly ahead.[22]

Although she had commented earlier on the friendly reception she received from her fellow tourists, Mrs. Cuneo got some strange looks from the locals who lined the roads to watch the tourists drive by. "All along the way the village people stared at me as if I had been a monster of some kind. In one town a young man with his best girl on his arm came up to the car and gazed at me searchingly, 'Say Bess, it is a woman all right,' he remarked reassuringly."[23]

According to Mrs. Cuneo, their main trouble on the trip had been tire failure, not surprising, considering the roughness of the roads. "Our right rear wheel was smaller than standard size," she commented, "and the tires we used kept slipping. We lost a lot of time fixing them, and then there was that accident where we skidded into a fencepost."[24]

Andrew Cuneo, who was present at the interview, then suggested she tell the reporter how she had helped the village smithy fix the axle. His wife laughed and said, "Good gracious, people will think I am a regular crank if you make me a female blacksmith too.... I love my home and my children but you may say I am speed mad too."[25] (In 1907, the word "crank" was commonly used to describe an annoyingly eccentric person or one who indulged in unusual activities with excessive enthusiasm.)

Finally, the reporter asked Joan Cuneo to explain why she found driving an automobile so compelling. "What's the fascination of a trip that you don't see anything of?" he asked. She replied, "That's hard to answer. I suppose it's the sense of mastery of a powerful force. The feeling that the great mass of energy carrying you along at express speed is obedient to the twist of your finger ... sometimes."[26]

In retrospect the 1907 Glidden Tour seems to have been more of an ordeal than a recreational jaunt through the countryside. However, many participants, like Joan Cuneo, were eager to repeat the experience the following year. Despite the curiosity that Mrs. Cuneo aroused as she drove through country villages in goggles and duster, the Glidden tourists had received a much more enthusiastic welcome than they had in 1905. However, not everyone had been won over to the automobile. Several shots had been taken at one of the cars, and a few tourists were hit by stones thrown by unhappy spectators. Yet overall the tourists had been cheerfully welcomed almost everywhere they traveled. They were again met by cheering crowds as they neared their final destination at Columbus Circle and 59th Street. Their autos were so covered with grime that as they inched forward through the crowds the spectators began to write their initials in the thick layer of dust that covered the tourists' tonneaus.

The *New York Times* reported:

If it hadn't been for the vigilance of the traffic police, Mrs. Andrew Cuneo's car would have been so densely packed by the throng, that she would have found it more difficult to make any headway, than was the case when she was ploughing through the mud holes of the roads in northern Ohio. Mrs. Cuneo's plucky driving, her unfortunate accident just before reaching Baltimore, when an axle broke, the quick repairs she had made at a rural blacksmith shop, and her arrival in Baltimore at midnight were apparently known to all.[27]

Although she hadn't been able to get the perfect score she wanted in 1907, Joan Cuneo had gained the respect of all the Glidden tourists. They quickly raised money to purchase a silver cup, which was then engraved and presented to her at the Glidden awards banquet, in the ballroom of the Astor Hotel that evening. According to the *Times*, "the presentation was a complete surprise and she was cheered heartily as she accepted the souvenir."[28] Mrs. Cuneo was well on the way to becoming a national celebrity; the Washington, D.C., newspapers needn't have worked so hard to create a mythic background for her. She had already captured the public's fancy because of her unvarnished exploits as tourist and racer.

It probably is impossible for a modern reader to imagine the truly awful state of the roads Joan Cuneo and her fellow Gliddenites endured during the 1907 tour. *Outing Magazine* published an article titled "The Worst Roads in America" in November 1907, which may help readers understand just how tough and determined Mrs. Cuneo was, how much she loved driving, and how amazing her accomplishments really were.

M. Worth Colwell, its author, was an experienced automobilist who had already traveled thousands of miles. He rode along on the 1907 tour as a member of the press and wrote about the road conditions from firsthand experience. On July 10, a beautiful clear Wednesday morning, the 81 cars carrying three hundred passengers eagerly awaited the starting signal. However, before they had traveled five miles it was apparent that what they thought would be any easy drive had turned into a nightmare. The huge clouds of dust churned up by 81 vehicles was so thick, according to Colwell, that it was difficult to see more than ten feet ahead in the choking clouds. By the end of the day, all participants suffered from dry throats and nostrils; they were also sunburned on any exposed skin. Besides being extremely dusty, the road was also rough, and many tourists had to change their inner tubes before the end of the day.[29]

A heavy rain overnight promised to make their next day's run easier, but such was not the case. Instead the hapless tourists were met by oceans of mud, "slippery, slimy, treacherously dangerous ooze." Although the roadbed was hard, it "was covered with slime from a foot to two feet deep ... the cars floundered around in it like so many mired pigs ... for miles."[30] Most of the cars were equipped with anti-skid chains on all four wheels, and while the chains gave the wheels some traction, they didn't prevent the cars from skidding and sliding, often into giant mud holes. To make matters worse, the Tour Committee had set the driving time from Toledo to South Bend, a distance of 166 miles, at 9 hours (18.4 miles per hour). Any driver who didn't make it in time would be penalized.

83

Colwell felt that the time limit was suicidal under these conditions. In fact, he believed it was directly responsible for the death of one driver who turned over his car. The Otis family, who had been trapped under their car after skidding into a ditch, also suffered serious injuries.[31] Despite attempts by the AAA to convince entrants that the tour was not a race, it is obvious that all participants were determined to make the time and were willing to risk serious injury to get to South Bend in nine hours.

Charles J. Glidden spoke about the terrible road conditions in Ohio and Indiana that night. Glidden, who had traveled around the world by automobile, said angrily, "Seventy per cent of the roads encountered on this tour would, by any European government, be closed to travel and marked, 'Use at your own peril.'"[32] Glidden blamed the poor road conditions for the accidents and serious injuries to the participants but felt one benefit of the tour so far had been to make the public aware of the terrible conditions of the American highways. He made no comment about not allowing enough time for the day's travel.

The tourists were hopeful that the worst conditions were now behind them, but such was not the case. As they neared Chicago, Colwell and his fellow Gliddenites complained bitterly about the road conditions in the urban streets of South Chicago. He remarked on "the black, oozing filth and foul smelling mud ... a regular thing ... the natives are used to it and the children wallow in it ... it is hard to believe that such conditions of hub-deep filth can exist in such a large city when only a short distance away ... the parks present roads as fine as any in the world."[33]

On the return leg of the tour, as they drove through Ohio, the tourists were lulled into thinking that it would be an easy drive back to New York City, but they were yet to encounter the worst roads of the tour. The reality, according to Colwell, was that they met the hardest driving of the tour from Canton to Pittsburgh, due to the overwhelming number of dips (thank you, ma'ams) and water breakers at intervals from 20 to 100 feet apart. Reading Joan Cuneo's account of the tour, it may have seemed that she had exaggerated the road conditions through Pennsylvania, but evidently this was not the case. Colwell interviewed some of the local people, who said that many of the water breaks had been there when Pennsylvania was still a British colony. The inhabitants had constructed these bumps by placing a line of rocks across the road and covering them with dirt and stones, or logs were placed across the road and covered with stones. Over time, these impediments became permanent features of the road. Although invented to drain the hill country and prevent horse-drawn wagons from going downhill too quickly, the bumps were a nightmare for the tourists. Joan Cuneo and her fellow drivers were forced to ease over water breaks ranging from six inches to two feet high with their feet on the brakes and then slowly increase their speed until they reached the next one. It was not surprising that brakes, springs and axles needed replacement, while gears and transmissions were also abused. The passengers in the rear seats suffered torment; some were ejected over the hoods of their cars as the vehicles bumped their way downhill. Others took to riding on the running boards or walking alongside to get some relief. Although the drivers had the slight advantage of being able to hold on to the steering wheel, Mrs. Cuneo and her male counterparts had no time to relax on these treacherous roads. Colwell concluded that the only reason that there hadn't been more accidents was the skill of the drivers.[34] The last day of the drive on the macadamized road between Philadelphia and New York must have been heaven for the survivors of the extreme conditions they faced during the 1907 tour.

Even a glutton for punishment like Joan Cuneo must have been glad to spend some time at home with her children after her experiences on the tour. Pleased that her skill as a driver had been acknowledged by the other tourists, she was already beginning to plan ahead for the 1908 tour. However, at end of the year she was faced with a lawsuit resulting from a vehicle accident near her home. Although she was on her way to becoming a national celebrity and often mentioned in the automobile gossip columns; neither the accident nor the lawsuit was mentioned in any major New York paper.[35] Evidently, early in 1907 Mrs. Cuneo was driving down Jamaica Avenue on Long Island when she ran into a horse and cart also driven by a woman. The summary of the incident reads like a comedy of errors, but Joan Cuneo would pay dearly for her actions that day, however well intended.

> The plaintiff [driving a horse and cart] was going east along the right hand side of Jamaica avenue behind a meat truck [horse drawn] decorated with branches and flags, and carrying a picnic party. As she [Edith M. Peters] turned out from behind it to the left, to go close along side of it and pass it, she testifies that she saw the defendant [Joan Cuneo] coming with her motor car directly toward her fast on the same side of the middle of the street, and about 300 feet away, that the defendant continued on toward her until the motor car came near the heads of the horses of the cart, when the plaintiff in alarm turned to the left to go to the left of the motor car, whereupon the defendant turned her motor car to the right and thus ran into the plaintiff. She corroborated this. The defendant testifies that the motor car was in the middle of the road and as it got to the line of the horses' heads the plaintiff suddenly appeared for the first time from behind the truck, whereupon the defendant turned to the right to avoid her, and again to the left when she saw that the plaintiff was crossing the street diagonally. She was corroborated in this.[36]

It appears that Mrs. Cuneo was driving along at a good clip on Jamaica Avenue, a fairly wide road, when Ms. Peters, going the opposite direction, pulled out to pass a large wagon. While both tried to avoid each other, they each made a serious error of judgment, which resulted in a collision and injured the driver of the horse cart. Ms. Peters then sued Mrs. Cuneo to be compensated for the injuries she suffered in the wreck. A careful reading of the transcript shows that Ms. Peters may actually have been at fault. Instead of staying close to the side of the vehicle she was passing, she panicked and turned to the left, crossing the street on a diagonal. Joan Cuneo, well known for her quick reaction behind the wheel, initially moved to the right side of the road to avoid Ms. Peters, then quickly turned back to the left, hoping to avoid the frightened woman who had turned her horses straight towards her. If both women had stayed in their lanes, the accident might have been avoided. However, the jury didn't see it that way. The initial jury trial verdict went against Joan Cuneo. The jurors awarded Ms. Peters $2,500 in damages. This was a huge sum, worth $62,775 today. In 1907, the average workman made $10 a week. There is little doubt that Joan Cuneo's fame and wealth and her love of fast driving did not help her case. However, the judge revealed the current, widely held public opinion of automobile drivers in his following statement: "Persons in their place of security and power in motor cars should remember that their rapid and close approach may make a person think he or she is about to be run over, when that may not be the case. They should turn out reasonably."[37]

Mrs. Cuneo appealed the verdict, rightly believing that she was not to blame or that, in the worst-case scenario, both drivers had been equally at fault. However, despite or perhaps because of her fame and social standing, the verdict went against her at all levels. Stubbornly, Mrs. Cuneo took the case all the way to the New York State Supreme Court, but her appeal was denied, as was her petition for a new trial. Despite deciding against Joan Cuneo, the Appeals Court judge complimented her lawyer, saying that "the case was briefed and argued with unusual clearness and ability," rather curious considering his final decision.[38]

Putting thoughts of the trial behind her, Mrs. Cuneo looked forward to driving in the next Glidden Tour and other endurance runs and hoped for new opportunities to race. She was a daily visitor at the Eighth National Automobile Show held from November 2 to 9 in Madison Square Garden. Her name was mentioned in the newspapers along with the Vanderbilts, Jay Gould and many other notable New York attendees. Huge crowds eagerly paid an admission of 50 cents, and even more came after they raised the cost to one dollar. The amphitheater was packed with a dazzling display of the latest models, more than 30 gas engine cars and 10 electrics but only one steam-powered vehicle, the White.[39] Motorcycles were also on display for the first time, and the latest-model trucks could be found in the basement. At the show, much like today, motorists could also look at displays of auto parts and accessories of all kinds.

Joan Cuneo was particularly interested in the latest development in automobile tires. In 1907, all tires had inner tubes and changing a punctured tube was a difficult and time-consuming process. Her Rainier had suffered many punctures on the Glidden Tour, one blowout sending the Cuneo party into a ditch and causing a broken axle. Flat tires and blowouts were accepted as a fact of life by motorists in 1907, but tire manufacturers constantly worked on ways to make the tire-changing process faster and easier. At the show, Mrs. Cuneo was impressed by the new Fisk removable rim tire system. More than ever determined to finish the 1908 tour with a perfect score, she wanted to change her tires as quickly as possible. She decided to have the new 50 hp 1908 Rainier that she planned to order equipped with the Fisk removable rims, along with a set of spares, already inflated and bolted in place. Even though the car listed at a base price of $4,500, the removable rims were an accessory. With a set of the new Fisk equipment, she thought she would be able to take off a punctured tire rim and replace it with another rim and inflated tire in five minutes or less.[40]

She was not disappointed in the performance of her new Fisk tires, which greatly

MRS. CUNEO SAYS:

"In the selection of tires for track racing, two factors are of paramount importance—*first,* absolute SAFETY in tires combined with mileage durability; *second,* QUICKNESS in manipulating necessary tire changes. I find no mistake was made in my selection of Fisk Bolted-on Tires with Fisk Removable Rims, as, when driving with this equipment, I always have a feeling of perfect safety, never fearing an accident can possibly happen because of tire trouble "

We have many such voluntary tributes as the above to the splendid serviceability of

THE FISK REMOVABLE RIM

With the Fisk Bolted-On Tire

This equipment is today recognized as vitally essential to the up-to-date car. It adds wonderfully to the pleasure of motoring by eliminating annoying delays on the road and by giving at the same time an assurance of absolute safety which no wise motorist will overlook.

We have already equipped over 15,000 cars with the Fisk removable rim—come to our nearest branch, see a demonstration and you will understand why.

THE FISK RUBBER CO.

Chicopee Falls, Mass.　　　　　**Branches in 17 cities**

The Fisk Tire Company lost no time in using Mrs. Cuneo's purchase and endorsement of their tires and rims in their advertising (circa 1909, courtesy of Carl Ballenas, Richmond Hill historian).

reduced the number of punctures on the road, and praised them extensively. Fisk gave her comments top billing in the following 1909 advertisement:

Mrs. Cuneo Says:
"In the selection of tires for track racing, two factors are of paramount importance—first, absolute SAFETY in tires combined with mileage durability: second, QUICKNESS in manipulating necessary tire changes. I find no mistake was made in my selection of Fisk Bolted-on Tires with Fish Removable Rims, as when driving with this equipment, I always have a feeling of perfect safety, never fearing an accident can possibly happen because of tire trouble."[41]

The company, based in Chicopee Falls, Massachusetts, was quick to add that Mrs. Cuneo's praise of their tires was not solicited by them. However, as she was nationally famous and had been born and raised in Massachusetts, they were quick to take advantage of her favorable comments.

Joan Cuneo kept up with the automobile news that could be found in the daily papers. The following headline in the *New York Times* must have caught her eye. "Auto Track Races May Be Stopped, AAA Appoints Committee to Determine Policy in Sanctioning Meets" trumpeted the paper on September 20, 1907. Evidently the increased horsepower (and speed) of the latest models, as well as the number of serious track accidents that occurred regularly, had caused some auto club members to consider banning racing on circular tracks. AAA president W. H. Hotchkiss thought the time had come to move forward on this issue.[42] If Mrs. Cuneo did not find this upsetting, she should have, because it heralded the beginning of an anti-racing movement within the AAA membership and among auto manufacturers.

Although there was still considerable nationwide opposition to automobiles in general and, more specifically, to allowing women to drive them, by 1907 women motorists had begun to form their own auto clubs. There were already women-only clubs in on the West Coast and in Philadelphia and Chicago. The Long Island Motor Club, one of the largest auto clubs in the country, had just opened its doors to women. In an article praising the skill of women drivers, published in the *New York Times*, the author clearly expected an increasing number of women to enter and even win their share of auto races and touring competitions such as the Glidden.[43] Unfortunately for Joan Cuneo and other women who enjoyed competition, a large and influential group of men had already decided women racers had to go. They had tolerated women drivers when they were relatively few in number and when many drove slow-moving electric cars. A woman behind the wheel of a powerful racing car was something else entirely, a danger to herself, of course, but also to all the other drivers on the track.

At the moment, leading members of the AAA and the Automobile Manufacturers Association who held these views kept them undercover. However, just as more women had begun to enter local races on a regular basis, male opposition to female participation had begun to grow. Unbeknown to Mrs. Cuneo, membership in the movement to exclude women from racing now included some men on the AAA Contest Board who had the power to keep them out.

6

Queen for a Day

Even though she had not gained the coveted perfect score hoped for in the 1907 Glidden Tour, Joan Cuneo was proud of her performance and ready for more. Even more confident in her ability, she entered another endurance run set for New Year's Day, 1908. The Quaker City Motor Club announced a two-day trial over open roads from Philadelphia to Allentown, Pennsylvania, starting on January 1, and returning on the second. Despite the discomfort of driving an open car in the dead of winter, Mrs. Cuneo entered a 40 hp American Standard Renault in the run, as soon as it was advertised. The *Times* listed her as an entrant as late as December 29; however, she was not mentioned in a lengthy article on the results. It is likely that she decided to bypass this event, due to either bad weather or family demands.[1] Because of her celebrity status, her performance on the run would have been mentioned in the papers. The Quaker City run went off as planned, even though it was reported that many entrants crashed and slid all over the icy roads.

Perhaps she should have made the effort to complete the Quaker City Motor Club trial. AAA Contest Board members, who hadn't seen her handle a car, might have thought Mrs. Cuneo was not up to a tough challenge when she failed to show up on January 1. However, she did mail off her application for the Briarcliff Road Race, scheduled for April 24, 1908, at the beginning of January, with no inkling it would be rejected. By January 11, she had already driven the Westchester route of the proposed race. She commented to reporters that the course was a fine one and would require skillful driving by the participants. Cuneo believed the winning car would likely average about 35 mph, but bursts up to 60 mph were possible on the straight stretches. However, shortly after she sent in her application she heard rumors that some members of the committee were opposed to her participation in the race. Unfazed she demanded to be allowed to compete, saying she had already proved herself in numerous speed contests, as well as two Glidden Tours.[2]

Perhaps she should have tried honey rather than vinegar in her response to the committee's actions. A few days later, the *New York Times* reported that "after a considerable discussion over the entry of Mrs. John (Joan) Cuneo who sent in her check for $500, being the first payment of the $1000 entry fee, the Briarcliff Cup Committee decided it would be best to decline the entry and politely returned her check."[3] They did however recognize that she was a capable driver and agreed that she had the nerve, skill and experience to compete in such a dangerous high-speed contest. The *Washington Post* provided more information regarding the reasons behind their decision:

That Mrs. Cuneo has the necessary skill in driving a car has been shown in the past, when the promoters of races actively recruited her to enter their events. Now however as the stock car race will be a particularly difficult one there has been some argument over her entry, not because of the desire to bar women out of the race but because they did not wish to appear to be allowing a woman to take great risks.... Should Mrs. Cuneo meet with a serious accident, a wave of horror would go through the community and the committee would be severely censured for allowing a woman to take part in the contest.[4]

From her home on Richmond Hill, Mrs. Cuneo responded:

I have heard that there is some objection to my driving in the contest ... but I really can't understand why my sex should prove a bar. I have been in enough other contests, I think to have gained some experience in avoiding accidents. As a matter of fact, I have always felt that there would be some objection to my riding in the race, because if some accident did happen, the men would surely say, "Just like a woman," and that is a thing I hate to hear. I feel that I am perfectly competent to drive a car in any sort of race. As a matter of fact, I am perfectly at home in my car, and automobiling appeals to me purely for the sport there is in it.... It may be that as most of the drivers who ride in races are making their livelihood by so doing, they may feel that I am an intruder. But that side of it never struck me forcibly as they are equally in the race to find out which is the best car and who the best driver is and on these things the real sport depends. Accidents are likely to happen but in my past races I have always made it a rule to turn out when I heard another car coming up behind me. Besides I cannot take the risks that the men take. I never forget my husband and children when I am in a race and that alone makes me very cautious.[5]

Anyone who had observed Joan Cuneo racing or touring knew she was stretching the truth when she said she was always careful when racing. Insisting her thoughts were always on her husband and children when she was racing was a flat-out lie. Of course, her comments were calculated to soothe the fears of many readers that a woman might be injured or killed while racing. A year later she was more realistic in her response to similar questions, but then she was focused on her upcoming race.

A few days before the New Orleans Auto Carnival, Homer George interviewed Joan for *Collier's Magazine.* In the ensuing article appropriately titled "Shaking Dice with Death," George asked her why she was so successful at driving fast on a track. She responded "that I am able to accomplish the feat by putting aside all thoughts but speed.... Thoughts of danger have never bothered me, I do not credit it to particular bravery or caution in driving. Somehow it has just not occurred to me to think what might happen if I should drive into a fence or suffer a serious accident. It's peace of mind I suppose."[6]

Obviously she had the ability to put all of her focus on driving fast, totally in harmony with her car, as did Ralph De Palma and Barney Oldfield and the best of her male counterparts. Racing is one of the few sports today where the best women can compete with the best men if their skill, nerve and experience are equal. The members of the Briarcliff Committee seemed to realize this, admitting that Joan Cuneo had the "nerve, skill and experience" to successfully compete at Briarcliff. Yet prevailing attitudes of the male-dominant society of the time categorized women as the weaker sex whom men were expected to protect. Committee members couldn't bring themselves to allow her to take the risk.

Unfortunately for Joan and the other women who wanted to race, the belief that women were weak, dependent creatures existed mainly among middle-and upper-class WASP males. The membership of the AAA Contest Board and some other race-sanctioning committees came mainly from these groups. Joan's husband, Andrew Cuneo, was not a WASP and he supported her in her racing endeavors, although he may have encouraged her so that he could pursue his own interests. Louis Disbrow was from a WASP family but because of his shady past was considered somewhat of an outcast by many in Richmond Hill. Because Disbrow had been Joan's mechanic for years, he knew she was a skilled driver and also supported her endeavors. It didn't help Joan Cuneo's cause that away from the race course she looked like the petite, soft-spoken, well-dressed society woman she was, rather than the strapping mannish female people expected to see. The *New York Evening World* later reported that Mrs. Cuneo was eager to race at Briarcliff. The paper said, she almost "wept like a woman" because her entry was rejected "because she was a woman."[7] If Joan Cuneo did shed tears after she learned her entry had been rejected, they were surely tears of anger and frustration.

The Briarcliff race was the first ever held in Westchester Country. Driving eight times at speed around the 32.4–mile circuit was certain to challenge the skill of the best drivers. It promised some smooth sections along with a fair share of bumps, dips and curves. No doubt, the varied terrain was one of the reasons Mrs. Cuneo wanted to race at Briarcliff, as she loved a challenge. Because of its proximity to New York and other large cities, the Briarcliff race drew huge numbers of spectators, many of whom were hard put to find accommodations in the largely rural area. As a result, race fans turned viewing areas alongside the road course into one gigantic picnic for several days.

Among Briarcliff's 22 entries were a variety of "stock cars" from the United States and Europe, including Fiat and Isotta Fraschini from Italy, Renault and Panhard from France, Benz from Germany. and American makes such as Stearns, Apperson, Lozier and Simplex. The cars would be driven by some of the world's best drivers, including American professionals Barney Oldfield, whom Joan had terrified at the Dutchess County Fair, Ralph De Palma, George Robertson, and Louis Strang, the eventual winner, and noted amateur Louis. G. Bergdoll. Among the foreign drivers was Emanuel Cedrino, who had turned white after his near miss of Joan's car.[8] So keen was the interest in this race that the Marconi Wireless Telegraph Company broadcast bulletins about the current leaders. The Marconi company set up its wireless equipment at the Lozier race headquarters near the road course. From there, they sent news about the race to the tower of the Times Building in New York City. The Briarcliff race ranks among the first sporting events ever broadcast, albeit to a very limited audience, as the results were posted only on the *Times* bulletin board.[9]

Unfortunately, Joan Cuneo was only able to read about the race. Not surprisingly, her evaluation of the track and prediction of the average speed agreed with those of Barney Oldfield and other members of the racing fraternity. She had been rejected mainly because the Race Committee believed it couldn't take the chance of a woman suffering an injury in the race. However, Joan had already proved that she could handle her Rainier at speed on rough terrain during the 1907 Glidden Tour and in the one-hundred-mile race at the Bennings Track.

As much as she loved track racing, Joan Cuneo had a powerful desire to drive in a road race. Despite her rejection by the Briarcliff committee, she immediately sent in her entry for the Savannah Automobile Club road races. Racing would come to Savannah for the first time on March 18 and 19, 1908. To Mrs. Cuneo's dismay, she was yet again denied a chance to race by the Savannah club race committee, which responded to her application in the negative, saying "they did not care to establish such an innovation."[10]

The Savannah Auto Club was successful in its attempt to hold road races in 1908, including the "Grand Prize" race sanctioned by the ACA. Savannah's leading citizens hoped to make the city an important stop on the racing calendar, which would help the economy of the city. Unfortunately, just as Joan Cuneo failed in her attempt to race there, Savannah's attempt to bring racing to the city fizzled out after three years, mainly, I believe, because northern interests considered Savannah a small backwater. Perhaps Savannah would have done better if they had allowed Joan Cuneo to race. New Orleans would actively court female drivers for their Auto Carnival, held in conjunction with Mardi Gras, in 1909. The more conservative Savannah Auto Club had no desire to take a chance on having a woman participate in their inaugural race program in the spring of 1908.

Mrs. Cuneo received yet another rejection when she sent in her entry to a sanctioned event that would be held near her Richmond Hill home. A series of races was proposed for Jamaica, Long Island, in conjunction with the Subway Celebration on June 6, 1908. Exclusion from the Long Island event so close to her home was especially painful. Curiously, the *Los Angeles Herald* reported "that the committee refused her entrance in accordance with the rule of the racing board that barred women from participating in racing events of all kinds."[11] The paper went on to say "the ruling is substantially the same as that was made in Europe, where women have been barred from all competitions of this character."[12] It is not clear just what "racing board" the *Herald* referred to. It could have been the AAA Contest Committee, which was now responsible for sanctioning most races in the United States. However, the AAA had, as yet, made no public announcement that the racing competition rules had been changed to eliminate female participants. Had some secret agreement already been made that was leaked to the Los Angeles paper? The AAA Contest Board meetings were not open to the public. In addition, the debate and decision to banish women from racing was never mentioned in the Contest Board minutes that still exist.[13] Consequently, it is impossible to determine if the AAA Contest Board had already decided to eliminate women competitors from racing in 1908, without setting a date for this change. Fortunately, Mrs. Cuneo would score her greatest racing triumph in February 1909, before any public announcement was made. Since rumors about banning women from racing that had already surfaced early in 1908, Joan Cuneo's success at New Orleans could not have been the original reason for changing the rules. The decision was already in the works.

It is clear that Joan Cuneo's desire to race against the best male drivers, whether professionals or skilled amateurs, ruffled the feathers of the male establishment — and those of some women, too. However, the reasons for growing anti-female racer sentiment held by the middle- and upper-class members of the AAA and the Automobile Manufacturers Association were deep rooted and complex. They went far beyond the lingering influence of Victorian values. Some members of the upper class were concerned about the increasing professionalization of the sport. Initially, wealthy sportsman and car manufacturers had driven their cars for either the thrill of competition or a desire to promote their product. By 1908, professional drivers heavily outnumbered amateurs in sanctioned races, although nearly every race meeting included a series of less competitive events for amateur drivers. Even the prizes awarded were gradually changing from silver cups or gold medals to cash. Professionals had no need for silver cups or gold medals: they raced for a living. Gradually wealthy amateur sportsmen and manufacturers either retired from racing or were killed or seriously injured while competing. By World War I, almost all the men who drove in sanctioned races in the United States were skilled and experienced professionals.

By 1908, many men involved with auto manufacturing and sales had begun to believe that auto racing was no longer the best means to promote their products racing as a sport. They thought the mounting number of drivers, mechanics and spectators who were killed or injured at races had a negative effect on sales. Other manufacturers thought racing had outlived its usefulness as a promotion tool for the automobile, and a few believed the current cars were just too dangerously powerful to be raced.

In the end, despite these fears, the faction that wanted to eliminate auto racing could not kill the sport, even though it is still extremely dangerous. Too many members of the male establishment either loved racing or had a vested interest (profiting from racing) in seeing it continue. As a compromise, the AAA literally threw Joan Cuneo and other women who hoped to compete on even terms with men "under the bus" by not allowing them to race. Despite the growing number of articles touting the skill and ability of women behind the wheel, the AAA Contest Board seemed to believe that trading on the old fears regarding the frailty and incompetence of women was the best way to save racing. All of these arguments would be expanded and further developed when the Automobile Manufacturers Association entered the battle for the control of American racing later in the year.

Did Mrs. Cuneo see this coming in 1908? It is hard to say. Despite the growing number of times she was turned away from competitions, she kept on challenging the male establishment. From comments she later made, Joan Cuneo eventually came to believe that women had been banned because men didn't want to lose to women. Many other men and women also believed this at the time. It gradually became the standard answer for why women were banned from racing. Today Joan Cuneo is still blamed for getting women banned from racing in books about the early days of racing, especially those dealing with women racers. However, the elimination of women from auto racing would actually result from a number of factors, which came to a head at the end of 1908.

To the members of the Contest Board, who loved racing, banning women seemed their best option if auto racing was to be saved as a sport.

Despite the rejections she received that spring, Mrs. Cuneo enjoyed both growing national fame and increasing respect for her accomplishments behind the wheel from her fellow competitors. Because of her celebrity status, she was asked to write about her driving experiences and explain why women made good drivers for *Country Life Magazine.* The resulting article, which appeared in March 1908, was titled "Why There Are So Few Women Automobilists."[14] A *Country Life* photographer came to the Cuneo home on Richmond Hill and took a series of photos of Mrs. Cuneo, wearing a grease-spotted dress, at work on her car in her garage. The photos accompanied the article. A lady to her fingertips, Joan Cuneo never wore trousers or overalls when she worked on her cars.

In the article, Joan Cuneo gave several reasons why women initially might be afraid to drive an automobile and then explained why they shouldn't hesitate to take up driving, which she considered a wonderful sport. First, she stated, most women had a natural disinclination to get dirty and many believed they didn't have the ability to understand machinery. However, Mrs. Cuneo believed that the main reason women were afraid to get behind the wheel was that they lacked confidence in their ability to learn how to operate a complex machine. Implied in this statement was the male reluctance to support the participation of women in an occupation considered to be masculine. Obviously, none of these caveats applied to her. She admitted to having already owned seven cars, which she had driven for a total of eighty thousand miles. The accompanying photos proved she didn't mind getting dirty working on her car.

Mrs. Cuneo was aware that not all women, or men for that matter, were capable of learning to drive a car well. However, she continued, the obstacles that kept women from "having the keenest enjoyment of the greatest sport of to-day" were easily overcome.[15] She did not believe that timid or overly excitable women could become good drivers. In fact, she thought they had no moral right to drive, because they could not be trusted with the lives of their passengers. However, self-reliant women who could keep their nerves under control at all times and were capable of making a quick decision would do well.[16] She recommended that they start with a small (and relatively slow-moving) electric car to learn the basics of steering and rules of the road, then move on to a more powerful gasoline car. Joan Cuneo believed that women were more cautious by nature (although she didn't seem to possess this attribute) and therefore were less prone to accidents caused by reckless driving. Finally, she assured those women who worried what might happen if their car broke down that there were always motorists around to lend a helping hand and that it really wasn't that difficult to change a tire.[17]

Although some cities had begun issuing auto licenses including number plates at this time, there was no sort of test associated with getting one, besides proof of ownership. People simply bought a car and headed out on the road, often getting no instruction whatsoever. As a result the number of automobile accidents began to climb as fast as the number of automobiles in the country increased (there were 550,000 automobiles in 1909) and the horsepower and speed of these automobiles grew just as rapidly as their numbers. The problem was compounded because automobiles shared the road with and were often outnumbered by horse-drawn vehicles of all sizes. Horses disliked noisy automobiles, and their drivers often overreacted when meeting an auto. These factors caused a variety of collisions similar to Mrs. Cuneo's unfortunate accident the preceding year. Finally, the quality of the roads almost everywhere in the country ranged from poor to awful, as had been demonstrated on the Glidden Tours, and most roads were more suited for horse-drawn vehicles than automobiles.[18]

In the spring of 1908, Mrs. Cuneo also gained nationwide notice as a result of a newspaper venture designed to publicize the most important automobile event New York City had held to date. In 1907, the New York Automobile Trade Association announced that an Auto Carnival would be held in April 1908 to celebrate the tenth year of the automobile trade in the city. While the carnival itself was organized by a special committee of the New York Trade Association, the *New York Evening World* took charge of a contest to elect a King and Queen "to reign over" the highly publicized event. Printed ballots soon appeared on the automotive page of the *World*, and while votes trickled in slowly at first, by the end of March hundreds of thousands of ballots had been cast. The votes were distributed among a long list of male and female candidates, who had been nominated by the readers.

A number of actresses currently performing in New York received votes; no doubt their supporters thought they would add a dash of glamour to the event. To be fair, many female stars of the stage did own and drive sporty cars, but most were not experienced motorists. To complicate the issue, auto manufacturers were afraid that actresses would use the cars the manufacturers sold to promote their own careers by racing or touring. These conservative gentlemen believed that publicity of this sort would give the wrong impression of their product and hoped an actress would not be elected Queen. However, the contest was open to the public and men of all ages thought that there was nothing wrong with having a beautiful Queen, even if she didn't know how to drive. Elsie Janis, a pretty ingénue, did have some connection to automobiles, as she had starred in a play about the Vanderbilt Cup in 1906. Other female stars who got votes seemed to have no connection to the automotive world besides driving or riding in a car. Eva Tanguay, a vaudeville star known for her flamboyant personality, received many votes, as did Edna May Spooner and Beatrice Morgan, who were currently performing in New York theaters. Pitted against them and a number of other women was Joan Newton Cuneo. At 32, she was not quite so young and pretty, but she was nationally famous because of her skill behind the wheel.

The list of male vote getters was much more eclectic. It ranged from Buffalo Bill Cody, the Wild West showman, to local businessmen, including F.W. Clinton, head of the Danbury Hat Company, Judge J. H. Faulkner, several automobile company executives, including Colonel K. C. Pardee of Maxwell Motors and Leonard K. Clark, the young and handsome superintendent of the New York Transportation Company. Surprisingly, no race car drivers received any votes, although Barney Oldfield was so well known that his name was already synonymous with fast driving.

A week before the balloting closed, the *Evening World* interviewed Mrs. Cuneo at her home and the article, titled "Glidden Tour Trophy Winner May Be Queen," appeared the next day.[19] It seems the *Evening World* favored her to win, as they printed more about Joan Cuneo than they did about all the other candidates combined. In the interview, she again promoted automobiling for women, saying that

> automobiling does not spoil a woman for her natural duties. I think a woman shines in no other relation of life as she does as a mother. My two children, Antonio Newton Cuneo, nine and Magdalena [sic], seven, are my most frequent companions in the car. Sonny is not venturesome but his little sister loves to drive the car sitting on my lap with her little hands on the wheel, and she is becoming quite expert. I do not know how it happened that I was voted for the queen of the carnival but I should appreciate the honor. I suppose some other woman will win it however.[20]

But she was wrong. After the final ballots had been tallied, including more than half a million that were cast in the last hour, Joan Newton Cuneo was elected Queen of the carnival, receiving 280,764 votes, while Leonard K. Clark won the race for King with similar totals.[21] The King and Queen would have the honor of presiding over the most highly publicized event of the six-day-long carnival. This was an illuminated parade of over fifteen hundred automobiles of all kinds, including over one hundred flower-bedecked cars driven by their owners, hoping to win prizes for their decorative efforts. The flower-bedecked car Queen Cuneo was to drive was a Mora, a relatively unknown make that would be marketed for only five years.[22] There would also be a number of other events requiring the presence of the King and Queen, including several banquets, a tour, and a hill climb. In addition, the automobile dealers of New York had set up eye-catching displays of their latest models along "automobile row."

The news of Joan Newton Cuneo's election as Queen of the Auto Carnival was heralded in the *Holyoke Transcript*, which stated that her picture adorned the front pages of all the New York papers. Although the Auto Carnival was widely covered in a number of newspapers across the country, the only newspaper that had extensive coverage of the Queen and King was the *New York Evening World*. It was their contest, after all. The *Transcript* went on to say that Joan Cuneo was "rated the most intrepid woman auto driver in the country, if not in the world"!!![23]

Although the parade of more than fifteen hundred vehicles was late in starting, the more than half a million spectators who lined the parade route waited cheerfully.[24] One of Queen Cuneo's attendants, "Prince Antonio Cuneo," age nine, was missing from the Mora when the parade was about to start. After more than an hour's frantic search of the vicinity, Antonio was finally found. He was playing jacks with Billy, a bellhop, in the cloakroom of the hotel where the car was parked. As the Queen's car would roll off second in line after the grand marshal's car and the little prince was to participate in the coronation ceremony that preceded the parade, they had to find him. By the time Antonio was back

Joan Cuneo and her son, Antonio (Sonny), ready to lead the Auto Carnival parade during her reign as queen. They are sitting in a rose and lily-bedecked Mora automobile. Sonny had just been located after going AWOL to play jacks with the hotel bellhop and he is not happy (courtesy of the National Automotive History Collection, Detroit Public Library).

in his place, an hour and one-half had gone by. No one seemed to mind the delay, especially since all the vehicles would be visible in the dark, because of special efforts made to illuminate the cars.[25] Finally, the grand marshal's car slowly began the drive along the parade route, between crowds of cheering onlookers.

Motor World provided the best description of the flower-bedecked cars of the carnival royalty:

> The royal chariot in which Queen Cuneo, her two small children and attendants sat [Joan Cuneo did not drive the car] was arranged as a throne, with a crown-shaped canopy decorated all over with American beauty roses and Easter lilies. The wheels were concealed by clusters of roses. Immediately following the queen was King Clark—who in everyday life is a taxicab superintendent—garbed sumptuously in crimson robes, with heralds, carrying long trumpets, standing on the footboards.[26]

As it turned out, the parade was worth the wait. After the flower-bedecked cars of the grand marshal and the carnival royalty came a line of the latest racing machines, with the noted AAA starter Howard [*sic*: Fred J.] Wagner as grand marshal of this division. The snorting, belching cars were driven by well-known racers such as Barney Oldfield and Emanuel Cedrino. The old-time models came next. The first in line was the oldest car in the parade, an 1893 Haynes, driven by Elwood Haynes himself. The "peculiar little car" was followed by ten more Haynes autos, showing the advances the company had made in the last 15 years.[27] It may seem strange today, but in 1908 the public already considered autos built a few years earlier as ancient curiosities, so quickly had the automobile industry progressed. There was much interest in the early models and the racing cars that evening, and people crowded around them during their wait for the start of the parade.

Elwood Haynes, who many credit with building the first American automobile, drove it to New York from Washington, D.C., where it had been on exhibit at the Smithsonian, for the parade. When he reached New York City, Haynes was promptly arrested by a bicycle policeman for driving without a license number showing. The overzealous policemen hauled him before a magistrate. After Haynes explained that the Smithsonian Museum had loaned him the car to drive it in the New York parade, the magistrate allowed him to drive his car in the parade without penalty or license.[28] Undoubtedly the most unusual vehicle among the historic cars was the wind wagon of Dr. Julian P. Thomas. The wind wagon was a motorized tricycle or three-wheeled car. Its motor powered not a driveshaft or a chain but a large propeller at the rear of the vehicle that produced a strong current of air. The whirling propeller drove the car but also blew dust and street debris over the crowds lining the street as it passed before them. The contraption created quite a stir, but most were glad to see it move out of sight.[29]

After the historic cars came a display of the latest-model pleasure and commercial vehicles of all kinds. Last in line were at least a hundred strikingly decorated cars driven by their owners in competition for prizes in various categories. A string of commercial displays and floats ended the lengthy procession which had taken more than an hour and one-half to pass any given point. Near the end of the parade, an automobile-drawn wagon carrying a cart horse trundled along. On the wagon was written in large letters "Farewell the Horse!" a prophecy with which many spectators readily agreed. When the last vehicles of the grand procession finally reached Columbus Circle, it was long after 11:00 P.M., and spectators and participants slowly headed for home. Even then people were reluctant to leave and kept congratulating the promoters on organizing the first of what they hoped would be an exciting annual event. Many likened the crowd along the parade route that night to those who gathered in the city to celebrate New Year's Eve.[30]

On Wednesday evening, King Leonard and Queen Joan and their retinue, along with the "automobile Magnates" in town for the carnival, were feted at an elaborate theater party held at the Majestic Theater. Mrs. Cuneo, clad in an "exquisite pink chiffon gown," was accompanied by her husband, Andrew Cuneo, and her children. The entertainment included some special touches added to entertain the automobile-loving audience.[31] Thursday morning, many of the automobilists in town for the carnival drove out to Fort George to witness a hill climb organized by the Carnival Committee. Queen Joan and King Leonard presided over the event, but Mrs. Cuneo would have much preferred to be a participant rather than a spectator. In the evening, Miss Edna May Spooner, currently starring in David Belasco's *The Wife*, played homage to the little woman who had defeated her in the contest for queen, by hosting her and her retinue in "royal boxes" at Blaney's Lincoln Square Theater. After viewing the play, the royal party, including Prince Antonio and Princess Maddalena, were treated to a reception held on the stage.[32] By the end of the carnival week, everyone agreed that it had been a huge success and the manufacturers association was already planning to hold another the following year.

The automobile-related activates of Mrs. Cuneo, during the spring and early summer of 1908 brought her both disappointment and pleasure. She did not get to participate in any of the sanctioned races she had tried to enter. However, she would have been an unusual woman indeed if she had not enjoyed her brief reign as the Queen of the Auto Carnival. Although she hadn't yet competed in any sanctioned races in 1908, she had the Glidden Tour to look forward to and she hoped there would be other opportunities to race in the future.

The 1908 tour was scheduled to start on July 9 and finish on July 23, taking a roundabout route of 1,669 miles from Buffalo to Saratoga, New York, by way of Pittsburgh, Philadelphia, Boston and the White Mountains.[33] Making a good showing in the tour had become increasingly important to the automobile manufacturers, who now entered teams of their machines, as well as some of the larger motor clubs, which entered teams of their own. This made it increasingly difficult for individual motorists to win any kind of award. Even Joan Cuneo, who planned to drive her new 50 hp Rainier, joined a motor club team to enhance her chances. The major tire companies, including Goodrich, Diamond, Fisk and Empire, also had a stake in this venture and had begun to feature testimonials from participants like Mrs. Cuneo in their advertising. The dominant influence of the manufacturers was an important factor in the demise of the Glidden Tour a few years later. Another was that the original purpose of Jasper Glidden had been accomplished. Automobiles were growing in popularity by leaps and bounds, as was their reliability and ease of use. More and more couples and family groups had begun to tour the country on their own and later wrote travel books about their experiences. Emily Post, much better known for her books on etiquette, published an account of her auto tour to California in 1915.

M. Worth Colwell was again along to report on the Glidden Tour and commented at the beginning of his article that "the AAA almost concluded that women shouldn't be allowed to play in its little games, but then relented, and Mrs. Cuneo was there with her Rainier."[34] Colwell must have been privy to information about banning women from competition. In fact, although Colwell said Mrs. Cuneo was there "to uphold the claim of the fair sex to recognition as 'safe and sane' operators of motor cars in competitions," there would actually be two women in the 1908 tour.[35] Mrs. E. W. Shirley of Jamestown, New York, entered her Overland runabout in the competition for the Hower Trophy.[36] Although Mrs. Shirley would also be cheered by the crowds as they passed through towns en route, her activities were not monitored as closely as Joan Cuneo's. After she had gained some demerits, Mrs. Shirley was hardly mentioned in the newspapers.

Despite the publicity she generated for Rainier, the *San Antonio Light* reported that Mrs. Cuneo had a difficult time recruiting an observer. The Rainier Motor Car Company provided no support for her entry, even though this would be the second time she drove one in the tour. She finally managed to recruit an observer from the ranks of the many newspaper reporters who followed the tour, but he would not actually ride in her car. Mrs. Cuneo would only have a woman companion, Mrs. E. S. Berwick, and a mechanic (Louis Disbrow) with her. Again, "the little woman "would be the only one to drive the car the entire length of the tour.[37]

On July 12, the *New York Daily Tribune* reported that Mrs. Cuneo had been served with a summons when the tourists stopped for the night in at the Hotel Schenley in Cambridge Springs, Pennsylvania. Allegedly, she had run into the car of one James Haines, a local resident, during the 1907 tour, causing $50 in damages. A later account in *The Horseless Age* gave a different version of the incident. According to *The Horseless Age*, on the run to Bedford Springs last June Mrs. Cuneo had smashed into Haines' car, which had been pulled up alongside the road for repairs. Haines had been under the car when she hit it and had been badly hurt. His wife and another woman traveling with them had been sent back up the road to warn oncoming tourists of the disabled car. The Haines party said that all the tourists except Mrs. Cuneo slowed down, "but she dashed on at a high rate of speed and crashed into the car and then drove on without waiting to see what damage was done; consequently they were suing her for $500 damages"[38] Because she had not responded to his lawyer's demands and Haines had learned that she would pass through the area again as a Glidden Tourist, he made arrangements to serve the papers when the tourists stopped for the night.

Mrs. Cuneo's account was quite different from that of Haines. She recalled that only the top of her car struck the other one as she rounded a turn last year, but as she thought no material damage had been done, she continued onward. She told her fellow tourists that she would have her lawyer look into the matter.[39] As a result, Mrs. Cuneo left Cambridge Springs the next morning with the rest of the tourists, without appearing at court to answer the charges.[40] She didn't want to lose any time on the day's run to Bedford Springs, which she knew from the preceding year was an extremely difficult one.

In a similar vein, in another account of the 1908 tour she was reported to have driven at 40 to 50 mph on the leg between Johnstown and Harrisburg, "where she sent the big Rainier over the mountains at an alarming pace," saying that she really had to "beat it" for more than 40 miles in order to have some spare time at Albany. According to the newspaper, "such driving has gained [her] a universal reputation in the driving world.[41] The paper didn't mention just what kind of reputation they meant!

On July 15, Mrs. Cuneo had another close call behind the wheel that would have seriously shaken up most people. As she approached a railroad crossing near Coldenham, New York, the flagman on duty motioned her to cross the tracks. Then he saw to his horror that an express train was coming fast and he dropped the gates. Joan Cuneo, with a typically quick reaction, put her foot down on the pedal and drove across the tracks just as the gates were descending. The crossing gates tapped the rear of her car as the Rainier cleared the tracks, just missing the express train as it flashed by. This was yet another instance of Joan Cuneo's famous luck, but she again reacted with typical coolness. As the *New York Times* reported, Mrs. Cuneo "did not seem to be worked up over the occurrence."[42]

When the tourists reached Albany, New York, Mrs. Cuneo still had a clean score, although Mrs. Shirley had acquired a few faults and dropped out of contention. Now Joan Cuneo was greeted by crowds, whenever they saw the big Rainier driven by a little woman wearing an elaborate hat. They had made up a verse, which they sang to the tune of "Mr. Dooley" whenever she appeared:

> O Mrs. Cuneo, O Mrs. Cuneo,
> The greatest woman driver that we know;
> She keeps a-going, she makes a showing,
> Does Mrs. Cuney-uney-uney-O[43]

The 1908 tour had its ups and downs, in the quality of both the roads traveled and the food and accommodation available to the tourists. A few nights they had to deal with very poor or nonexistent lodgings, and they went without a few suppers and lunches. At other stops, they were entertained royally and treated to fine meals. The stop in Boston was particularly memorable for the tourists, as they enjoyed a clambake and shore dinner and then a series of amusing speeches. At the end, Mrs. Cuneo had to respond to a unanimous toast. She replied with a smile that "women must always have the last word, but nevertheless, it was not least," and her audience then serenaded her for several minutes with the "Mrs. Cuneo" song.[44]

On the twelfth day of the tour, a number of the cars encountered difficulties, even the chairman, the stern and proper Mr. Hower, and Mr. Glidden. They were riding in the tonneau of the official's car, a Pierce Great Arrow, when the car "flew into a ditch" and both gentlemen were thrown out. Their driver, Mr. Wilkinson, had tried to avoid a team of horses without frightening them and ended in the ditch instead. Although neither gentleman was hurt, it took 35 minutes to get the car out.[45] Others had a variety of mishaps, and Mrs. Cuneo was one of this group. Despite her new Fisk tires with detachable rims, she had tire trouble. To make matters worse, the Rainier broke a fan belt. She was forced to make up the one hour and fifteen minutes she had lost, driving hard on rough and narrow mountain roads. M. Worth Colwell reported that "when she reached the control, she seemed about exhausted, and was suffering from a strained knee."[46] Joan had kept her clean score, but it had taken a tremendous toll on her amazingly strong constitution. The night before the tourists were to reach their final stop at Saratoga, there were 27 contestants left with a clean score, 22 for the Glidden and 5 for the Hower. Only three of the ten contesting auto clubs were still in competition. On Mrs. Cuneo's team, Chicago Motor Club 2, one of the three members had only 942 points, while she and the other Chicago team member had perfect scores of 1000.

The tourists were happy to reach the beautiful resort town of Saratoga on July 23.[47] At the conclusion of the tour, her fellow participants commented on Mrs. Cuneo's sportsmanlike behavior and good humor, as well as the strength of the small, gentle, slightly built woman. Again she had driven every inch of the route while men drivers often grew exhausted and were forced to rest and be relieved.[48] After it was recorded that Mrs. Cuneo was the first (and only) woman to complete a Glidden Tour with a perfect score, she was again presented with a silver cup by the other contestants, who "admired the skilful little woman's pluck."[49] In addition, she received a gold medal from the AAA for finishing with a perfect score and a handsome cup from the Chicago Motor Club for her contribution to their team.[50] She responded with her customary innate modesty:

> It has been my ambition for years to make a perfect score in the Glidden Tour and I am supremely happy now that I have finished perfect. All along I have felt confident of doing so. My car was running every bit as well as if I was putting it in my garage at home and having it locked up every night. This is pleasing because it is a new 45–50 HP Rainier that I bought this spring and it had not been thoroughly tried out before starting on the tour.[51]

Ironically, the *New York Times* reported that "the combination of expertness as a driver and womanly modesty exhibited by Mrs. Cuneo ... will go far towards opening ... other contests to women. Even those opposed to women as drivers ... were won over by her uniform good nature and sportsmanlike conduct."[52] Instead it seems to have had exactly the opposite result. Another rather ironic result of her achievement on the tour was that shortly after the tour ended the Rainier Motor Car Company began to feature Mrs. Cuneo's exploits in a number of advertisements in the *New York Times* and other automotive journals. However, the company had not supported her participation in the tour and her expenses had been heavy. The following ad appeared on September 20, 1908: "The same Rainier '50' which Mrs. Joan Newton Cuneo drove for 2000 miles in the Glidden Tour of 1908 with an absolutely perfect score was entered by her in the Long Island Efficiency Contest September 16th and 17th, carrying five passengers, all women, and again finished without a single penalization."[53]

Mrs. Cuneo hoped to encourage other women to take up automobiling as a sport by her exploits on the Glidden and was encouraged when she read about four ladies from Elgin, Illinois, who traveled alone from Elgin to New York City and back by themselves with no male help. She answered those who felt their venture was foolhardy by saying:

Why should they not do that. I have shown that it is possible for a woman to do these things and I sincerely hope that others will take hold and open up the blessed country for women in a motor car. Why should they drive around cities all the time with the attending dangers when the sweet smelling country is before them with all these beautiful mountain views ... these beautiful resorts ... and so on ... say to the ladies that touring is a rest and not work ... that they may undertake country driving without fear, providing they will but make the effort. The country has no terrors for me and need have none for other women providing they will use judgment and go about the trips with the utmost care at first. Confidence in themselves will soon come and ultimately we shall see healthier and better women and all will be due to the blessed opportunities provided by the motor car bringing my sex into the open air of the mountains and the plains.[54]

Joan Cuneo, although always denying she was a feminist, chafed at the limitations placed on middle-class women by the societal conventions of the late Victorian era. While she was comfortable in her drawing room entertaining callers, she loved to spend time outdoors and often drove long distances in all kinds of weather. She appreciated the freedom that automobiling gave her and wanted other women to gain self-reliance and freedom through the sport of automobiling as she had. In addition, she believed motoring would improve their general health as they spent more time outdoors.

In April of 1908, Andrew Cuneo bought two lots in New Orleans at the corner of Tchoupitoulas, Saint Peter, Market and St. James.[55] He again visited the city in August of 1908 to attend a meeting of the Oyster Commission.[56] Cuneo had several business interests in New Orleans by this time, not surprising because he had many friends among the city's large Italian community. When he returned to New York City, he told his wife that the New Orleans Auto Club was planning a series of races in February 1909 at the end of Mardi Gras. Thus Joan Cuneo had time to think about what races she might enter in New Orleans and what car she might bring and perhaps even shop for a new one. In the meantime she spent time with her children and participated in several tours.

In September, she entered the Long Island Efficiency Run mentioned in the Rainier ad. This must have been an easy drive for her and her five female passengers, as she was very familiar with the roads on Long Island. However, some of the male competitors had trouble with the deep sand and mud holes along the route. Again, she was the only female entrant. However, her mechanician, Louis Disbrow, who usually accompanied her on tours, drove another Rainier in the run, and both finished with a perfect score. Disbrow's car may have been furnished by the Rainier Motor Car Company, or it might have been Joan Cuneo's first 35 hp 1907 Rainier.

Early in January 1909, she would enter a similar event, an endurance run exclusively for women drivers. This event was to start from the Plaza Hotel in New York City and end at the Walton Hotel in Philadelphia, with the ladies returning the next day. Besides Mrs. Cuneo, who was to drive the Lancia "Lampo," a sporty red race car that had just won the light-car race at Savannah, the event attracted a dozen skilled or semi-skilled

Joan Cuneo with a lady friend, beaming as she sits behind the wheel of the bright red Lancia Lampo that had just driven to victory in the light-car class at Savannah in 1908. They are ready to start the Ladies Endurance run. Although Joan wasn't eligible to win the main prize, she got to their destination first. Notice the series of holes drilled in the frame of the car to reduce its weight (courtesy of Jack Deo, Superior View Photos).

female drivers. They included Mrs. Alice Huyler Ramsey, driving a Maxwell, Miss Harriet Quimby in a Cadillac, six-foot-two Mrs. Evelyn M. Buckman in a Renault, and half a dozen other women. Unfortunately, there is some discrepancy between the entry list and the record of those who finished the event. Miss Quimby, who later gained fame as an aviatrix, was listed as an entrant but not as having completed the tour. On the women's tour, 21-year-old Alice Huyler Ramsey would impress C.W. Kelsey so much by her driving skill that he would recruit her to drive across the country in a Maxwell later that year.[57] Miss Mildred Schwalbach, who became a particular friend of Mrs. Cuneo, was listed among those who completed the run but not in the list of entrants.[58] Not surprisingly, Joan Cuneo managed to reach Philadelphia first, arriving more than an hour ahead of schedule. On the return trip, Mrs. A.W. Seaman was so determined to reach New York ahead of Joan Cuneo that she bumped into the pilot car several times "in a vain attempt to get ahead of Mrs. Cuneo," narrowly avoiding an accident, and was criticized by some of the participants. However, Joan Cuneo excused Mrs. Seaman's actions as those of a novice. She said self-righteously, "If she had been an experienced driver like myself, I would have expected her to be penalized or reprimanded, but she is evidently hazy on the ethics of the sport."[59]

7

The Great Mardi Gras Races

Early in 1909, Joan Cuneo would achieve her greatest success as an auto racer. Surprisingly, it would not happen at a track near her home or on the beach but in New Orleans. Because Andrew Cuneo traveled to New Orleans on a regular basis, Joan learned about the proposed New Orleans Auto Carnival when it was in the planning stage, so she had time to prepare for the competition. Although she had achieved success with her Rainier on several tours, it was reliable rather than fast and had performed poorly in the Bennings race. In order to be competitive at New Orleans, she needed a faster car. She finally selected another four-seat touring model that had already make a name for itself in racing circles: the Knox "Giant." The 50 hp Knox would be built at Springfield, Massachusetts, not far from her old home at Holyoke. The Knox, although not specifically built for racing, had a reputation as a well-built and fast machine. Mrs. Cuneo visited the factory several times to check on her Knox during the construction process and was thrilled with her new car when she picked it up that winter. A major reason for Joan's success in New Orleans would be that she now had a car that compared favorably to most of those that would be raced there by the professional drivers.

Before the Civil War, New Orleans had been a financial and trading powerhouse, as well as a bustling port. Now it was quickly losing ground in these areas to fast-growing western cities like Chicago, Cleveland and Detroit and had actually declined in population in the last 50 years. Men like the New Orleans Auto Club president, T. C. Campbell, and Homer George hoped to boost its economy by promoting the Crescent City as a vacation destination. New Orleans already hosted one annual event that drew many visitors, Mardi Gras. The Mardi Gras season began after the feast of the Epiphany, January 6, and ended at the beginning of Lent, usually sometime in February. Mardi Gras featured a series of parades and balls, held by a number of krewes, or social organizations. The carnival season usually lasted about a month but could be longer, depending on the date of Easter, which varied from year to year. Mardi Gras formally drew to a close after the Rex Parade on Shrove Tuesday, the day before the Catholic penitential season of Lent began on Ash Wednesday. Its timing could not have been better. Mardi Gras drew people to New Orleans when the city's weather was at its best. In the days before air-conditioning, not many people came to hot, humid New Orleans in the summer unless they absolutely had to.

New Orleanians had long enjoyed horse racing and had been quick to appreciate the faster automobile. In 1904, Barney Oldfield visited New Orleans and set speed records at the Fair Grounds horse track. Why not, thought the New Orleans Automobile Club (NOAC), combine the two events, holding an auto carnival featuring the nation's leading drivers on the last days of Mardi Gras? The auto enthusiasts could watch thrilling races

during the day and dance the night away, if they had an invitation to an exclusive Mardi Gras ball. Adding a race program would answer critics who complained there was little to do during Mardi Gras except attend carnival-related events.

At the Auto Carnival, Joan Cuneo would get her chance to race mainly because of the risk-taking mentality of Homer George who put together the race program. Banking on the New Orleanians' love of (horse) racing and New Orleans' civic pride, he was ready to do anything, including inviting women to race, to bring people to New Orleans. The city fathers desperately wanted to bring back the prosperity their city had enjoyed in the antebellum period and they hoped the race carnival would be a start.

New Orleans boasted several tracks built for horse

Joan, after giving her brand-new Knox Giant a trial run in January 1909, at the Knox Factory at Springfield, Massachusetts. The fenders are off and she is wearing racing goggles and a duster (courtesy of John Y. Hess, president of the Knox Motor Car Club, original photograph from his personal collection).

racing: the historic Fair Grounds, a one-mile oval dirt track, and another at City Park. Both drew substantial crowds every year during the racing season. However, in 1908 the appropriately named Locke Law was passed by the Louisiana legislature and signed by the governor. A majority of the people of Louisiana outside New Orleans, as well as the still powerful Catholic Church, supported this bill, which ended racing and betting in New Orleans for seven years. Many ordinary citizens were tired of the wholesale corruption that permeated the sport. A similar disgust of racetrack corruption had already caused racing to be banned in a number of states. Ironically, the Fair Grounds would indirectly benefit from the national movement against horse racing. Not realizing racing would soon be banned in their city, too, the Fair Grounds management bought a fancy grandstand from a St. Louis racetrack. The track had gone out of business after racing was prohibited in Missouri. The Fair Grounds owners had the attractive building, which included a lovely covered Palm Court, reassembled in New Orleans. The Palm Court gave the city its largest covered auditorium to date. Fortunately, the addition of the grandstand was quite a draw, even during the ban on racing. The French Fete drew fifteen thousand people to the Fair Grounds in 1908, and the venue would be used for many other events before horse racing finally returned to New Orleans.[1]

The NOAC saw the temporary demise of horse racing as a golden opportunity for automobilists. These ardent city promoters planned to schedule an automobile carnival during the last three days before Mardi Gras in 1909. They immediately contacted other AAA clubs to notify them of the carnival and asked them to generate publicity. They also wrote to racing notables including well-known starter Fred Wagner and wealthy race promoter William K. Vanderbilt for advice and suggestions. The promoters also planned a series of promotional pieces to advertise the carnival.

First, however, they had to decide what kind of races they would hold, which drivers to invite, and how they would prepare the track for auto racing. Initially preparing the track seemed the easiest. New Orleans Auto Club president T. C. Campbell decided not to purchase *glutern* (a mixture of oil and tar often called taroid), which the eastern tracks used to keep down the dust and harden the track surface. Campbell believed they could save money at the Fair Grounds by using the refuse from Louisiana sugar mills called bagasse. Bagasse consisted of bits of cane stalk left behind from sugar refining. It was free for the taking and readily available in huge, moist heaps. For some strange reason, Campbell believed sugarcane waste could serve exactly the same purpose as glutern, although the only characteristic bagasse shared with glutern was high moisture content.[2] If spreading bagasse on the track worked as well as he expected, the canny Campbell thought that they could easily develop a market for this useless by-product of the sugarcane industry selling it to keep the dust down at other dirt tracks.[3] However, Campbell soon realized his mistake and used taroid instead.

Unlike almost all other auto race promoters in 1909, Campbell and George wanted to recruit women drivers for the New Orleans meet. They believed that watching women " duel with death" on the track as eagerly as their male counterparts would be a huge draw. According to NOAC publicity, New Orleans would host the most notable event ever arranged in auto-racing history by adding a race for the women's championship of the United States. The *Picayune* trumpeted: "Ladies to Flirt with Death with Same Enthusiasm as Men Drivers World Renowned!"[4] Campbell and George then contacted Fred Wagner in New York to see if he knew any women who might be willing to take up the challenge. Wagner knew Joan Newton Cuneo well; he assured them that she was already interested and that Alyce Byrd Potter of Elgin, Illinois, said she would enter.

Not nearly as well known as Joan Cuneo, Alyce Byrd Potter was a relative newcomer to the sport. In 1907, she had gained fame at the Harlem Track in Chicago when she set a new women's record rumored to be faster than Cuneo's in a "90 hp racing car."[5] Potter, born to an upper-middle-class family, had been bored with playing golf and tennis at the country club. She took up driving after firing her chauffeur when he arrived to pick her up at the country club under the influence of alcohol. After driving her car home, she developed an interest in touring and working on automobiles. Besides her unopposed victory in the Ladies' Championship of the West in Chicago, she established a new record for driving from Chicago to Boston and back. Potter beat the previous record, established by a man, by four hours. She had three female companions with her and took complete care of her Haynes automobile. Mrs. Cuneo had been in Chicago in 1907 when Alyce Potter set her record at the Harlem Track. She knew and liked Miss Potter and looked forward to racing against her.[6]

Campbell believed the publicity gained from recruiting these two women might lure even more female racers to New Orleans. He had heard of a few other easterners, including Mrs. Rogers and Mrs. Fitler, who might also want to compete for the women's championship. The club planned to donate a handsome silver trophy for the winner of the women's event, augmented with a floral piece in the shape of a seven-foot-long automobile, to honor their female sensibilities. Non-professionals would have an opportunity to compete for the amateur championship of America, open only to *gentlemen*. The Klaw & Erlanger theater group had pledged a trophy worth $500 for the winner of this race. George had come to New Orleans as a press agent for the Tulane and Crescent Theaters owned by the Klaw & Erlanger syndicate and he coaxed them into donating the trophy.[7]

Getting the word out regarding the Mardi Gras races was critical. T. C. Campbell and Homer George were determined to follow the lead of the Savannah and Ormond Beach race organizers, who advertised their events all over the country. Largely at their own expense, Campbell and George ordered one hundred thousand copies of a "handsome six page folder printed on heavy enamel paper and superbly illustrated."[8] The folder was to be distributed to hotels and businesses in 30 cities in the Northeast by George. In addition, the club handed out thousands of window cards. They also hoped that newspapers throughout the country would promote the Mardi Gras Auto Carnival as eagerly as the *Picayune* would.[9]

Articles about the Auto Carnival began to appear in the *Picayune* in January 1909. Soon readers were greeted with a barrage of information about the carnival on an almost daily basis. They learned that wealthy Chicago sportsman Arthur W. Greiner had notified the NOAC that he would drive a special racing car in the amateur events. Greiner assured the club that he had secured the entry of Alyce Potter, who would drive a Haynes in the women's championship against Joan Cuneo and her Knox. Unfortunately, Greiner would not make good on this promise. The article also promoted Miss Potter's racing experience, saying that "she had competed in many events with it [her Haynes]" when in reality she had only raced once, driving unopposed.[10] However, Greiner did enter his National in the Mardi Gras race carnival and said he had chartered a private railroad car to bring his party to New Orleans.

On February 4, the *Picayune* announced that the NOAC had decided against holding a two-hour race, instead focusing on "speed, speed, speed." The truth was that the track insurers forbade the club from holding night races at a track that had "vast quantities of gasoline and oil laying around in storage."[11] The insurance company had a point, as large quantities of these flammable liquids would be needed to light the track. Campbell concluded, correctly, that shorter events that featured professionals (drivers), women and amateurs, would be more exciting for the spectators.

Having given up the idea of using bagasse, workmen had already started preparing the track. After scraping off vast quantities of sand, they would pour thousands of gallons of oil on the track.[12] Today's concerns about oil spills and pollution of groundwater were not a consideration for the racetrack owners in 1909. Oiling a dirt track to keep down the dust was common practice at the time, and thousands of gallons were poured on dirt-track surfaces all over the country before auto races.

On February 7, the *Picayune* printed a picture of the Klaw & Erlanger trophy, inscribed *World's Speed King.* It was flanked by cameo portraits of Fred J. Wagner, the referee and starter; Mrs. Joan Newton Cuneo; T. C. Campbell; and Homer George. Although Miss Potter was still mentioned, Mrs. Cuneo was identified as the only woman in the race. The article went on to list the top three male entrants and the cars they would drive. They were George Robertson, the winner of the Vanderbilt Cup race, and his Simplex, Lewis Strang, the winner of the Savannah, Briarcliff and Lowell races, in his Isotta, and Ralph De Palma, holder of the world's speed records from one to five miles, and his Fiat Cyclone. Then the less distinguished pilots and amateur drivers were listed along with a few New Orleans car owners who hoped to try their luck in the amateur races.[13]

The newspaper then wrote about an ongoing feud between George Robertson and Lewis Strang. Robertson was the "daredevil pilot" and Strang the "brainy and nervy "driver. Both, according to the *Picayune,* could lay claim to being the best race-car driver in America but might have to give way to the relative newcomer Ralph De Palma. Only Robertson planned to drive an American-built car, the Simplex, during the race meeting, as many racers thought European cars were more reliable and faster.

The next day, the newspaper played up the formal entry of Mrs. Joan Newton Cuneo and dropped a bombshell. Before she mailed in her entry form, Mrs. Cuneo had checked not only the women's championship race but every other event on the auto carnival entry form as well. The *Picayune* gushed that "it was hard for even a calloused automobile race follower to realize that a frail woman is possessed of such daring and nerve ... to undertake to pit her skill and courage against the strong men who are reckoned as the greatest drivers in the world."[14]

Joan Cuneo remained a reserved and modest woman despite her celebrity status and had sent no publicity photos along with her entry. George and Campbell were forced to find their own photos "of the wonderful woman." This was not difficult because many photographers, including the famous sports photographer Lazarnick, had taken her picture by 1909. The article also went on to mention that Mrs. Cuneo drove because she loved to race and her husband, a wealthy New York banker, spent thousands a year on her hobby, "just to gratify her desire to speed along the fast stretches of the road and track, and show her skill in making the turns."[15]

The *Picayune* concluded with a story of Mrs. Cuneo's success in the long-distance race at the Benning Track in Washington, D.C., in 1907, where she defeated several male competitors at a very dangerous track.[16] This, according to the newspaper, was the reason why the AAA began to reject female entrants. But unlike other clubs, the NOAC had the courage to brave the AAA and add a women's event, which would be the premier event of the carnival.[17] However, most race promoters seem to have already decided to exclude women. In a small article printed on February 11, the Savannah Auto Club, which would again hold races in March, once more rejected the application of Mrs. Cuneo to race in their main event, as "the committee did not wish to establish such an innovation."[18]

Unaware of this setback, Joan Newton Cuneo arrived in New Orleans by train on the same day, accompanied by her husband, Andrew, and her son, Antonio (Sonny). Although Mrs. Cuneo had never visited New Orleans, her husband was well known in the city. As a result, her accomplishments as a daring female driver were already celebrated among New Orleans society. Before traveling to New Orleans, she had visited the Knox Factory in Springfield, Massachusetts, to check on the progress of the new 50 hp Knox, "Giantess," she would drive in the races.[19]

In an interview with the Cuneos the *Picayune* printed an intriguing story of how Joan Cuneo got into auto racing. Parts of it are inaccurate; her first car was listed as an electric, but it actually was a small steam-powered car, and her second vehicle was not a gasoline-powered car but a more powerful White Steamer. According to the *Picayune*, when his wife complained of being covered with dust as she was constantly passed by faster cars Andrew Cuneo, an indulgent husband, willing to provide her with any luxury, ordered a *huge machine* for her! However, he was afraid that she wouldn't be able to handle the new vehicle and secretly hired a chauffeur to maintain and drive the car for her. The chauffeur may have been Louis Disbrow, who had been her riding mechanic for the last five years. Over the years, Joan Cuneo and Louis Disbrow grew comfortable in their friendship. In at least one race at New Orleans, he had to hold her in the car when she negotiated sharp, flat turns at speed.[20]

Again the reporter, like most people who saw Joan Newton Cuneo for the first time, was startled by her size and demeanor. Expecting an Amazon, he met a small female a little over five feet tall and weighing less than 125 pounds. The impression she gave was more of a woman who was at home at the family fireside or in society drawing rooms than one who loved a sport "in which nerve, daring and strength are required to a great degree."[21] That she had brought her young son along and they had enjoyed attending a performance of *Buster Brown* at the Crescent Theater, while her husband was entertained by business associates, only reinforced this impression. The Cuneos were probably interviewed at the Grunewald Hotel, the finest in New Orleans at the time, where they would stay for over a month.[22]

110

In 1909, most of the drivers shipped their cars to New Orleans by boat or train. According to the *Picayune*, the race cars of Lewis Strang, Ralph De Palma, Jimmy Ryall and Joan Cuneo were scheduled to arrive on the Morgan Line steamship *El Paso* on February 12. Strang and Ryall had also arrived in the city, and Bob Burman and De Palma were to arrive shortly.[23]

The *Picayune*'s relentless promotion of the Auto Carnival indicates that interest in the Auto Carnival had not been as strong as the NOAC had hoped. The newspaper praised the quality of the entrants, saying that "leading drivers of three lands would compete." However, no foreign drivers would actually drive in any of the race carnival events. Ralph De Palma was consistently referred to as "the foreigner" although De Palma's family had immigrated to the United States when he was a boy and De Palma was an American citizen. Louis Chevrolet was indeed Swiss, but although his name was on the entry list, he would not drive in any races. Foreign cars there were, and one particularly good one, De Palma's Fiat Cyclone, but the carnival would not "bring together the leading drivers of three lands."[24] Barney Oldfield, the most popular driver of the time, had expressed no interest in racing against his rival Ralph De Palma in New Orleans.[25] No wonder the NOAC did not waver in allowing Joan Newton Cuneo her big chance to drive against her male, rivals when other clubs were turning her down; the daring female driver had become their biggest draw.

The *Picayune* also carried much information about the trophies that would be awarded to the amateur drivers. In 1909, auto racing still attracted a few wealthy amateurs like Louis Bergdoll, Caleb Bragg, Arthur Greiner, and Foxhall Keene and, of course, Joan Cuneo, who raced because she loved speed. Campbell and George also hoped that local drivers would want to show off their fast cars. Many amateurs enjoyed displaying the silver cups, medals and trophies they won on their mantels or in their smoking rooms. Professional drivers like Strang, Burman, Robertson and De Palma much preferred cash prizes, as racing was their job. Recognizing this, the NOAC would award cash prizes for the professional and open events.

In a 1909 article, Frederic J. Hoskin claimed that a talented racing chauffeur could make between $25,000 and $50,000 a year if he was lucky.[26] By 1909, the meaning of the word "chauffeur" was changing. In 1900 it meant any male (or female) who drove or raced a car, but increasingly it referred to someone who was hired to drive a car. Even $25,000 seems too optimistic an amount in winnings, except for the most successful drivers. The winners' purses generally were small, although contestants could enter a number of races every day. Today, most of the drivers at the highest level race only once a week during the season, unless there are heats or qualifying laps to determine the starting order. In 1909, most race programs featured a number of short races each day. The last race was the featured event, usually 25 to 50 miles long, and the winner usually received a more costly prize. The programs were set up the same way as horse race meetings, which often had eight or nine events of varying lengths. Depending on the season, racing moved south and to California in the winter months and was popular in the Midwest and Northeast during the summer and early fall. Automobiles, unlike horses, could run at top speed more than once a day, as long as nothing on the car broke. Nevertheless, the drivers had to keep their cars in repair or pay a mechanic to do so, buy tires, and pay for travel expenses and their mechanics' salaries. Drivers might also be forced to take time off because of injuries suffered in crashes, which happened regularly. Auto racing was a blood sport in 1909. After watching a few events, locals who signed up for amateur races often got cold feet, failing to show up or hiring professionals to drive for them in the race.

Five days before the race, the *Picayune* listed the following participants in an advertisement: George Robertson, Ralph De Palma, Lewis Strang, Bob Burman, Al Denison, Schelfler (no first name), Arthur W. Greiner, Chevrolet, Ryall (Jimmy), Mrs. Joan N. Cuneo, Miss Alyce Potter and other stars. Admission was $1.00, which included access to the grandstand, and tickets would be on sale before the race at Grunewald's music store.[27] By February 17, most of the professional drivers and some of the amateurs had arrived in New Orleans and spent time tuning up their cars on the streets and in the countryside around New Orleans and visiting the Fair Grounds track.

On February 16, Mrs. Cuneo and a lady passenger in her Knox had turned onto Canal Street from the West End road when Jimmy Ryall in his Vanderbilt Cup racer, with T. C. Campbell as passenger, came up behind her. Ryall expected her to pull over and let him pass, but she stepped on the gas, challenging him to a race. Ryall immediately let the throttle full out, but although he was able to gain on her, he couldn't pass Cuneo's Knox. When the speeding cars reached Claiborne Avenue, they both let up because of the traffic. Poor Ryall spent a good bit of time afterwards telling everyone how he would have passed Mrs. Cuneo, but in fact, he hadn't, and this gave her considerable credit among racing fans in New Orleans.[28]

Despite all their hard work, NOAC members were disappointed over the amount of entries they had received, as registration would close on the 18th. It looked like very few New Orleanians with fast cars were willing to race them on the Fair Grounds track, nor were the city's automobile dealers eager to race their latest modes.

On the day before the races, Joan Newton Cuneo invited Homer George for a practice ride in her Knox. George was nervous about speeding down the road with "a little, frail woman ... with tiny hands and feet handling the controls." He later wrote that "she is the nicest-looking woman imaginable. She is so nearly a typically 'cute' woman that one wonders at her nerve and ability when it comes to handling automobiles."[29] With Joan Cuneo, appearances were deceiving, especially when she got behind the wheel. She enjoyed taking unsuspecting people for ride in one of her race cars and had been trying to lure George into her Knox for several days. He finally ran out of excuses, and they headed out to Lakeview Road. It had, at that time, several straight and level two-mile stretches built of hard-packed shell where the drivers could let their cars out. Poor George clung to the car in fright; the wind whistled past him as the stripped-down car hurtled along the open road. Joan Cuneo, however, "managed the monster like it was a child and complained because it was impossible to let the monster out to its greatest speed."[30] George claimed she got the car up to 90 mph, but it was capable of more than 100 and Mrs. Cuneo did her best to get it there on the straightaway.

During their outing, she admitted to George that she most wanted to win the amateur championship, and the Klaw & Erlanger trophy more than the women's championship. She said:

> I came here with that ambition uppermost in my mind, and I will not be satisfied if I am not successful. I do not fear any man in the world if I am given a good car, in the Knox Giant I have a wonderful machine and whoever wins the trophy will certainly have to do miles in much less than a minute each if that person is to beat me. I have walked all around the track several times and am thoroughly familiar with it. I think I will be able to not only win this amateur championship but set a new mark for 5 miles amateur racing.[31]

Homer George and Mrs. Cuneo were accompanied on the trip by Louis Disbrow, her riding mechanic, and young Antonio Cuneo, who rode in a second car during the speed trial. Nine-year-old Sonny was very proud of his mother's ability to handle a race car, planned to watch her race, and would be the first to congratulate her if she won. After his session in the Knox, George was convinced that Joan Cuneo would win more than one of the races. "She is little short of marvelous," he exclaimed.[32] He was right.

The first day of racing was bright and sunny and a crowd of five thousand locals and tourists assembled in the grandstands at the Fair Grounds to view the spectacle, while dozens of gaily decked cars filled the infield. According to the *Picayune*, the presence of Mrs. J. Newton Cuneo driving her Knox Giant lent a

Publicity photograph of Joan Cuneo that appeared in the New Orleans *Picayune*, probably taken at the Knox factory when she picked up the car. She is dressed in a velvet suit, not ready for driving (courtesy of John Y. Hess, president of the Knox Motor Car Club, original photograph from his personal collection).

Joan Cuneo, Louis Disbrow and her son, Antonio, age ten, after taking Henry George for a fast ride on Lakeview Road outside New Orleans (courtesy of Jack Deo, Superior View Photos).

sensational flavor to the three events (out of six) in which she participated on the first day. "The men cheered her enthusiastically at all times as she would flash past the stand ... but the women, the pretty girls, as well as the older ladies, rooted for De Palma, Strang, Jimmy Ryall or other dare devil fellows ... although they did not always chivalrously slow up when Mrs. Cuneo came within striking distance and tip their hats."[33] At first, most of the New Orleans women in the stands didn't approve of Joan Cuneo's exploits on the track, although later on they began to support her. Even the newspaper thought the other drivers ought to respect her femininity during a race. This was the last thing Mrs. Cuneo wanted on the racetrack.

The first event on Saturday was a one-mile free-for-all time trial to lower Ralph De Palma's world speed record of 51 seconds for the mile, which he had recently set in his Fiat Cyclone. It was easily won by De Palma, with Ryall coming in second in his Matheson, Robertson third in his Simplex, and Mrs. Cuneo fourth in her Knox. The new Orleanians hoped that at least one new world's record would be set at the Auto Carnival. Although De Palma didn't break the mile record, he did better Barney Oldfield's record in the ten-mile speed trial, while Mrs. Cuneo broke her own women's record for five miles in 5:05. Mrs. Cuneo's best showing was in the 50-mile free-for-all, where she finished second behind De Palma. Only De Palma had started from scratch in this race; all the other drivers were given more than half a minute's handicap, with Schelfler, clearly outclassed in his Jackson, getting over a minute's head start. While De Palma drove rings around the others, Joan Cuneo hung in there gamely, finishing second in 52:40.35 to De Palma's 51:37.45. Robertson had a blowout, and Strang withdrew.[34] The five-mile race for New Orleans cars was postponed, as only Anthony Monteleone showed up ready to race with his Thomas. Schelfler won a five-mile event for stock cars in a walkover when Bob Burman withdrew his Buick.

The second day of racing was Joan Newton Cuneo's best. She won the amateur championship, earning the Klaw & Erlanger Trophy despite Jimmy Ryall's crash into the fence as he was going for the lead.[35] She then won the Klaxon Signal ten-mile race, beating a Packard entered by Donnelly, whom she had beaten earlier in the amateur championship. By this time, the crowd was with her and cheered her triumph enthusiastically. She then went on to attempt to lower her mile record to under a minute and just missed, driving the mile from a standing start in just over a minute (1:00⅕). Although she expressed excitement in bettering her previous record, she must have been disappointed to just miss. Joan Cuneo then stated she would not compete in the last two events (ten- and one-hundred-mile races), as her stock of Fisk tires was low and she wanted to save them for the final day's racing. In the ten-mile race De Palma won yet again, while Bob Burman won the one-hundred-mile race in his Buick in a record time of 1:43.39⅖ over Robertson in his Simplex.[36]

The good weather of the first two days was replaced by mist, rain and drizzle on Monday. Although attendance was down the crowd was still large even though Rex, the King of Mardi Gras, was about to parade before thousands of spectators lining the streets of the city center on Fat Tuesday.[37] The first race at 3:00 P.M. was yet another five-mile exhibition by Mrs. Cuneo, who drove unopposed to better the women's championship record. "The plucky woman driver, her fingers decked with diamonds but dressed plainly on account of the oil and dust, lowered the record she had set Saturday by 3 seconds." In the five-mile race for the T. C. Campbell Trophy, she finished third behind Robertson and Burman, with Strang finishing fourth. Mrs. Cuneo also won another five-mile amateur race, again defeating Donnelly's Packard, and Schelfler's Jackson. Probably the most interesting event of the day was the fifth race, a ten-mile handicap. Only De Palma started the race at scratch. Mrs. Cuneo, Strang, and Burman got a 50-second handicap, while Robertson's was 45 seconds. De Palma quickly passed everyone but Burman, who got a fast start. Their cars collided when De Palma moved to pass, and Burman's Buick got the worst of it. Mrs. Cuneo by careful driving managed to finish second, ahead of Robertson and Strang, who had similar handicaps, while the damage to Burman's car forced him to withdraw.[38] Only in the finale, a 50-mile race won easily by Ralph De Palma, did she falter, finishing ten miles behind De Palma, although Strang was five miles behind and Robertson six. Determined as she was, Joan Newton Cuneo did not have the strength to keep up with her male rivals at the end of a long day's racing. At the start of the 50-mile race, she had already muscled her car around a rough track for more than 30 miles at speeds of 50 mph or more.[39]

The final comments of the drivers after the conclusion of the meet were revealing: De Palma, "Treated fine here, but would have broken more records with smoother track"; Mrs. Cuneo, "Just splendid and enough excitement to last a long time"; Robertson, "Car was too heavy for the track"; and Strang, "Hard luck but no complaints, and will drop this losing streak before long," Bob Burman seemed pleased with his victory in the one-hundred-mile race, while Fred Wagner remarked, "One of the best managed meets I've ever attended and some of the greatest driving, all things considered."[40]

On February 25, the NOAC held Automobile Night at the Klaw & Erlanger Tulane Theater and the winners of the major races received their awards. The newspaper commented: "The victories of Mrs. Cuneo in the amateur championship race and other events made her the most prominent figure in the automobile world today. She broke a number of world's records in her racing and defeated the most daring of male contestants in almost every race in which she participated. *Her* driving was really the most astonishing feature of the carnival."[41]

Unfortunately, the Auto Carnival did not turn out to be one of the great annual track-racing events in America, as referee Wagner proclaimed at the start of the meet.[42] Only Ralph De Palma, Bob Burman and Joan Newton Cuneo came away with heightened reputations. De Palma was on his way to becoming the most successful racer of his era, winning every race he entered at New Orleans and setting several speed records. Joan Newton Cuneo won the amateur championship and the Klaxon Signal race and gave her male rivals a run for their money in the others. However, less than a month later all women drivers would be formally banned by the AAA from sanctioned racing. The Mardi Gras Auto Carnival was her swan song, although it was a spectacular one. She had performed beyond the expectations of most, especially since her Knox Giant was not a custom-built race car, although she drove it well. Thrilled, she dashed off a telegram to the Knox Company at the conclusion of the carnival informing them of her success.

Campbell and George should have been proud of their preparation of the track, as there was only one accident with only minor injuries to the driver. However, they were disappointed at the response to their extensive publicity. To them it was only an indifferent success, although they met their expenses. Only four top drivers actually showed up for the races. The size of the purses might have been a factor, as the largest cash prize offered to any winner was $100. Even the amateurs who raced for fun didn't flock to New Orleans. Arthur Greiner, the Chicago sportsman whose arrival was touted, did not race. Carl G. Fisher did not honor his initial commitment to enter the amateur races, nor did William K. Vanderbilt and his wife respond to the New Orleans club's invitation to the Auto Carnival.[43] Jimmy Ryall and F. E. Schelfler, semi-professionals, with some experience, did compete, along with a few lesser-known drivers. Unfortunately, in most of the races, only a few drivers on the entry list actually finished or even started the race. Some of the male amateurs may have been scared off by Mrs. Cuneo's success. None of them would have wanted to be beaten by a woman. The only driver who consistently outraced Mrs. Cuneo was Ralph De Palma, as he won all his races. She managed to come in ahead of Strang, Robertson, and Burman at least once, and they were considered among the top drivers of the day. The belief that they would cut her some slack and "let" her win is interesting but not likely. Her Knox was as fast as any car in New Orleans except for the Fiat Cyclone, and she drove it with confidence. They might not want to run her off the track or "tip their hats to her," but they certainly would not have wanted her to pass them. Finally, Fred Wagner, an experienced starter, gave her the same handicap as two of her male (professional) counterparts for the ten-mile handicap. The men recognized her very real talent as a racer.

Today's tracks are smooth. A caution flag flies if there is an accident and the drivers slow down. Any debris that has fallen off a car is picked up. Although NASCAR'S Sprint Cup cars aren't as easy to steer as the family sedan, they are 100 percent more responsive than the cars of 1909. In addition, they have much better tires and four-wheel brakes. The Knox car that Joan Cuneo drove was hard to steer, with none of the advantages of the modern race cars. The tracks she drove on were reasonably smooth at the beginning of the day. By the last race, they were pitted with ruts from the day's pounding by the heavy cars and littered with debris from accidents or simply with nuts, bolts and car parts that fell off as the drivers roared around the track. She wore goggles but no helmet, and there were no seat belts to keep her in the car. It is no wonder she telegraphed the Knox Motor Car Company on February 23 with news of her success. She wrote: "Hurrah for Knox Giant! Three days events, won three firsts, two seconds, besides making woman's word's records."[44]

Despite the relatively poor turnout, Campbell and George believed that next year's auto carnival would be better, as the Auto Carnival had been widely publicized, mainly due to the efforts of Joan Cuneo and Ralph De Palma. However, Campbell and George were particularly disappointed that the local auto dealers had provided little support. Only Buick and Packard responded to their attempts to fill the stock car races with every make sold in New Orleans. However, even though Buick cars did perform creditably in several events, the Buick Company did not send a noted woman driver from Detroit to drive against Joan Cuneo in the woman's race as they had stated they would in January.[45] They probably realized that there were no women drivers in Detroit who had Mrs. Cuneo's level of skill. Even the "free for all race open to New Orleans drivers" went to Anthony Monteleone by default. He had his Thomas ready to go at the start of the race, while Mr. Lindrose in his Oldsmobile and Mr. Schwartz in his Buick were no-shows. Several others, who had bragged about their fast cars, failed to enter the events open to them. Although the race was initially postponed, when no more drivers showed up the next day starter Wagner finally decided to award the trophy to Monteleone by default.[46]

On the 25th, a mass exodus of drivers and officials from New Orleans began as they headed for the next competition. Most, including Fred Wagner, the starter, would travel to Daytona. Only Mrs. Cuneo remained in New Orleans, bitterly disappointed, because she had finally heard that women would be banned from sanctioned racing the following month. Blocked from competition, she had her touring car shipped to New Orleans and spent some time exploring the area around the city with her son, while her husband completed his business. No doubt she was thinking hard about where and how she might continue her racing career.[47]

Despite the efforts of Campbell and George, the Mardi Gras races would not become an annual tradition in New Orleans, and there would be no more women entrants in sanctioned events for decades. Even the risk-taking NOAC could not allow women to compete or their races would not be sanctioned by the AAA. The NOAC held two more meets at the Fair Grounds track, but only one of these was during Mardi Gras. The second Mardi Gras race carnival drew only three thousand spectators. There were many complaints about the small number of events and participants, so there were no attempts to schedule another. In 1915, horse racing resumed at the Fair Grounds. New Orleans, despite the heroic efforts of the NOAC leadership, would not become an important site of auto racing in the South.

8

Banished!

When Joan Cuneo finally returned to her home at Richmond Hill in March of 1909, she was both elated at what she had accomplished in New Orleans and angry about the underhanded actions of the AAA. She had learned that the Contest Board had quietly changed the rules for 1909, without any public discussion of why women would be eliminated from competing in sanctioned events. Even then, she had a hard time believing that this change in the rules applied to her. She thought she had finally shown decisively by her performance in New Orleans that she was equal to the challenge of competing against male professionals. True, Mrs. Cuneo had not defeated Ralph De Palma at the Auto Carnival, but he was behind the wheel of a Fiat Cyclone, at that time one of fastest cars in the country, and her Knox was no match for the Fiat. She had already decided to make another visit to the Knox Factory at Springfield, Massachusetts, to order a new model, built and painted to her specifications. She planned to pick it up a few months later at the factory. Unfortunately, while this new Knox model, called the Giantess, in honor of Mrs. Cuneo, did prove to be a fast racer, she would never drive it in a sanctioned competition.

A modern reader might ask what kind of relationship Joan Cuneo had with her husband and children during this tumultuous period of her life. She obviously spent a good deal of her time with automobiles, whether touring in the country, competing in events, or working on her cars. While there is quite a bit of information on her public life tucked away in old newspapers across the country, Mrs. Cuneo didn't talk much about her private life. She had daily help, like all women of her class, so she was not responsible for household chores or cooking. She also had a nurse or nanny for the children when they were small, and when they were older they went off to school, although Maddalena's deafness probably required some special education and care. Joan took her children with her whenever possible; both Antonio and Maddalena rode with her in the flower-bedecked Mora during the New York City Auto Carnival. She was obviously proud of young Antonio, or Sonny as she called him, as he was prominently present in several family photos and in New Orleans. Newton family photo albums have yielded no pictures of Maddalena as a child, but she was also a big part of her mother's life as well; she was thrilled by Maddalena's budding skill behind the wheel. Joan Cuneo loved children and was increasingly involved with charity events for orphans while she lived in New York. A woman of her class was expected to fulfill her civic duties in regard to the less fortunate members of the community. However, Mrs. Cuneo did seem to genuinely enjoy loading one of her large cars full of orphans for excursions to amusement parks or a drive into the country. She later said that providing the orphans with a day of freedom had been one of her greatest pleasures in automobiling.[1] Ninety years ago, 97-year-old Alice Newton Childs met cousin Joan Cuneo for the first time. Alice fondly recalled her kindness to a little girl, and she still cherishes Rosa Belle, the doll Joan Cuneo brought her that day.[2]

Andrew Cuneo was often away on business, as he had been since their marriage, but this was expected of the Victorian businessman. Although he did accompany Joan during her first ventures into racing and touring, he had hired Louis Disbrow as her mechanic by 1904. By 1908 she often spent more time with Disbrow, especially on her automobile-related adventures, than she did with her husband. Andrew Cuneo did accompany her for the entire length of the 1905 Glidden Tour and was a member of her party on the 1907 Glidden. He also took pride in her accomplishments, but in 1908 her companion was Mrs. E. S. Berwick, with Disbrow along as her mechanic.

Andrew was also an indulgent husband and provided her with sufficient funds to purchase any type of automobile or automotive equipment she wanted. He may have done this because he had a guilty conscience or because their marriage was dying and they were mainly interested in keeping up appearances. Before World War I, women of her class usually surrendered control of the money they brought into the marriage to their husbands. In fairness, Andrew Cuneo's wealth far exceeded the money that Joan Cuneo inherited from her father, John C. Newton, and Andrew Cuneo, no doubt, paid for her string of expensive automobiles.

Mrs. Cuneo did not lack for women friends and, despite her predilection for fast driving, was always able to recruit four or five women friends to accompany her on a tour or a drive. Mrs. Berwick or another female friend was needed as a companion to keep up appearances when Mrs. Cuneo's husband didn't travel with her. In 1908, it would not have been appropriate even for a married woman to travel alone with a man not her husband, even though they stayed in separate rooms. At the same time, she got along very well with the men she raced against, those who competed with her in Glidden Tours, and race organizers and officials she met (all men). Even after she could no longer compete, she drove a number of fast racing cars, such as the Lancia Lampo, that belonged to the racing fraternity, at their invitation. Quite a few men later voiced the opinion that she should have been allowed to keep on racing. They admired her not only because of her skill behind the wheel but also because she did not hesitate to get her hands dirty. She often changed her own tires, worked on her cars, and was photographed with prominent grease spots on her clothing, which further endeared her to them.

Just three months after her success at the New Orleans Fair Grounds, Joan Newton Cuneo was turned away from participating in the Fort George Hill Climb. As a reporter for the *New York Times* wrote, "An unpleasant incident arose just after the contest had started. Mrs. J. N. Cuneo had entered a Knox Giant ... to give a special exhibition of driving against time." It seems clear that at the last minute the race organizers had decided that they really didn't want her there, in any capacity. Strictly speaking, an exhibition was not the same as a competition. Her entry had been accepted by the Fort George Carnival Committee, and she had received special mention on the program. Prominently visible in large print was the following message: "SPECIAL EXHIBITION EVENT, Mrs. J. N. Cuneo will drive a Knox Giant against time."[3] Mrs. Cuneo had hurried back to New York from the Knox Factory at Springfield, Massachusetts, to participate in the hill climb, which of course involved stripping down her car beforehand.

When Mrs. Cuneo reported to the officials at the starting line, she was informed that the rules barred her from competing or giving an exhibition.[4] Barring her from giving an exhibition added a further twist to the change in the rules. One newspaper reported that the real objection was against allowing her to be timed by the official timing equipment, as it was reserved for those who were legally entered in the event.[5] This seems a pretty lame excuse, as they could have timed her with stopwatches.

The normally reserved Joan Cuneo was visibly distressed as she hunted down Colonel K. C. Pardee, the head of the contest committee. Pardee had been associated with the automobile industry from its American beginnings, first with Packard and then with Maxwell-Briscoe, and had participated in all the Glidden Tours. The reporter noted that Joan Cuneo seemed close to tears. She was well acquainted with Pardee and demanded an explanation of the committee's about-face in regard to her entry, as they had barred her from the competition after actually soliciting her entry. She tried to reason with him as best she could.

"I have been permitted to compete in contests heretofore, and it seems strange that I should be barred on this occasion," Mrs. Cuneo pleaded. Blinking away angry tears, she continued, "My entry fee was accepted and I have my car prepared for the exhibition I was to give. In addition I have come from Springfield to take part in the contests."[6]

Unwilling to be the "bad guy," Pardee passed the buck to a local official. An exasperated Joan Cuneo was sent to Robert Lee Morrell, the referee. He had the unpleasant job of telling her flatly that she couldn't compete in the hill climb. Morrell said there was nothing he could do because the event was sanctioned by the AAA. He went on to read her the rule that disbarred her. Of course Joan Cuneo was aware of the rule that limited competitors in AAA-sanctioned events to males 18 years and older. She hoped somehow to get around it, as she had when she entered her first Glidden Tour, especially as the organizers had accepted her entry fee. This would not be the case, as the officials told her politely that they "regretted the necessity of refusing to let her drive, but the rule which unfortunately covered her case, must be enforced."[7] Joan Cuneo, dressed in a "jaunty, loose-fitting khaki suit with auto cap and gauntlet gloves, watched wistfully as the other entrants drove up to the starting line."[8]

She still had hopes of entering the straightaway time trials that would be held the next day on Hillside Avenue, Jamaica, Long Island, close to her home on Richmond Hill. Stalking off the course, she consulted a lawyer and was ready to apply for a court order to compel the officials to let her drive . Then she learned that the manager of the Knox Company had quietly substituted the name of Al Dennison as the driver of the Knox cars in the time trials.[9] Dennison was one of the men who regularly drove Knox cars in competition. This underhanded move by a company for which she had provided much free advertising made it impossible for her to proceed further. Joan Cuneo was again relegated to the ranks of the spectators as she had been for the hill climb the previous day.

The Fort George Auto Carnival Committee had initially encouraged her entry into both the hill climb and the straightaway events, because Mrs. Cuneo was a huge draw. However, cooler heads prevailed and they had reversed their decision on the day of the event. She was not able to get them to change their minds because both were AAA-sanctioned events and they didn't want to risk being penalized by the sanctioning committee.[10] Although her application had also been denied when she tried to enter the 1908 Briarcliff race, her hefty deposit of $500 was returned At Fort George, she was turned away at the starting line, despite their acceptance of her entry and fees. Looking back, their actions seem exceptionally insensitive. To make matters even worse, Joan Cuneo later said that she had tried out the Fort George, Fort Lee and Wilkes-Barre hill climbs and made record times on all of them.[11] Joan Newton Cuneo and other women racers had become pawns in a power struggle between American auto manufacturers and the two most

Joan Cuneo and Louis Disbrow ready to take the Knox Giant for a trial speed run up Giant's Despair, with the car stripped for racing. This photograph was taken before Joan's drive up the hill shown in the following photograph, as Joan, Louis Disbrow and the Knox above are relatively dust free (courtesy of Jack Deo, Superior View Photographs).

Joan racing up Giant's Despair Hill Climb in 1909 with Louis Disbrow, her riding mechanic, keeping her in her Knox Giant (courtesy of the National Automotive History Collection, Detroit Public Library).

powerful auto clubs in the United States, over the regulation of auto racing within the country.

To understand what women racers were up against, it is necessary to take a brief look at the development of auto racing in the first decade of the twentieth century. Between 1900 and 1909, hundreds of auto contests were held in towns all over the United States. They fell into two categories: endurance runs or tours, to promote the reliability of the automobile, and speed contests of some kind. Thousand-plus-mile tours over the generally awful unpaved roads that linked American cities and towns were often very challenging. Even tougher were the obstacles faced by a growing number of people who drove from coast to coast because of the yet unbuilt infrastructure. Obviously people who attempted these long drives were attracted to tough, durable vehicles.

Many men and more than a few women quickly fell in love with speed. Fanatical race fans of the day were called speed bugs, while fast drivers were called scorchers. Speed events were very popular with both speed bugs and scorchers. Races were held on city streets, horse or bicycle tracks, or the flat sands of Ormond Beach, Florida, or Atlantic City, New Jersey. As the cars became more powerful, speed events became more dangerous. Finally, timed hill climbs and assorted fun events called gymkhanas provided a different and often less serious kind of competition.

Before 1910, most races were only loosely regulated in regard to entries and timing.

Their promoters' primary purpose was to entertain both speed bugs and newcomers to the sport, while making a profit. Cheating and hipping (use of drivers who did not get the prize money but a salary) of races was common, and the speed records that resulted were often dubious. Most of the spectators didn't realize that the races were fixed or that many events were choreographed to provide the most excitement for the fans. Once the Contest Board took control of racing, it made a strong effort to eliminate hipping and cheating in AAA-sanctioned races. Even today, it is extremely difficult to totally eliminate cheating in racing. However, in 1909 cheating and hipping was a common practice in many non-sanctioned events across the country, and it went on for decades. A lot of the early records that were set were probably inaccurate for several reasons in addition to cheating and hipping. Racing was a relatively new sport and the race promoters were inexperienced at starting and timing and keeping track of the laps run in the events they organized. Another problem was that if several cars were competing in a close race the amount of dust they generated on a dirt track often made it difficult to determine the winner.

It is not well known today that the Automobile Club of America (ACA), with mainly upper-class membership, the middle-class American Automobile Association (AAA) and the American Motor Car Manufacturers Association (AAMA) all sanctioned races during the first decade of racing.[12] The ACA and the AAA had already been feuding for several years over which group would sanction and set the rules for the important auto competitions in the United States. As a result, there had been little progress in developing rules and regulations that would apply to all types of racing in the United States. The absence of racing standards allowed Mrs. Cuneo and a few other women to compete at a variety of tracks, as in New Orleans, where the promoters were willing to take a chance on female racers. However, this laxity regarding racing rules was about to change.[13]

In the fall of 1907, the AAA held a meeting at its New York headquarters to discuss the future of racing in America. Present along with AAA officials were representatives from the National Association of Automobile Manufacturers, the American Motor Car Manufacturers Association and the Importer's Salon. All agreed that although track racing was necessary to promote the auto industry, there were too many races held on tracks that were dangerous to both contestants and spectators. The AAA put forward a plan that involved granting sanctions only to member clubs or other well-established organizations. To address safety issues, they would require a photo of the turns on each track where a race was to be held along with a certificate stating that the track had been thoroughly examined and found to be in good repair. If the track met these conditions, the AAA would then send a referee who would have the power to approve the track and the competitors. The referee could also reject an entrant with a reputation for reckless driving.[14]

In May of 1908, the American Automobile Manufacturers Association supported the AAA in its dispute with the ACA over the sanctioning of the Vanderbilt Cup and the addition of so-called international races.[15] What the AAMA really objected to was the

ACA's close ties to the Automobile Club of France, which controlled Continental racing. They feared that the ACA would be influenced by the French club, which, not surprisingly, favored French manufacturers, as the managing director of the Panhard Company was the chairman of their Contest Committee.[16] All of the manufacturers' groups believed that there was a need for a national body that would sanction racing in America; it didn't matter to them if it was the AAA or the ACA. However, the manufacturers would not be happy with any auto club sanctioning group unless their representatives were allowed to attend its meetings, and put forward their concerns. If they were not allowed to participate, the manufacturers decided to establish their own national sanctioning body, as they were required to "pay the bills," researching and developing new and more competitive models."[17]

During 1908, the more broadly based AAA slowly increased the number of races it sanctioned, as the ACA positioned itself to sanction international competitions because of its affiliation with European clubs. The ACA's role would eventually have diminished anyway, because of its relatively small membership, and the club seemed satisfied with its involvement in international racing. However, although the auto manufacturers wanted an American sanctioning body, they didn't like the new rules the AAA had developed in 1907. Also worrisome to the manufacturers was that the AAA had abolished its Racing Board and replaced it with a Contest Committee. This seemed to indicate that the AAA was close to abandoning the racing field except for tours, hill climbs and similar contests.[18]

By the end of 1908, Percy Owen, the chairman of the Committee of Manufacturers and president of the Liberty Motor Car Company, proposed that it might be best if the manufacturers established their own racing board. It would be made up of representatives from the most successful automakers of the time. Their next step would be to replace the AAA as the chief American race-sanctioning body. They would take this next step if the AAA didn't cooperate with the manufacturers and agree to all their suggestions for the regulation of racing.[19] Why were the auto manufacturers upset with the AAA in 1908? They believed that the AAA provided little structure for American racing. The manufacturers were also appalled at the current state of racing. They were convinced that if regulations were not expanded and enforced, the accidents and deaths resulting from unrestrained racing might tarnish the reputation of their automobiles, causing the failure of their companies. In addition, they didn't like the AAA's decision against sanctioning races on tracks of a mile or less in circumference.[20] In 1908, the majority of tracks in the United State had a circumference of one mile, a half mile, one-third a mile or even a quarter mile and had originally built for bicycle or horse racing. In 1908, there were as yet no tracks built for auto racing, although speedways would soon be opened in Atlanta and Indianapolis and others were planned. If short-track competition was not allowed by the AAA, it would effectively kill track racing at least temporarily.

The growing number of women who wanted to race also worried the manufacturers. Dozens of (male) drivers and riding mechanics had been killed or seriously injured in races during the last decade. As a result, there had already been several unsuccessful campaigns to ban auto racing. The manufacturers were unwilling to take a chance on what might happen if a woman driver was killed or maimed and pushed the AAA to limit racing to males. Given the law of averages, the manufacturers believed a woman driver would eventually be injured, especially if more women took up racing. No one seemed concerned about the large number of spectators who were also killed or maimed at the races. At the same time, most manufacturers believed that winning races or receiving awards for their vehicles' performance in tours was the best possible advertising in an extremely competitive market.

Alfred Reeves, the general manager of the American Motor Car Manufacturers Association, said in 1909, "No one can deny the good that comes from races and touring contests, for besides lending a certain element of sporting interest to automobiling, they add materially to the knowledge of cars on the part of the buying public and on the part of the manufacturer himself. It would, indeed, be regretful to see any waning of interest on the part of the manufacturers."[21]

The business of building automobiles really was a competitive nightmare in 1908. Literally hundreds of entrepreneurs and mechanics had already produced or were trying to build their own version of a self-propelled vehicle. To complicate matters even further, the gas engine automobile had yet to establish its dominance over steam and electric vehicles. However, despite the odds, a relatively small group of manufacturers had surged to the forefront, building and selling more cars every year. Ford and Olds led in the entry-level category and sold the largest numbers of cars overall. Manufacturers in the middle- and high-priced brackets were still struggling for dominance. These groups benefited most from success in all kinds of competition, including tours, races and novelty events. However, they also had the expense of building specially designed race cars for these competitions, which required vastly differing specifications. To date, they had received little guidance from the AAA. Obviously these manufacturers had the most at stake in this battle, because they believed that winning races sold cars.

Because he believed that the AAA might eventually withdraw from sanctioning racing, Percy Owen, the chairman of the Committee of Manufacturers and a promoter of the 1908 Briarcliff race, put forward the idea of a national (auto-racing) body. It would have the authority to make rules and issue sanctions.

A suggestion was made that the governing body should be made up of the twenty-five auto manufacturers who have been consistently identified with auto racing in the past. [Listed were long forgotten marques such as National, Apperson, Lozier, Chalmers-Detroit and Palmer, along with the still familiar Renault and Fiat.] Along with a governing body of twenty-five manufacturers or importers, they would appoint a committee of two manufacturers' representatives and three experts in no way connected with the manufacture or sale of cars ... who would formulate binding rules and sanction races.[22]

The manufacturers felt that building race cars and supporting factory teams was costing them too much money because of the current lack of regulation and classification.

The Rules Committee of the manufacturers then created a list of five classes based on piston displacement, price and weight that would be applied to stock car events, along with two special classes. They also made some changes to the definition of a stock car. To the manufacturers, "a stock car [was] a motor car completely described in the manufacturer's catalog for the current or any preceding year which is manufactured in quantities of 25 or more, which is for sale by the regular selling representatives of the manufacturer and is manufactured ready for delivery to buyers."[23]

By February, the manufacturers had moved forward and planned to meet in Chicago to take another step towards forming a national sanctioning body. Their plan would then be submitted to representatives from all the manufacturers organizations for a vote. However, they had already changed the makeup of the governing board. It was now to consist of representatives from 25 manufacturers and importers that had raced cars in the United States in the last two years.[24]

Unexpectedly, only a few days later the *New York Times* announced that the manufacturers had decided to cooperate with the AAA rather than forming their own racing board. After moving towards trying to control racing, the manufacturers backed off. They probably realized that sanctioning racing might be more trouble than it was worth. After the Chicago meeting in February, they decided to wait and see how the AAA responded to their concerns.

Jolted by this challenge from the manufacturers, the AAA changed its tune and announced it would work with the automakers. The AAA must have realized that they didn't want the manufacturers to control racing, but gaining their support would strengthen the AAA's position. A few days later, the *New York Times* intimated that the AAA might not agree to work with the manufacturers even though it seemed the logical solution.[25] In the end, however, several leading manufacturers were appointed to the AAA Rules Committee and three representatives from the Manufacturers Contest Association were allowed to have some voice at the meetings of the AAA Contest Board. However, this did not initially satisfy the manufacturers or the auto club members.[26] Eventually the auto club contest board agreed to most of the changes that the manufacturers wanted, including a revival of track racing under AAA supervision. Besides the controversial new rule allowing only males to race, the AAA created a standardized entry form and a new schedule of fees based on the type of event sanctioned, although it offered a 50 percent discount for clubs affiliated with the AAA.[27]

The most surprising result of the agreement between the automakers and the AAA was the banning of women from sanctioned events. Despite a number of rumors circulating in the press, the new rule was not mentioned in any newspaper until the AAA members applied it to Joan Cuneo at Fort George. Neither group ever issued a statement saying that women would be banned from racing; they quietly made the existing rules more gender specific. At the same time that Joan was winning races in New Orleans, the AAA released a statement that "all races must be run under the existing rules of the AAA [which had just been developed by the joint efforts of the AAA and the Manufacturers Contest

Association] until new rules can be formulated by the special committee ... of the MCA."[28] This was the beginning of a long working relationship between the auto manufacturers and the AAA. As a result of their cooperation, however, Joan Cuneo would be turned away when she tried to enter races sanctioned by the AAA.

It is likely that the AAA would have eventually have banned women from racing, as had been done in 1904 on the Continent. Only in Britain would women continue to participate in a relatively few women's races and speed trials at their premier track, Brooklands, between 1910 and the 1920s.[29] There were still a few places Joan could test her skill after the AAA sanctions became the rule. Not all auto clubs immediately bowed to the authority of their parent club, nor were all auto clubs affiliates of the AAA. When the Harrisburg, Pennsylvania, Motor Club didn't get a response from the AAA regarding a sanction for a reliability run planned for March of 1909, they went ahead with their program without a sanction.[30] A few years later the International Motor Contest Association (IMCA) would be founded as an alternative to the AAA, although the best-known races were AAA-sanctioned events that drew the top drivers.[31]

As early as January 1908, there had been hints that women might eventually be excluded from racing in an article published in the *Washington Post*. On the society page, a reporter discussed Joan Cuneo's exploits on the track and her desire to compete in the upcoming Briarcliff Road Race.[32] The columnist then pointed out that the Briarcliff race was a high-speed, nerve-wracking three-hundred-mile road race almost as dangerous as the Vanderbilt Cup and "should Mrs. Cuneo meet with a serious accident, a wave of horror would go through the community and the [organizing] committee would be severely censured for permitting a woman to take part in the contest."[33] As it turned out, she wasn't allowed to race at Briarcliff or Savannah, but both Mrs. Cuneo and Mrs. Shirley were allowed to enter the Glidden Tour, despite M. Worth Colwell's inference that some were opposed to letting women "play games" along with the men (in the 1908 Glidden).[34] At roughly the same time, a Cleveland woman, Mrs. K. R. Otis, competed in and won a Cleveland hill climb; she then broke the record for driving between Cleveland, Ohio, and Buffalo, New York, in her powerful Stearns car despite the inclement January weather.[35] Mrs. Otis was one of several woman who had taken up automobiling as a sport within the last year. Having to deal with one woman competitor was bad enough; the AAA had no desire to support or encourage increasing numbers of women to participate in automobile competitions

In March 1909, the *New York Times* printed an article that intimated that the automakers also wanted to bar women from entering that year's Glidden Tour. which was in no way a race, and the AAA would probably agree to their request.[36] According to the *Times*, "The communication to the Contest Board asks that a regulation be made by which 'only males 18 years or over be eligible to take part as contestants or drivers' in the annual tour of the American Automobile Association."[37] Initially this seems strange, as manufacturers loved the publicity their autos gained from success in Glidden events and by 1908 factory teams dominated the tour. Joan Cuneo's exploits in the two tours she completed (she didn't finish in 1905 because her car gave out on the last day) had been widely advertised by the makers of the White and Rainer autos she drove. The tours were not any more dangerous than any other cross-country run, so why would the manufacturers want women excluded from these relatively tame events? Considering the available evidence, banning women from competition rested on the issue of the Glidden Tours having always been sanctioned by the AAA. Although women had already been excluded from sanctioned races, if a determined and influential woman, specifically Joan Cuneo, was allowed to drive in a sanctioned tour, she would undoubtedly argue that this set a precedent for her entry into other sanctioned events. A judge might then overturn the rule and the unthinkable would happen: women could return to competition. That the 1909 AAA decision to exclude women was driven by its desire to keep Joan Newton Cuneo from any kind of competition is supported by its actions in 1911. Although the Glidden Tours were sanctioned by the AAA until 1913 and women were still barred from competition, one woman driver was allowed to enter the 1911 tour and quite a few women rode along as passengers. Miss Birdie Marks, of Athens, Georgia, came back from Europe, where she had been touring, to enter the Glidden. Not only was she allowed to participate, but she finished with a perfect score and received a gold medal for her efforts.[38]

In 1909, several other women who had driven on tours or raced also protested the ruling. One was Mrs. Cuneo's highly touted rival at the New Orleans Auto Carnival, Alyce Byrd Potter.[39] In April, the *Los Angeles Herald* printed an article dramatically titled "Women Drivers in Arms Against Men: Scream Aloud Because of Being Barred." The article claimed women drivers were angry with men because they had banned them from the Glidden Tour.[40] Joan Newton Cuneo was quoted extensively in her support of Alyce Potter's desire for a national women's tour. However, while a few women-only touring events were held, nothing with the scope of the Glidden Tour was ever developed by any women's group. In fairness, it must be noted that by 1909 interest in the Glidden Tour was waning despite the publicity it had received. An increasing number of men and women now had the confidence to set out on their own, taking long automobile trips with family and friends. The AAA got more and more requests for travel information and began to produce brochures called *Trip Tiks*. The *Trip Tiks* provided motorists with information on road conditions, food and lodging en route, the location of garages and places to buy gasoline. AAA *Trip Tiks* were still provided for members in booklet form until a few years ago, but the proliferation of GPS devices and smart phones has made them almost obsolete.[41]

In 1909, there was only one gas station in the country and there were no motels or roadside diners. Locating fuel when traveling through rural areas required much planning and luck. It was a double concern if the tourist was driving a steam-powered car, which required a supply of water as well as gasoline. The first drive-through "filling station" in the United States (filling station was the common name for a gas station at this time) was built in 1913. However, the AAA *Trip Tiks* would make solo traveling much easier, even on bad roads, and more and more drivers felt comfortable going it alone, rather than on a Glidden or Good Roads Tour.

Some of the more skilled and adventurous female motorists, most of whom knew their way around a wrench, traveled extensively across the United States with other female friends. A few, usually young and good-looking outdoor types or actresses, were hired to drive across the country to publicize the toughness and reliability of a particular brand of automobile. Despite the outcry that resulted from the AAA and the auto manufacturers' opposition to women driving in AAA-sanctioned competitions, not all automobile executives wanted women banned. J. H. Willys, the president of the Overland Automobile Company, believed that women drivers should be encouraged rather than criticized or banned from racing. According to Willys:

> But lately there has been some difference of opinion as to women's success as drivers. To me this is a gross libel. If anything were needed to convince the average judge of car-driving of the futility of such a contention it is only necessary for him to consider the various important touring events in which women have participated. Women drive with rare discretion and good sense. I have observed that women who learn to drive a car are, as a rule, exceptionally capable after they have mastered its mechanical details. It may be true that they are not quite as daring as men in all emergencies but this, I believe, is rather a recommendation than a drawback.... I cannot see any just reason why women should not be allowed to enter all forms of race meets, hill-climbs and endurance contests. Certainly no man every drove a better race than did Mrs. Joan Cuneo in the recent Mardi Gras events at New Orleans. No woman has ever driven a better endurance contest than has this plucky little woman when she has been entered in the Glidden Tours. Certainly women are more capable of sitting behind the wheel of an automobile than are many male drivers who use the highways for speeding and reckless driving.[42]

Willys was not the only member of the Auto Manufacturers Association who felt this way, but he was one of the few who were willing to voice their opinions in print. However, men who wanted women to continue racing were in the minority, and most kept their opinions to themselves. As time passed, the changing of the Contest Board rules to exclude women was taken for granted, and as a result women would not race at the highest level in the United States until long after World War II.

However, Joan Cuneo was still a public figure even if she had stopped racing. Readers were given a glimpse of her life outside the automobile world in a brief article published in the *New York Times* in June 1909. The *Times* discussed her work in promoting a charity near to her heart, Orphan's Day, an annual orphans' outing to several local amusement parks. Being Joan, even her charity work involved automobiles. A charter member of the Woman's Motoring Club of New York, she headed the Women's Brigade, which was in charge of ferrying the orphans to and from the amusement parks. The ladies recruited members and friends who would loan or drive their cars full of orphans to Coney Island, Luna Park or Dreamland Park for the day. In the article, she informed New York automobilists that they would still be able to use their cars during the day after they had unloaded their cargo when the parks opened in the morning until 5:00 P.M., when the orphans had to be picked up. The automobilists needn't worry that they would have to watch the children at the amusement parks, as they would be in the charge of their teachers. According to Mrs. Cuneo, a veteran of this event, the children were very well

Mrs. Cuneo, with one of her large cars filled with orphans, talks to them as they get ready for their day at Coney Island (courtesy of Jack Deo, Superior View Photos).

behaved and would not damage the cars they rode in. Joan Cuneo herself provided two cars along with a large cash donation for the excursion, although stipulating that she would carry girl orphans only in the car she drove.[43]

In July, Mrs. Cuneo got yet another speeding ticket. She was arrested on Ocean Parkway in Brooklyn by a motorcycle policeman. No doubt the frustration over not being allowed to race was wearing on her. Motorcycle policemen in New York did not wear the traditional blue uniforms but instead wore pale gray outfits similar to those worn by professional chauffeurs. As a result, the policemen were often accused of trying to trap unwary motorists. Mrs. Cuneo was at the wheel as usual, with her husband, Andrew, and several friends in the car, when a motorcycle policeman spotted her. He had to chase her for some distance before she stopped. He charged her with going 30 miles an hour, on the parkway. In court she waived examination and was released after paying $200 bail.[44] Since she always drove as fast as circumstances allowed, she collected quite a few tickets while she lived in New York, but not all were mentioned in the newspaper.

On August 15, Mrs. Cuneo went to Springfield, Massachusetts, to pick up the Knox racer that she had ordered a few months earlier. The fact that she had ordered a new Knox after women had been banished indicates that she still hoped to race again; otherwise she would have had no need for another race car. Her new racer had been built according to

131

Joan Cuneo at the wheel of her brand-new 1910 Knox Giantess, which she has just picked up at the Knox factory, In the backseat are Louis Disbrow on the left and, a rare picture of her husband, Andrew Cuneo on the right. Standing next to the car is the president of the Knox company, Mr. E. Cutler (courtesy of Harriet Newton Draper).

her own specifications. A spokesman for the Knox Automobile Company said they considered the Knox "Giantess" that they had completed the finest car ever built at the factory. Although chassis, engine and drivetrain were the same as in their racing model, the Knox Giant, which she had driven at New Orleans, Mrs. Cuneo wanted the body altered to fit her petite frame. The driver's seat was several inches lower, with wide cushions and high backs, and the steering wheel and other controls were also adjusted to fit Mrs. Cuneo. The Giantess was also painted an original color, which she called a golden green-bronze, with upholstery to match. When Mrs. Cuneo took the car for a trial run she said it was the first car in which she didn't have to add cushions to create a comfortable fit.[45] Unfortunately, although Barney Oldfield had invited her to come to the opening of the Indianapolis Motor Speedway in July 1909, the Giantess was not ready until August, so she didn't go. Mrs. Cuneo might have taken her Rainier, but the new Knox was much the faster car. It had been rated at the factory as being capable of running a half mile in 25 seconds. She also may have been skeptical of the notice she had received from the Indianapolis Motor Speedway that she had been made eligible for speed trials from a kilometer to 50 miles.[46] Joan Cuneo would never have the opportunity to race her beautiful new car in an AAA-sanctioned race, although she eventually entered it in several races, with Louis Disbrow as the driver.

With no opportunities for competing in AAA-sanctioned races, Joan Cuneo was reduced to attempting to set new speed records at local athletic events and country fairs. The racing at these events was much more informal and flew under the radar of the AAA Contest Committee. In July, she tried to lower her times for one and five miles at the annual athletic games of St. Monica's Church at the Metropolitan Track , Jamaica, Long Island. Unfortunately, she didn't even come close to her best times there.[47] In October, she was recruited by the organizers of the Danbury, Connecticut, fair to attempt new records for five and one mile at the half-mile horse track on opening day. She broke the five-mile track record by nearly a minute, covering the distance in 7:19, and lowered the one-mile track record by 12 seconds at 1:16 and ¼. However, again she was not close to her own personal best. Her exploits received the bare minimum of publicity in the *New York Times*, although the automobile page provided more information, saying that Mrs. Cuneo drove a 45 hp Rainier, not the new Giantess, in this attempt.[48]

Despite the discouraging outing at the Danbury fair, Joan Cuneo's spirits rose when she was approached by the Atlanta Journal–New York Tribune Committee shortly afterwards. This group was in charge of the Good Roads Tour from New York to Atlanta that would culminate in a race meeting at the brand-new Atlanta Motordrome. Not only did they want her to drive the press car, but they also hinted that she would get a chance to "unofficially" try out the new track. As she loved auto touring and was eager to try out the reportedly fast track even in an unofficial capacity, she quickly accepted. Louis Disbrow, gradually gaining a reputation as a skilled race-car driver, would go along not only as her mechanic but also to drive in several events at the first scheduled Atlanta races.

9

Joan Cuneo's Swan Song — On to Atlanta

Little did Joan Cuneo know when she eagerly accepted an invitation to drive the press car in the New York to Atlanta Good Roads Tour in October 1909 it would be her last appearance in a nationally publicized auto event. In fact, the Good Roads Tour would signal the end of her nationally publicized career as an automobilist. Recruiting Joan Cuneo as a participant was a logical choice for the *Atlanta Journal* and *New York Herald* Good Roads organizing committee. In 1909, Mrs. Cuneo was at the height of her fame.[1] Her comments on a variety of automotive topics appeared regularly in newspapers and magazines, and she was the subject of several interviews in popular magazines. Although today she is remembered only as the woman responsible for the banning of women from racing, in 1909 she was a nationally respected authority on all things automobile.

By the time she was banned from racing, Joan Cuneo had competed in almost all of the major automobile-related events in the first decade of the twentieth century. She had raced on Ormond and Atlantic City Beach, participated in three Glidden Tours and competed in a number of races at fairgrounds throughout the Northeast, ending with her victories at the Mardi Gras race meeting in New Orleans. Even after she was banned from competition, she still had the respect of many of her male counterparts, including Barney Oldfield, who had invited her to Indianapolis that August. It is true she never got to drive in a Briarcliff, Savannah Grand Prize or Vanderbilt Cup race, but it was not for lack of trying on her part. Her advocacy of improved roads, and her national fame, made her an easy choice. Her presence would draw attention to the desperate need for improved roads in the United States and promote racing at the new Atlanta Motordrome.

Her fame was such that in 1909 her exploits in the 1908 Glidden Tour were featured in *The Weed*, a promotional magazine issued occasionally by the Weed Tire Grip Company. She shared space in the issue with the internationally famous magician and escape artist Harry Houdini. As a promotion for Weed, he had successfully escaped from a number of the company's tire chains that had been wrapped and padlocked around his body.[2] The telegram Mrs. Cuneo sent to the Weed company after the Glidden Tour was prominently featured on the last page of their magazine. She had written: "...used chains three wheels hardest day's trip — 130 miles over mountains — record time — an impossibility without chains."[3] Obviously, her participation in any motoring event generated considerable publicity in many newspapers. This would be the case in the first New York to Atlanta Good Roads Tour.

Although a number of Good Roads Tours were held during the first two decades of the twentieth century, the New York to Atlanta tour was the brainchild of a group of Atlanta businessmen and racing enthusiasts headed by Asa Griggs Candler Jr. and financially supported by his father, Asa Griggs Candler. In 1877, Candler Sr. (1851–1929), a druggist, bought the formula for Coca-Cola from John Pemberton and his associates for $2,300. Due to his business acumen and marketing ability, he made a huge fortune selling Coca-Cola, and the Candler name is still a familiar one in Atlantans. Candler Sr. was keenly interested in the further development of the city, and his second son, 29-year-old Asa Griggs Candler Jr. (1880–1953), worked for his father as a real estate developer. Junior, who became increasingly eccentric in later life, loved fast cars and auto racing.[4] Because of Candler's interest in the development of Atlanta, Junior was able to get his father's backing for the construction of a purpose-built racetrack near their city. As a result, Asa Griggs Candler Jr. and Carl Graham Fisher share the honor of initiating the construction of the first auto speedways in the country. Fisher's Indianapolis Motor Speedway was rushed to completion in the summer of 1909 and, despite an accident-ridden start, is still a successful venue. The more carefully built Atlanta Motordrome was completed a few months later. Although it was nearly accident free during its lifetime, the Atlanta track held only three race meetings before it was abandoned, eventually becoming part of Atlanta's first airport.[5]

According to the *Atlanta Constitution*, while driving in the Atlanta suburb of Hapeville early in 1909 Junior and his friend Edward M. Durant got the idea of building a purpose-built racetrack.[6] These young men, president and vice president of the Atlanta Automobile Association, believed a speedway would provide both a venue for thrilling racing and encourage tourism and economic development in the city. After convincing his father that it was a viable plan, Candler Jr. bought three hundred acres of land south of Atlanta for $77,674, to create a speedway south of the city.[7] As money seemed to be no object to the wealthy Candlers, the track was built quickly, sparing no cost, without cutting corners.

Candler's motordrome was 2 miles in length and 100 feet wide in the homestretch, while its banked curves were 60 feet wide with 10-foot banking and a radius of 500 feet. The track surface was a mixture of clay, sand and gravel with an asphalt binder. When it was completed, prospective fans would be able to view the races from either bleachers holding fifteen thousand, or a covered grandstand with twenty-five thousand seats. The *Constitution* reported that the track cost $400,000, which would equal $10 million today.[8] The motordrome had a somewhat unusual design, which may have contributed to its relative safety, as a substantial earthen berm separated the track from the spectators. The track surface was 12 feet below the grandstand level and had literally been carved out of red Georgia clay by two giant steam shovels, running 24 hours a day. This was a costly undertaking and the *Constitution* reported that each bite of the huge shovels cost Candler $2.50. After the surface was finally leveled, workers laid pipe around the circumference of the track. Then train tracks were built to its outer perimeter so that tank cars could easily deliver the oil that kept down dust and made the surface slick.

When the track was completed, a group of Georgia motoring enthusiasts traveled to New York City, along with representatives from the *Atlanta Journal*, to gain support for their first race meeting. At this time, Atlanta had two major newspapers, the *Constitution*, which came out in the morning, and the *Journal*, an evening paper. While both praised the construction of the speedway, the *Journal* was known for its support of the Good Roads Movement as well as its innovative sports coverage and was the best choice to represent the Atlanta interests in New York City. In New York, the *Journal* contingent got the *New York Herald* interested in their project. Together, an organizing committee from both newspapers decided that the best way to promote the motordrome would be to hold a Good Roads Tour. It would follow the national highway south, starting in New York City and ending in Atlanta, supporting the betterment of the nation's roads while calling attention to the new speedway. The tour would also bring a number of enthusiastic race fans and tourists to the city a few days before the races were scheduled to start. The committee rightly believed that the addition of celebrity drivers such as Ty Cobb and Joan Cuneo would generate extensive press coverage of the tour on its progression to Atlanta.

The Good Roads Tours shared some similarities with the Glidden Tours; both involved planned cross-country drives with the purpose of promoting automobile travel and road improvement. The Good Roads Tours did not encourage competition, although the entrants were referred to as contestants and the participants were expected to follow a set of rules. Glidden Tours offered few opportunities for sightseeing en route, while participants in Good Roads Tours traveled at a more leisurely pace and could visit some of the historic attractions along the route. Interacting with local residents who lined the roads to cheer on them on gave the participants many opportunities to publicize the need for new or improved roads. The highways that were eventually built, such as the Dixie and Lincoln Highways, encouraged even more automobile tourists to travel cross-country on their own.

The Good Roads Movement had been founded in 1880, not by automobilists but by a mixed group of bicyclists, bicycle organizations such as the League of American Wheelmen, and numerous bicycle manufacturers.[9] By 1900, the movement had aided its cause in several ways: first by convincing the notoriously conservative farmers that better roads would help rather than hurt them and second by getting both the federal and state governments to pass laws allowing their participation in road-building projects. However, despite the initial success of the wheelmen, interest in bicycle touring waned after 1900. With much work still to be done, the Good Roads Movement was taken over by automobilists who had similar interests.

In Atlanta, as soon as the speedway neared completion Candler Jr. and Durant sent invitations to a number of professional drivers, including all of the current stars, to try out their track. To gain as much publicity as possible, they also lured newspaper editors from five nearby states into visiting the track, with the promise of a Georgia barbecue.[10] They wanted to avoid the mistakes of Carl Fisher, the impatient promoter of the Indianapolis Motor Speedway. Fisher scheduled several events as soon as the Indy track was completed without adequate testing. As a result, the badly prepared track surface caused a number of injuries and several fatalities when the speedway opened in 1909.

Local residents were also invited to view the newly constructed track and five thousand Atlantans came to Hapeville on October 3, for the open house, by streetcar, auto and buggy.[11] The *Constitution* considered the turnout a first rate example of Atlanta spirit, especially since the people who toured the track had overwhelmingly positive comments. On October 15, Ralph de Palma, George Robertson and Charles Basle, who had shipped their race cars to Atlanta, tried out the new track under the watchful eye of AAA starter Fred Wagner. All three pronounced it first rate, as did Barney Oldfield. Before the start of the race meeting, at least 50 professionals had driven on the track with great success The Atlanta Auto Club also contacted Mrs. Cuneo and offered her an opportunity to test the new track in "an unofficial capacity the day after the tourists reached Atlanta."[12] Joan Cuneo, set to leave New York City behind the wheel of a tour press car, eagerly accepted their invitation.

When the officers of the Rainier Motor Car Company heard that Joan Cuneo would be a participant in the New York to Atlanta tour, they realized that her exploits would again offer them an excellent opportunity to publicize their automobiles. Mrs. Cuneo owned two Rainiers, which she had successfully driven in two Glidden Tours and a number of speed trials. She also had written a glowing account of her car's performance in the 1907 Glidden for Rainier. As a result, Rainier company officials offered her a refurbished and recently overhauled Rainier to use on the tour. Although the number 8 Rainier was by no means a new car, Joan Cuneo gladly accepted their offer, as then she wouldn't have to put one of her own cars through the beating it would take on the tour.[13] They also proposed that Louis Disbrow, who would accompany Joan Cuneo to Atlanta on the tour, should drive a factory-owned Rainier in the Atlanta races. Disbrow was quick to accept this opportunity to drive Rainier number 9 in a number of races at the speedway. This car was shipped to Atlanta by train. Rainier sent a representative along on the tour to record the details. The resulting story of the Good Roads Tour and the first Atlanta races, which included many photographs taken by Lazarnick, who also accompanied the tourists, was later published by the company. The Rainier was designated as a press car, and for much of the tour Mrs. Cuneo carried a full complement of passengers. However, most of the Lazarnick photographs in the Rainier brochure show only two passengers in the Rainier, Joan Cuneo and Louis Disbrow.

Joan Cuneo still hadn't accepted that she had been permanently banned from sanctioned competition. As soon as she took possession of the factory refurbished Rainer, she tried it on several local tracks, wanting to keep her hand until she could run a real race. Although the times she recorded at the Metropolitan track and the Danbury fair were slower than expected, she made no attempts with her faster Knox. She may have wanted to get her money's worth out of the Rainer company which had promised her a new car after her success in the Glidden but never followed through. However Mrs. Cuneo later ran a fast time with the same Rainer at Atlanta.[14]

On the morning of October 25, the procession of 43 tourist cars left from Herald

Square in New York City. They were scheduled to arrive in Atlanta nine days later on November 3. The contestants were escorted by at least 50 local cars to the Staten Island Ferry, where the locals would watch the tourists embark on the first leg of their journey south.[15] On the first day of the tour, Mrs. Cuneo carried a full complement of passengers, as she had been told to keep the newsmen at the front of the procession. Taking these instructions to heart, she put the pedal to the metal driving on the relatively good New Jersey roads and got to Philadelphia two hours before any of the other tourists. Spectators eagerly watching for the long parade of automobiles cheered her along the route to Philadelphia.[16]

When the rest of the tourists finally arrived, Mrs. Cuneo headed for Fairmount Park, which, among other attractions, boasted a 7.8–mile road course marked out on city streets inside the park.[17] Eager as always to drive on a road course, she put the Rainier through its paces on the Fairmount street course. It is not recorded if her passengers enjoyed being whisked around the winding, twisting street course at a high rate of speed.

The next day's destination was Gettysburg, Pennsylvania, and as the roads were in good shape, Mrs. Cuneo continued her quick pace. The checker's car, a blue Chalmers Detroit, driven by Ty Cobb, had left two hours ahead of the rest of the tourists. By the noon stop Mrs. Cuneo had overtaken Cobb, and she was soon out of sight. Arriving at Gettysburg well ahead of the others, she had time to drive over the historic battlefield with a full complement of eight passengers. Unfortunately, by the end of this second day, a majority of the tourists were upset by Mrs. Cuneo's fast driving. Because of their complaints, the tour referee firmly requested her not to run ahead of the pacemaker. Pleading that she had not understood that the speed of official cars was restricted (a likely story), Mrs. Cuneo agreed to comply with the rules (against speeding) for the rest of the trip. She later complained that driving at a slow pace was "the greatest hardship she had to endure on the Tour."[18]

For the next two days, the roads were quite good, but this would soon change when the tourists got to Virginia. There a combination of multiple toll booths and a growing number of water breakers made fast travel difficult. The difficulty of the drive was offset by the hospitality of the Virginians who lined the roads as they neared Staunton to cheer Mrs. Cuneo and Ty Cobb as they drove by. After Staunton, the tourists had no choice but to follow a series of narrow, winding roads along steep gorges and chasms as they worked their way through the Appalachian Mountains. Chains were strapped on to give the tires more purchase, and many cars overheated while forging their way up steep grades. For their efforts the tourists received a very enthusiastic welcome in Roanoke. Not only did a large crowd greet them, but they had made an impromptu series of welcoming banners that stretched across the road. One, claiming a speed limit of 120 mph, was laughingly approved by Mrs. Cuneo and several others.[19]

The roads leading from Virginia to North Caroline were much rougher and many cars broke down or had blowouts; however, the Rainier performed flawlessly for Mrs. Cuneo. The stretch from Winston-Salem to Charlotte added another degree of difficulty

Joan Cuneo and Louis Disbrow driving through a stream in the Rainier number 8 on the way to Roanoke, Virginia, on the 1909 New York to Atlanta Good Roads Tour (courtesy of the National Automotive History Collection, Detroit Public Library).

for the tourists, as they had to motor through 18 streams in a 30-mile stretch. Today we take for granted the many bridges we cross every day when traveling by car. That part of the nation's infrastructure had yet to be developed in much of the country in 1909, and drivers of cars and wagons alike were often forced to ford the streams that crossed the highway. The tourists found this to be quite an adventure, because the shallow streams often had steep banks covered with brush, while the deeper creeks had graded banks. Getting through these obstacles left all the participants soaking wet, as the water often went over the floorboards of the cars, and not a few stalled out in the middle of a stream. Mrs. Cuneo however, enjoyed the challenge, and she and her Rainier managed to clear all the water hazards without mishap.[20]

The tourists reached Charlotte late on October 30; fortunately, Sunday, October 31, had been designated as a rest day. Although even the seemingly tireless Mrs. Cuneo enjoyed a rest in Charlotte, she loaned out the Rainier so that a number of local residents could try it out. The next day, winding down the foothills of South Carolina to Gaffney, the tourists faced perhaps the worst drive of the trip. The roadway was narrow, with a crowned center, and very lumpy, as not all of the stumps had been completely removed.

These conditions posed problems for the tourists who drove European cars. They had been built for European roads, which were generally much better than those in the United States. Almost all American manufacturers of the time took the quality of the roads into consideration and produced cars that had a much higher road clearance.

On the ninth day of the tour, Mrs. Cuneo came to the rescue of a fellow tourist whose car had broken a crankshaft and could go no farther. Seeing the disappointment of the driver and passengers, she volunteered to tow the car to Commerce, Georgia. She and Disbrow had problems with the poor quality of their tow rope, which broke a number of times. However, they managed to tow the disabled car two hundred miles to their Georgia destination. While carrying a full complement of passengers, the Rainier still managed to average 20 mph. Joan Cuneo later commented that this was probably the most difficult task the Rainier faced on the trip.[21] Fortunately, the crew of the towed car was able to repair it overnight and they managed to get to Atlanta under their own power the next day.

On the last day of the tour, 20 cars full of enthusiastic Atlantans arrived to escort the tourists to their city and they were cheered along the way by excited spectators. When they reached Decatur, Georgia, another 200 autos were lined up to escort the tourists to their final destination in downtown Atlanta. Amazingly, city schoolchildren were let out and workers were dismissed early so they could enjoy the gala event, and the city echoed with the sound of the bells and whistles of the city.[22] The happy tourists were royally entertained by their Atlanta hosts when they reached their destination.

Mrs. Cuneo, while enjoying the festivities, was more interested in seeing the new track. Heralded as "the only woman who ever attempted to drive a racing car on a circular track in professional contests," she had been asked to give an exhibition on the new speedway Thursday morning. Due to the AAA ban on women racers, she was excluded from entering any of the amateur races on the program. Instead, she was to "perform" an exhibition time trial as part of the entertainment for the tourists. She would drive two race cars around the two-mile oval: a Pope-Toledo owned by Asa Candler Jr. and a Renault owned by Edwin Durant. In addition, Mrs. Cuneo decided to take her Rainier out on the track and try its paces . All those who watched her exhibition were impressed. The gentlemen who had entered the amateur races starting next Tuesday found her performance both challenging and intimidating. Not a few were probably glad the she had been barred from the competition. Joan Cuneo whipped Candler's Pope-Toledo around the track in a snappy 1:45 and Durant's Renault in 1:51.[23] She later said that she had never sat in either of the race cars before she took them out on the track to try their paces. Neither was there an attempt to adjust the cars to Joan Cuneo's small stature, which made her times even more remarkable.[24] Finally she took old number 8 onto the track. Though it carried full equipment, including four extra tires and rims, its top and a carload of passengers, she still managed the two-mile circuit in 1:56, a speed of more than 60 mph.[25] Again, it was not recorded how her passengers enjoyed such a quick trip.

All the tourists were allowed to try the new track after lunch. Although a number of cars were soon zipping along the speedway, Mrs. Cuneo had by far the fastest time. The *Constitution* mentioned that Ty Cobb, the Georgia Peach, was also expected to drive his Chalmers-Detroit in an exhibition as one of the program features the following Tuesday. As his time was not mentioned in the results, Cobb was obviously a much better baseball player than he was a race-car pilot.[26]

Her chance to drive at Atlanta over, Mrs. Cuneo spent a few days getting to know some of the other female auto enthusiasts who lived in the Atlanta area. Also included in the group was fellow New Yorker Mildred Schwalbach, the other woman pilot who drove the second press car in the tour. Joan enjoyed taking the Rainier out into the Atlanta countryside and driving around the city. She also stayed to watch the racing because her close friend Louis Disbrow was entered in a number of events.

The first Atlanta race meet was unusual in that it featured two two-hundred-mile races: one on the opening day, for cars of 301 to 450 cc displacement, and one on the last day of the program for the so-called big cars, of 451 to 600 cc. Most of the cars with engines of smaller displacement were also able to enter the big-car races, because they met the minimum weight requirement. Having two lengthy premier events was not the custom in 1909. As most of the races were short, a race of 50 miles was considered a long event. This is easily understandable for several reasons. The cars took a beating as they roared around the dirt tracks of the day. Shorter events allowed the professionals a chance to enter and win more races, and to the fans the finish was the most exciting part of the race.

The Atlanta Automobile Association had spared no expense on track preparation and the prizes and trophies they offered were larger and more expensive than the average. It is no wonder that some of the leading drivers of the day flocked to Atlanta for a chance to win as much as $1,000 for coming in first in just one of the races. Because the professional drivers routinely entered every race for which they had a suitable car available, Atlanta would provide a hefty payday for a lucky few.

The opening day feature race was a two-hundred-mile run for the beautiful Coca-Cola Trophy presented by Candler's Coca-Cola Company along with $600 in gold for the winning driver. It drew many of the top racers of the day and some lesser-known ones as well. Even Barney Oldfield brought his big Benz to Atlanta to try out the track, although his chief rival, Ralph De Palma, had not stayed to race. Louis Chevrolet, George Robertson, Charles Basle, Louis Strang, and Ben Kirschner rounded out the group of better-known professionals, while many aspiring professionals had also come to Atlanta to try their luck.[27] Oldfield, after losing his one-mile record to Strang, and his ten-mile record to John Aiken, broke a steering knuckle in his Benz and was forced to retire. He would not compete in any more events at Atlanta. George Robertson broke an oil pipe in his Fiat and would race no more the first day. The honors in the first two-hundred-mile race went to Louis Chevrolet, who won the Coca-Cola Trophy, setting a new mark of 2:46.48, an average of 72 mph for two hundred miles. He would have finished the race without any delays if his engine hadn't briefly caught on fire! When Chevrolet noticed smoke billowing from his engine, he quickly drove into the pits, and the fire was extinguished with no damage. Roaring back onto the track, he soon passed his closest rivals, who had gained a brief lead, and they were miles behind him at the finish. Only four of the nine entrants completed the race, a prime example of the high rate of attrition in auto racing at this time.[28] In 1910, the Coca-Cola cup race was reduced to one hundred miles, although the City of Atlanta Trophy race would remain a two-hundred-mile event.

Usually only one major trophy was awarded at any race meet, but the Atlantans had scheduled what they considered their premier event, another two-hundred-mile race for the City of Atlanta Trophy, on the last day of the meeting. The Atlanta trophy race again drew some of the nation's best drivers and fastest cars, because the winner would receive $1,000 cash while a beautiful silver-and-gold trophy worth $10,000 would go to the car owner.[29] Among those expected to contest for the Atlanta trophy were a number of drivers who had driven in the Coca-Cola Trophy race. They included George Robertson in his Fiat 90, Lewis Strang in another powerful Fiat, Louis Chevrolet in his Buick, Ray Harroun in a Marmon, and Charles Basle in a Renault 35–30.[30] One of the favorites was the "world's fastest automobile": the 200 hp Fiat, which broke Barney Oldfield's record for the mile on the first day of the meet with Strang at the wheel.[31] Louis Disbrow, in his 50 hp Rainier, was not expected to contest for the win. The Rainier, although known for its reliability, was not a particularly fast car and had not performed well in the Coca Cola Trophy race. Disbrow knew his car was at least 5 mph slower than the Fiats and Chevrolet's Buick , so he decided to drive his own race, holding the Rainier steady at about 70 mph, hoping that attrition would allow him to eventually take the lead. This was the same strategy Ray Harroun would use to win the first Indianapolis 500.

The race started just as Disbrow expected with Strang and Chevrolet speeding to the front of the pack. George Robertson was the fan favorite, as the crowd knew that Asa Candler Jr. had purchased his Fiat before the race in hopes that the trophy would stay in Atlanta. On mile 85, Chevrolet had transmission trouble and had to retire from the race, while Strang, plagued with tire trouble, fell out of contention. This left Robertson and Disbrow running neck and neck in the front except that Disbrow was 6 miles or three laps behind. However, luck was on Louis Disbrow's side that day in Atlanta. With less than 25 miles to go, the Fiat broke its chain, and before it could be replaced Disbrow's Rainier was 8 miles ahead of the field. Although Robertson drove the wheels off his Fiat, he could not catch Disbrow. The City of Atlanta Trophy went to the lightly regarded Rainier with Disbrow at the wheel in a time of 2:53.07.[32] He didn't set a new record, but he did win $1,000. For some reason, the idea of a golden trophy worth $10,000 excited the imagination of the general public so much that the Rainier Motor Car Company decided to exhibit the City of Atlanta Trophy at a number of locations throughout the Northeast.[33] Although he had already had some success as a driver behind the wheel of Joan Cuneo's cars, this was the first major win for Louis Disbrow. It came at a very good time, because Mrs. Cuneo was now excluded from sanctioned races and no longer had much need for a riding mechanic. Although she was very happy for his success, Joan

Louis Disbrow and fellow auto racers leaning against a large chain-drive race car. From left, the men are Bob Burman, Disbrow, Tower and Grenon (no first names). The last two may be riding mechanics, as their names aren't familiar and it was customary for drivers to wear a white shirt and tie when racing (Library of Congress Print and Photographs Division, Washington, D.C.).

Cuneo would have loved to drive in the races herself. Instead, she could only cheer on her friend.

At the end of the Atlanta meet, Joan Cuneo headed back to her family at Richmond Hill. There she continued to work on her cars and drive in an occasional exhibition until the Cuneo family moved to Scarsdale a few years later. Joan Cuneo and Louis Disbrow would remain friends. Disbrow would accompany her to a few more races and speed trials; however, he would begin a new career as a full-time professional driver in 1910. The Rainier company, recognizing his ability and familiarity with the Rainier, gave his budding professional career a boost by letting him drive their factory-owned car in Atlanta. Much to their delight, he brought the City of Atlanta Trophy home to the Rainier company in Flushing, New York. His success at Atlanta led to other offers, and by 1912 he would be a successful race-car driver with a national reputation. Disbrow returned to Atlanta in 1924 to run on the Lakewood track. Unlike most of his peers, he was still racing at the age of 48. The state-of-the-art Atlanta Speedway was long gone; by 1924 it had become part of what is now Hartsfield-Jackson Airport. By 1911, Candler Jr. and the Atlanta Automobile Club had lost interest in the track, and the new management was not able to make a go of it.

No longer able to compete as a "driver of large racing cars," Joan Cuneo still remained a national celebrity in 1910 and was often quoted in the newspapers. In February, she was interviewed by the New *York Times* about organized touring, and the Glidden Tour in particular. Not surprisingly, since she could no longer compete in sanctioned tours like the Glidden, Mrs. Cuneo was critical of the events. Speaking from personal experience, she commented that the rigid schedule and competitive aspects of the Glidden Tours made it impossible to enjoy the scenery or even know what towns the tourists were passing through, because of their focus on earning a perfect score. According to Mrs. Cuneo:

> They are required to rise at uncomfortably early hours to stand in line waiting for breakfast room doors to open and then to gulp their meal, so as not to cause an instant's delay at the starting line.... Once they get under way they are forced to trail along in someone else's dust and arrive at the noon and night controls coated with dust within and without. At the night stops their cars are taken from them and locked up in garages to prevent any work being done on them. It is a case of rush and eat twice every day for the schedule must be made whether the sun burns like a furnace or the wind blows a gale or the rain falls in torrents. There is no fun in it and no real touring in it.[34]

She went on to say that she had met some people at the Madison Square Garden Auto Show who recognized her because they had seen her drive through their town on the last Glidden Tour. Although she smiled and nodded, she later confessed that she had absolutely no recollection of ever being in such a place. The type of touring show she now preferred, since she could no longer compete, was one that provided route information and accommodations and also allowed the tour members freedom to travel at their own pace.[35]

10

Winding Down

Early in 1910, three writers interviewed Joan Cuneo for their publications; two were well-known figures in the automotive world. Although she had been interviewed and quoted widely in the press for years, each of these articles provides fresh insights into her life and character, connecting more pieces of the puzzle that was Joan Cuneo's life. The first interview appeared in the *New England Automobile Journal*'s February 26 issue as part of a section titled "Women in the Motor World." It was written by the prominent female automotive columnist Mrs. A. Sherman Hitchcock. Mrs. Hitchcock came from the same social class and background as Joan Cuneo and shared a similar love of automobile touring. As a result Mrs. Cuneo felt comfortable with the writer and shared information that she thought would be useful for women interested in automobiles.

The section started with a discussion of what "fashionable women motorists" might wear while driving in the "Sunny South" or in a snowy New England winter. Mrs. Hitchcock was a proponent of having well-tailored driving outfits made of good materials and textures. She felt it was necessary for the woman motorist not only to be a skilled driver but also to be becomingly and smartly attired to appear well on the road.[1] Recognizing that an increasing number of women continued driving through the winter months, Mrs. Hitchcock praised the long fur coats and fur-lined garments as being very stylish and recommended a fur turban or bonnet to complete the ensemble.

Her interview with Joan Cuneo was prefaced by the now familiar list of her accomplishments. Mrs. Hitchcock couldn't resist describing her subject saying "a more dainty, petite, refined little lady would be difficult to find. She is a decided aristocrat, with a most charming personality."[2] Like several others who were charmed by Joan Cuneo, Mrs. Hitchcock was treated to a ride, in her Knox Giantess on a winter day when the roads were covered with snow. Unlike most, Mrs. Hitchcock enjoyed her ride, saying:

A ride as a passenger with Mrs. Cuneo at the wheel would convince even the most skeptic [*sic*] [of her skill]. Such was my own experience on a day when road conditions were truly awful because of the heavy fall of snow just previous, and her splendid control of the large high-powered car under such adverse circumstances was remarkable for a woman operator. When in her seat behind the wheel there is little visible except her head and shoulders, and as you hear the roar of the mighty motor and watch the tiny hands manipulating the wheel you realize what a woman can achieve in motoring providing she is possessed of determination and courage.[3]

Mrs. Hitchcock then asked if Joan had any advice for fellow female motorists and she replied:

When I decided to drive long distances and to be entirely responsible for my car I decided to try to learn the little things which mean so much to good service of a car. *I even washed my car several times so as to be able to know when it was properly washed or just rubbed or wiped off!* I kept the engine clean and oiled and realized for the first time what it meant to have the brass always bright and shining. I learned how necessary it was to watch every bolt and nut, how much depended on the proper lubrication and even how to grind the valves. I love a clean engine and the satisfaction to me of knowing the inside of my car is cleaner than the outside is very great.

She then went on to discuss de-mountable rims, "a godsend to women," and how the invention of a self-starter for gasoline engines would encourage hundreds more women to take to the road. Cuneo would soon get her wish, as the first self-starter appeared in the Cadillac that same year. Finally she talked about the different driving styles of men and women, insisting that women had a more delicate touch on the clutch and did not have the habit of slamming on the brakes when they came to a crossing, which she attributed to 80 percent of male drivers. She also suggested to women readers that if they learned how their cars worked they would be much less likely to be taken advantage of by unscrupulous dealers and mechanics.[4]

At the end of the interview, she commented that " the greatest task was learning to look out for other users of the road, and suggested that they [women] not do anything foolish behind the wheel that would cause men to exclaim, "Just like a woman."[5] Again proving that she was a conventional woman of her class who just happened to be addicted to fast driving, she advised woman drivers "in dress and manner be womanly, abhor all things freakish and be comfortable and look comfortable while driving."[6]

The next article appeared in April 1910. By Robert Sloss and titled "What a Woman Can Do with an Auto," it has often been quoted in recent years as a major source of information about Joan Cuneo's career as an automobilist. One of the most often quoted passages has been Mrs. Cuneo's denial of any feminist proclivities. "Would that I could cultivate some suffragette tendencies and fight for my rights. But I can't — having instead always tried to keep the woman's end in automobiling sweet, clean and refined. I drive and race just for the love of it all."[7] Automotive historians have argued that her comment proves she was in no way a feminist. Throughout her life Joan Cuneo was always careful to conceal her innermost feelings. Yet there were several times during her racing career when she was sorely tempted to hire a lawyer and fight for her rights after she was turned away at the starting line. Joan Cuneo also drove the Briarcliff road course and several hill climb roads informally at full speed for her own satisfaction and to prove that a woman could do it.

While most of the Sloss interview deals with her exploits as an automobilist, it also included several hitherto-unpublished anecdotes of interest. Mrs. Cuneo remarked that she had received two compliments during her career that she valued highly. One was from a woman she had just met who said, "...you're the woman I saw driving down the street the other day; I thought at the time you looked as if you just grew in that automobile. Most women have such a hunched-up, worried look, just as when they drive horses they lean forward anxiously as if pushing on the lines."[8]

The second was from the famous Italian tenor Enrico Caruso. Mrs. Cuneo took him for a drive one morning when he was appearing in New York City. Caruso exclaimed, with his usual exuberance, that he had never ridden in an automobile until that morning. When she asked why he felt that way, as surely he had an auto of his own, Caruso replied, "Ah, I have three, but now I know that I have never really ridden in any one of them. I see that my chauffeur does not know how to drive them at all. He starts with a jerk that nearly throws me forward from my seat; he stops with a bump that almost breaks my neck over the back of it. He should run a trolley car — nothing else! But this — this is like sailing on the ocean or in the air!"[9] After this florid compliment, Mrs. Cuneo recalled, she stepped on the throttle, as she loved doing that to an unwary passenger, and "scared him into silence."[10]

Joan Cuneo at work in her garage; she didn't mind getting dirty but always wore a dress covered with an apron, as well as her jewelry. Note the AAA entry numbers hanging on the wall (courtesy of Harriet Newton Draper).

The third article, titled "Out-door Women," was written by Richard Duffy and appeared in the June issue of *Good Housekeeping* magazine. Perhaps to give the article more authority, it was prefaced with the comments of a professor of physical science at Columbia University. Dr. Thomas Denison Wood was at that time an authority on women's physical education with decided views on when and how women should exercise. Wood proclaimed that the more education a woman had, the more she benefited from physical training in moderation, "especially during the ripening years."[11] Wood did include a caveat that "women as individuals are temperamentally more inclined to overdo" and should not be trained by a male."[12] Wood did not believe that playing sports and games made a woman "mannish" as long as she became proficient in sports that were suited to her, but he encouraged women to get their exercise outdoors, whenever possible.[13]

Quickly moving past Wood's comments, Duffy discussed a number of the new "athletic women," who had mastered outdoor sports such as swimming, tennis, golf, horseback riding and the new sport of automobiling. Recognizing Joan Cuneo as the foremost woman automobilist in the United States, Duffy allowed her an opportunity to explain why she felt driving an automobile was an excellent sport for women. She eagerly responded:

> Motoring breeds self-reliance and responsibility in a woman and keeps her out of doors the year 'round in all kinds of weather. The woman motorist can always get quickly in touch with her friends, can be a more constant companion of her husband and children and can learn more about her own country.... If for no other reason, an ambitious woman would learn to run her own car to "save the cost of a chauffeur and the extra expenses and petty forms of graft some chauffeurs impose."[14]

Here she again betrayed an upper-class bias against the integrity of working-class mechanics and chauffeurs, implying that they often overcharged their customers. Earlier, she had made a similar comment to Mrs. Hitchcock, stating that she had washed her car herself several times so she would know if the person she had hired had done a good job. Mrs. Cuneo, though wealthy, was careful with her money, as were many others of her class.

Asked whether all women made good drivers, she responded that only those who were willing to give driving their full attention would be successful. Mrs. Cuneo said, from personal experience, that automobiles were not as forgiving as the family pony if their female driver happened to be distracted by a display in a store window. She did feel that women had an advantage over men in one area. Women according to Mrs. Cuneo were not as prone to bravado as men. Then, somewhat tongue in cheek, she added, "I won't say they are not subject to speed fever, but even when they have it, they hardly take the foolish risks of men."[15]

She then commented on her accomplishments as a racer, saying that she was an exception as a woman motorist because of the many cups, medals and ribbons she had won. This statement prefaced her explanation of why she believed women had been banned: "Now I am no longer allowed to compete with men ... under the laws of the AAA. This may be due to consideration for me and my sister motorists or it may be self-appreciation on the part of the men."[16] The tone of this statement implied that she believed the latter reason to be the correct one, although she never publicly criticized the actions of the AAA. In none of her interviews did she mention her friendship with Henry Ford or the fact that he had asked her to design the interior of the first sedan built by Ford Motor Company.[17]

Although proud of her records, silver cups, medals and ribbons, Mrs. Cuneo was most interested in advising women of the health benefits they would gain from motoring. However, she didn't suggest that the average woman should drive in lengthy and strenuous

Joan Cuneo photographed at the wheel of one of her cars at the time of her interview by Sloss circa 1910. She is wearing a fashionable military-style driving outfit, quite different from the shirt-waist or dress she usually wore while driving.

competitions like the Glidden Tours. She commented that she had lost 26 pounds during the course of one tour without suffering any ill effects, due to her strong constitution, implying that the tours were strenuous events. Nevertheless, she couldn't help poking fun at her masculine counterparts on the Glidden Tour, after watching with amusement "the great parade of rubdown, massage and medical precaution most of the men drivers went through at the close of a day's run." Mrs. Cuneo continued, "I used to lie down in a quiet, darkened room for a while and let every single idea flit from my consciousness except the will to rest. It seemed to me I got just as much benefit from my plan and surely I had less inconvenience."[18]

She admitted to never training for a race but instead living the regular outdoor life that she had enjoyed since she was a girl. She reiterated, as she had said many times before, that she had entered a number of competitions because she loved the sport but then added something new: "*and because I like to prove that women can do big things.*"[19] Yet in the next paragraph, she admonished women not to dress like a freak in a car.[20] Throughout her public life, she said over and over again that she was not a feminist or a proponent of women's rights. However, in her own quiet way, she inspired and influenced thousands of women to take up an outdoor sport/pastime that would make them more independent. She was indeed her father's daughter.

When she was not giving interviews to a series of reporters, Joan Cuneo continued her struggle to regain her place in the now masculine world of automobile racing. Although Mrs. Cuneo was no longer able to race officially, she still had the regard and esteem of the racing fraternity and was included by her fellow drivers in an event honoring Fred J. Wagner, the perennial starter for sanctioned AAA events. A large group of the prominent drivers of the day, including Bruce-Brown, Robertson, the Chevrolet brothers, and Mrs. Joan Newton Cuneo, "America's premier woman driver," attended a theater party for a performance of Elsie Janis's new musical play. There they surprised Wagner with "a silver loving cup as a token of their esteem."[21]

However, in May Joan Cuneo, along with Mrs. Evelyn B. Buckman, Miss Mildred Schwalbach, Mrs. Peter Back and Miss Alice Heyes, had their applications to enter the New Jersey Run denied. The five women, all experienced motorists, were refused because the event was sanctioned by the AAA rules, which allowed only men to compete in sanctioned competitions. The organizing committee felt that the women would not try to buck the rules because they had an interest in the welfare of the sport, adding that they could drive in the reliability run if they chose but would not be recognized as "official entrants, contestants or drivers."[22] Since this was not what the women had hoped for, they declined the opportunity to just go along for the ride.

In June, Joan Cuneo was forced to watch while Louis Disbrow drove her beloved Knox up Summit Hill in less than a minute to win the Upper Westchester Automobile Club's annual hill climb event for cars with 801–601 cubic inches displacement.[23] The following week she was again a spectator as Disbrow, driving her Giantess, faced off against Ralph De Palma in another hill climb at Port Jefferson, New York.[24] On July 4, she returned to St. Monica's Field Day held on the familiar Metropolitan Race Track, Jamaica, New York. Here she could only attempt another women's mile record, with Disbrow again acting as her riding mechanic.[25]

The most fun she had behind the wheel of her new 90 hp Knox Giantess that summer was putting on a show for the crowds that had gathered to celebrate "Old Home Week" in Wilmington, Vermont. The Cuneo family was well known in Wilmington. Joan's father and three of his brothers had been instrumental in developing the area and still owned property there, while Mrs. Cuneo owned a cottage at Lake Raponda. The organizers of Old Home Week had no trouble recruiting one of their most famous residents to speed through the town in her powerful race car. They laid out a mile course on the unpaved street between the post office and the blacksmith's forge and Joan Cuneo made the run at a speed of 72 miles an hour, much to the admiration of local residents and visitors. Neither her husband nor Louis Disbrow accompanied her to Wilmington. Instead a local businessman, Verne L. Adams, rode with her as she roared through the town laying a trail of dust. Joan later recalled, with a smile, "that Verne Adams hair has never laid flat on his head since the day he rode with me."[26] She had also brought along her children, Sonny and Dolly, and she later let Dolly guide the big car down Wilmington's Main Street after she had driven her speed run.

Old Home Week in Wilmington, Vermont, 1911. Joan Cuneo guides her daughter, Dolly, as she drives the big Knox Giantess down Main Street. Dolly is sitting on her mother's lap and Sonny is perched in back (courtesy of Julie Moore, President, Wilmington, Vermont, Historical Society).

In October, Mrs. Cuneo again made the automobile page as the driver of a new 25 × 35 Renault American Special touring car. The *New York Times* reported that she had just completed a tour from New York through the Berkshires, stopping at Wilmington, Vermont, and then continuing through the Green Mountains. Mrs. Cuneo evidently gave the car a good shakedown drive. Most of the route she chose meandered through remote mountain areas; the narrow, steep, winding roads she traveled had plenty of rocks, sand, and water breakers.[27] The Renault automobile company capitalized on her reputation as a skilled driver when they advertised their new model. Their ad featured a picture of Mrs. Cuneo behind the wheel, along with her testimonial of the Renault's performance.

At the end of 1910, the Renault car company capitalized on Mrs. Cuneo's fame as "America's premier woman driver," to advertise their new 25–35 hp American Special. In the ad, she was pictured behind the wheel of the touring model, which sold for $5,800, wearing one of her elaborate flowered hats. Her photo was accompanied by the lengthy testimonial that follows:

Gentlemen:— My "American Special" Renault has given such wonderful service and satisfaction that I feel only too happy to write and tell you about it.

From Sept. 7th, the day of its delivery to me, until the 28th the car has covered over 1500 miles without the least bit of trouble to me of any kind. Being driven from New York to Wilmington, Vermont, 266 miles in one day—thro' the Berkshires and up into the wilds of the Green mountains, she was left to my care and attention in this garageless town. I drove her over these country roads, abounding in water breakers, sand and rocks and steep, winding grades. The way she responded to every demand of steering wheel and throttle, as well as her marvelous riding qualities, was a revelation to every one. After being able to handle the car in the congested streets of New York with the utmost ease, then to find her the same on these rough mountain roads, makes me indeed enthusiastic over my Renault car with its long stroke motor and its wonderful balance and superb riding qualities.

Thanking you for your many courtesies and kindness in making the car so satisfactory in every way, and looking forward to many more miles of the same kind of service and pleasure, I am,

Most sincerely,
Joan Newton Cuneo.

In March of 1911, Mrs. Cuneo was again a spectator, as she and her husband watched Louis Disbrow drive his Pope-Hummer (Pope-Hartford) at Pablo Beach, Jacksonville, Florida. This five-mile beach course is barely remembered today, as it was only in operation for nine months in 1911. However, during several days in March the Atlantic–Pablo Beach organization held a Speed Carnival, which drew a number of the better-known drivers of the day, including Wilcox, Burman and Strang, besides Disbrow. Louis Disbrow had some success at Pablo Beach, as he won the three-hundred-mile race in his Pope Hummer, as well as several other events.[28]

It was here that Joan Cuneo first got to drive Disbrow's fast car. Her unofficial speed trial on the beach was the source of a comment she made after being arrested for speeding

Close-up of the trophy given to Joan Cuneo by Louis Disbrow after she set a women's unofficial speed record in his Pope-Hummer on the Long Island Motor Parkway (photograph courtesy of Kathy Cuneo).

in Yonkers, New York, that May. Mrs. Cuneo was quoted as saying that "she did not consider the speed at which she had traveled as fast as she had gone at the rate of 112 miles an hour in a race at Palm [Pablo] Beach." As she pleaded her case by phone, it would have been easy for the person on the other end of the line to mistake "Pablo" for "Palm."[29] There never was any racing on Palm Beach because Henry Flagler, who developed the island, hated automobiles and wouldn't allow any on his beach.[30] A few weeks after the Pablo Beach races, Joan Cuneo had an another opportunity to drive Louis Disbrow's Pope-Hummer on the Long Island Motor Parkway. As she tried for a new women's (unofficial) record with the support of her (male racing) friends, Louis Disbrow again acted as her riding mechanic. She was able to get the big race car to a speed of 109 mph. Mrs. Cuneo made two half-mile runs from a flying start. With four watches on the car, she managed to set times of 17 and 16.5 seconds according to the AAA timers, driving faster than any woman had done in the United States up to that time. However, because AAA rules prohibited women from participating in racing, the record did not count as official.[31] Several other newspapers had her driving even faster, as the *Washington Times* and the *Suffolk County* (NY) *News* both listed her speed as 112 mph; the *Times* also listed her half-mile time as 16.5 seconds.[32]

Having just had several opportunities to again drive a big race car with the pedal to the floor, Mrs. Cuneo, who was indeed addicted to speed, found it difficult to drive the streets of Yonkers at a sedate pace. Although she would not have considered 43 mph fast, most of her peers would not have agreed with her. It was not surprising that she was arrested for speeding in Yonkers, not far from her home in Scarsdale, shortly afterwards. However, there was a more to the story of Joan Cuneo's Yonkers arrest than the paragraph printed in some newspapers. Motorcycle patrolman Alexander Read had to chase her for two miles before she finally stopped, and by this time he was covered with dust, as he had driven as fast as he could along the unpaved road, shouting for her to stop as he tried to catch her. Initially, Mrs. Cuneo, who was driving by herself, laughed at his threats, but finally she stopped and surrendered. After Patrolman Read formally arrested her for speeding, she suggested that he put his motorcycle in the tonneau of her car and ride back to the station with her. This he gladly did, as he had no desire to eat her dust on the way back. Reacting true to form, as soon as the patrolman was in the car Joan Cuneo stomped on the gas pedal and drove him back to the station at a "breathtaking pace."[33] There she pleaded with the police lieutenant in charge to let her off, saying "she would never speed again," but Lieutenant Connelly, recognizing a lie when he heard one, said only the judge could let her go.[34] Judge Beall paroled "the prisoner" until the next day, and she then dropped the patrolman off at the spot where he had arrested her and went on her way. The next day Mrs. Cuneo pleaded her case by phone but could not escape a fine of $10.[35]

In 1911, two years after being barred from competition, Mrs. Cuneo was still a newsworthy celebrity. In January, her picture made the front page of a dozen newspapers for a reason totally unrelated to automobiles: because of a wager made by her husband. The bet resulted from his belief that his wife could do anything she set her mind to. Andrew Cuneo, her banker husband, had lunch one day with several friends near his office on Mulberry Street. Initially, his companions laughed at one of their fellow diners because he had ordered only half of a squab (pigeon), a very small bird. He responded that squab was one of those dishes you could only eat so much of and would turn one's stomach if one had to eat it every day for a month. Andrew Cuneo replied that eating squab 30 days in a row was not an impossible task; it all depended on mind control. If one controlled one's thoughts and didn't dwell on the fact that one had to eat squab, one wouldn't develop an aversion to it. When his friend asked him if he could do it, Cuneo responded that while he might not be able to, he was sure his wife could. His friend then bet him $100 that she couldn't do it. When her husband told her about the bet, Joan Cuneo accepted the challenge and the bet was made.[36] The outcome of the wager was not reported, but anyone aware of Joan Cuneo's strong will and determination would not have bet against her.

Mrs. Cuneo was also indirectly involved in another contest that involved consumption of food, in this case spaghetti. The stunt was again initiated by her husband, Andrew Cuneo, the owner of the Atlantic Macaroni Company, as a publicity stunt to increase sales. In 1911, Cuneo's business interests had taken a downturn. Joan and Andrew Cuneo and their children had moved from their large Victorian to an attractive but smaller house in Scarsdale. Trading on his wife's friendship with the racing fraternity, Andrew Cuneo invited 50 prominent racing drivers to take part in a different kind of race, a spaghetti-eating race. The drivers happily assembled at the Bridge Club in New York City for a spaghetti dinner on April 12 to watch Louis Disbrow, Arthur Chevrolet and Paul Snutsel put away pasta. The pasta course was preceded by a plentiful selection of hors d'oeuvres, which the healthy young men quickly demolished. Then four contestants moved to center stage. Initially, Chevrolet, Disbrow and Snutsel had accepted the challenge to see who could down the most spaghetti in the shortest time. At the last minute, Ralph De Palma asked if he could also participate. Andrew Cuneo happily obliged, as the presence of De Palma, considered the top driver in the country in 1911, would garner even more attention. As the only Italian-American in the group and one who had eaten pasta all his life, De Palma had a decided advantage. With Andrew Cuneo acting as referee, the four racers set to their task. It was not a surprise that De Palma quickly finished his first plate and asked for seconds, while Chevrolet and Disbrow were still struggling manfully to finish their first dish of pasta. Chevrolet finished slightly before Disbrow, but both flatly refused to attempt a second serving, while Snutsel couldn't even manage one plate. As the reporter gleefully noted, this was De Palma's first victory on his eastern tour.[37]

The year 1911 was one of emotional highs and lows for Joan Cuneo. The most nerve-wracking drive she made during her life occurred that year not on the race track but during a family vacation. In September, Mrs. Cuneo and her children spent time at their cottage at Lake Raponda, near Wilmington, Vermont.[38] On Wednesday, September 6, her 12-year-old son, Antonio, was hit by several shotgun pellets that had ricocheted off a large rock.[39] Young Antonio and a group of his friends were trying out a shotgun in the woods near the Cuneo cottage. Lacking a target, they had tried shooting at the rock when

The Cuneo cottage at Lake Raponda where Joan, Antonio and Dolly stayed in the summer. Today it is surrounded by second-growth timber, but in 1910 the area around the cottage had been close-cut and was used for pasture and farmland (courtesy of Julie Moore, President, Wilmington, Vermont, Historical Society).

Antonio was accidentally hit. Of course, all the boys were afraid to tell Mrs. Cuneo what had happened and she didn't find that her son had been shot until he came home for dinner, dirty and miserable. Quickly assessing the situation, Joan Cuneo bundled Antonio into her Renault touring car and headed for the Wilmington office of Dr. L. F. Page. After a quick examination, Dr. Page found that there were indeed several pellets embedded in the boy's leg. Although the wound was not life threatening, the doctor believed there was a real danger that Antonio might develop blood poisoning. Although there were several closer hospitals, Dr. Page believed that the facility at North Adams, Massachusetts, 24 miles away, would provide the best treatment. Mrs. Cuneo bundled both Antonio and Dr. Page into the Renault and headed the car towards North Adams in full darkness, her path lighted only by the headlamps of the touring car.[40]

Here her experience driving on rough mountain roads in several Glidden Tours surely helped her to safely negotiate the narrow, winding roads, made worse by a recent rainstorm. She had also recently put the Renault through its paces driving through the Green Mountains and at least knew how the car handled on bumpy roads. When she headed for the hospital, the tree-lined road was lighted only by the headlamps of her big car. These hazardous conditions made driving at speed on a road considered one of the worst in the state even more dangerous, but Joan Cuneo never faltered, as her son's life might be at stake. The physician later commented "*that he had had one fast automobile ride!*" They made it safely to the hospital in little more than an hour, an amazing time considering the conditions. Antonio Cuneo received prompt treatment and the surgeons assured his anxious mother that her son was no longer in any danger. Mrs. Cuneo was allowed to bring him home in the morning, although she took a trained nurse home with them to supervise his care. Thanks to Mrs. Cuneo's skill, nerve, and ability to make quick decisions, her son suffered no lasting harm from his accident.[41]

If this near tragedy wasn't enough, nine months later Mrs. Cuneo's auto struck a young boy who attempted to dart across the street in front of her car. In this case, the story did not have a happy ending, as the injured child was not expected to live. According to the *New York World*, Mrs. Cuneo had just picked up a new electric brougham. She then drove it to Central Park for a photo shoot.[42] Taking the photographer back to his studio after they had finished and driving at a slow speed, she was startled to see a child running towards her vehicle. The boy fell to the ground and lay motionless, after bouncing off the mudguard of the brougham. Mrs. Cuneo immediately stopped the car and picked up the boy. Handing him to her chauffeur, John McWilliams, she quickly drove to Roosevelt Hospital.[43] The attending doctors told her the child was severely injured, having both a concussion and internal injuries, and was not likely to survive, but she told them to spare no expense in his treatment. Leaving the hospital, Mrs. Cuneo then drove to the West 68th Street Police Station to report the accident. The incident left her shaken and upset, especially since the physicians held out little hope for the child's recovery. It was ironic that the accident happened as she was driving at an uncharacteristically slow pace. Several eyewitnesses to the mishap agreed that she was not at fault, as she was driving at about five miles per hour when the child ran into her vehicle.[44] Perhaps due to the emotional stress she suffered from injuring a child (the *Washington Herald* reported that she had been distraught after the accident), Mrs. Cuneo did not give any public exhibitions of fast driving during the rest of 1912.[45] The media did not report the ultimate fate of the child.

In spring of 1912, Mrs. Cuneo traveled to Europe, no doubt to observe the latest European model automobiles.[46] She got back to New York just in time to drive to New York City from her home in Scarsdale to see the Simplex Midget Racer that had recently been driven by Ralph De Palma. As she said, "I just wanted to try the car out." While there, she also attended the Brooklyn Automobile Show, which she pronounced to be "charming."[47]

Mrs. Cuneo was still considered a national authority on highway improvement and was often called upon to speak on this topic. She believed that women could play an important role in promoting better roads, as did the growing number of female motorists. She was asked to give several talks at the Woman's Industrial Exhibition, which opened in New York City in March at the Grand Central Palace. She explained to her audience that by promoting better roads women could participate in a growing movement that would benefit not only automobilists but society at large. The exhibit, catering to the rapidly growing number of women automobilists, included a number of displays of automobile accessories and motoring apparel that appealed to women, besides various programs on driving.[48]

Although not actively engaged in politics, Joan Cuneo was a member of the Women's Democratic Club of New York. Women would not get the vote until 1920, but many middle- and upper-class women were active supporters of both the Democratic and Republican parties in 1912. Joan Cuneo received an invitation to a victory luncheon held for Mrs. Woodrow Wilson at the Waldorf Hotel in New York. Although Mrs. Wilson had requested only a simple luncheon, the members of the Democratic Club made elaborate preparations and 14 courses were served that day. Mrs. Cuneo had a place at the head table along with the club president and Mrs. Wilson, indicating that she had more than a little interest in political affairs and was a valued member of the club.[49]

In January of 1913, Mrs. Cuneo again took to the Long Island Motor Parkway to try to set another "unofficial" speed record. She had hoped to drive the Jay-Eye-See race car occasionally driven by Louis Disbrow, in an attempt to break the world speed record. This metal monster was built in 1912 by the J. I. Case Corporation, a major farm equipment manufacturer. It was probably the only race car that was named after a racehorse, the champion trotter owned by Jerome Increase Case, the founder of the company.[50] Unfortunately, the rocker arm on the Case machine broke while she was warming up the car before attempting the mile run. The cause was attributed to trying to open up a high-powered car in cold weather, but in reality race cars often broke down before and during races in 1913 for a variety of reasons. Disappointed, she then drove another three-hundred-cubic-inch car (make unknown), attaining a speed of 96 mph, not even close to the 112 mile record she set in 1911.[51]

A few days later, Mrs. Cuneo was asked to make a series of tests in New York City's Courtland Park, to see how quickly a high-powered car could stop at various distances. Many motorists as well as the Automobile Dealers' Association had asked her to undertake this challenge. Joan Cuneo was a popular choice for this trial, as she was a known proponent of speedy motoring. The tests were planned as part of a protest by drivers and dealers against a new ordinance limiting the speed of automobiles within the city to 15 mph. They felt that it was possible to stop an automobile safely even when traveling at a high rate of speed. Given the quality of the brakes on the automobiles of the time, this seems overly optimistic, but Mrs. Cuneo gamely accepted the challenge. Driving her Knox Giantess, with Louis Disbrow again beside her as riding mechanic, she tested the braking power of the Knox at 8, 15, 20, 25, 30, 35, and 40 mph. Charles A. Stewart, the general manager of the New York Automobile Dealers' Association, and several other interested motorists acted as referees. At 8 mph, she was able to stop the car in half the car's length, about 6'1", but at 40 mph it took 108'5" to stop.[52] The results were not particularly supportive of the motorists' claims and no more was said about the protest. This would be the last time Joan Cuneo participated in an automobile-related event that was reported in the *New York Times*.

11

Bankruptcy, Scandal, Divorce

Rumors of war as the new year dawned did not stop Joan Cuneo from traveling to Britain on the Cunard liner *Mauretania* early in 1914. She stated she was going abroad for a rest and to look at the new European automobile models. Her 39-year-old husband, Andrew, did not accompany her. He celebrated his February birthday with friends in New York, while she traveled abroad.[1] For the last few years, the Cuneos' marriage had become one of comfort and convenience rather than one of true companionship. Now 38, Joan Cuneo had been a public figure for nearly ten years, but although she was still keenly interested in auto racing, the sport had passed her by. Her children were growing up and away at school most of the time, and Louis Disbrow, her close friend during her auto-racing years, was now pursuing his own career as a race-car driver. She was at a point where she was undoubtedly thinking about how she would spend the rest of her life. As it turned out, in little more than a year this decision would be made for her, due to circumstances beyond her control.

Before she set sail for Europe, she wrote an article for *Country Life in America* that was published in January of 1914. Perhaps the most interesting information she provided in this article was a list of the 18 cars she had owned to date. Unfortunately, she doesn't name all the makes and models she owned and drove; two are identified only with tantalizing snippets of information. First she recalled that "in 1904, I had a short and sad experience with a gasoline touring car, the whole tonneau of which had to be lifted to get at the engine," and the second was "one of the first seven side-entrance seven passenger touring cars in New York in 1906, also a gasoline runabout."[2]

While she was abroad, Andrew Cuneo, for the first time in his 20-year career as a banker and businessman, suffered a series of severe economic reverses. The first indication that his financial problems were serious came in February. There was a run on the Cuneo Bank on Mulberry Street, which still served the Italian community of Little Italy. The run lasted five days. Andrew Cuneo, in New Orleans on business at the time, hurried back to New York, but by the time he returned, his employees finally had the run under control. Nevertheless, at the height of the crisis depositors had withdrawn over $200,000 from their bank savings deposits. Many members of the Italian community had deposited their life savings in the Cuneo Bank for the last 20 years, but now they withdrew them, in fear that the bank might go under.[3] While some re-deposited their money after they were reassured that the bank was sound, others did not. The event had shaken the confidence of the Italian community in the privately held Cuneo Bank, which they had relied on for a generation. It also did not bode well for the future of the bank, even though it boasted over $2 million in savings deposits and an even larger amount in its checking accounts.

By August, Andrew Cuneo's creditors had petitioned to the New York State District Court that he be declared bankrupt. The creditors claimed that Cuneo's assets would not cover his liabilities.[4] In December, Cuneo finally petitioned the court in response to the original petition, saying that he would repay his creditors all that they were owed. In reply, the District Court appointed three executors who took who took over the administration of Cuneo's assets and properties, including those he had received as part of his wife's dowry.[5] In December, Cuneo's creditors again met at the District Court and were informed that they had been offered a repayment of one hundred cents to the dollar. They would receive part in cash and part in notes on a new corporation to which Cuneo's remaining assets would be transferred and liquidated.[6] At this time, Cuneo lost control of his privately held bank and the Atlantic Macaroni Company.

Initially the publicity gained by Ralph De Palma's victory in the spaghetti-eating contest had done little to help the sales of Cuneo's pasta in the United States. However after World War I had broken out in Europe in August 1914, it became increasingly difficult to import pasta products from Italy, and the sales of the Atlantic Macaroni Company had picked up. The bankruptcy court felt that if Cuneo's creditors were willing to wait, they would soon be compensated from dividends paid on the large block of stock Andrew Cuneo still held.[7]

Although the Cuneo's had to cut back their spending after this setback, they still maintained a more than comfortable lifestyle. Joan Cuneo, at least, had not been shunned by her social set and she continued her charitable work with the orphans of New York City. In the summer of 1914, she had again thrown her energy into raising money for the orphans. Not only did she take charge of the annual Orphan's Day Run, which carried orphans to one of New York's three amusement parks for a day's entertainment, but she was also in charge of organizing a charity ball to raise money for the orphaned children.[8]

However, on January 26, 1915, Joan Cuneo was stunned to read in the *New York Times* that her husband was being sued by a young woman for breach of promise, as he allegedly had promised to marry her. As Joan quickly scanned the article, she learned that her husband had met 21-year-old Yvette de Von, of Italian and French ancestry, in New Orleans in 1911, three years ago. Before the young woman began a relationship with Andrew Cuneo, she had worked as an artist's model, while supporting an invalid mother. Miss de Von stated that Mr. Cuneo had promised to marry her in New Orleans, in May of 1911. He had passed himself off as a bachelor when he was actually a married man. However, instead of going through with the marriage, Cuneo sent his alleged fiancée to Florence, Italy, to study acting, and prepare for a stage career performing with an Italian company. De Von did not finish her course of study in Italy but instead came back to the United States and established residency at the Park Avenue Hotel in New York City.

When Andrew Cuneo learned that de Von had returned to New York, he was very worried that his wife would learn of their affair. He also feared that his beautiful mistress might blackmail him. Cuneo called on de Von at her Park Avenue apartment and pleaded with her to return the hundreds of love letters he had written to her over the last four years. De Von initially refused to return the besotted but still-wily banker's letters but finally agreed to give them up for a payment of $3,000. Cuneo eventually decided to give in to her demand for money on July 18, 1913. However, he insisted that she sign a statement to the effect that she had returned all the letters and had no more in her possession.

Shortly after Cuneo got his letters back, the still-infatuated banker coaxed the model into resuming their affair. He then persuaded her to give him back the $3,000 payment for him to hold for her, arguing that he would take good care of the money! Foolishly, de Von gave him the $3,000, even adding $2,000 of her own money for him to invest. He might have been smitten by De Von, but Andrew Cuneo was now short of funds and needed cash to stave off his creditors. The $5,000 would come in handy.

After the story broke, reporters descended upon Andrew Cuneo in droves. When he was first questioned, Cuneo refused to comment on Miss de Von's lawsuit. However, the reporters who followed up the original story didn't take the time to try to uncover more facts. The same information about Cuneo's affair that had been published by the *New York Times* was re-printed and embellished by several other newspapers in the next few days.[9] The *New York Evening Telegram* referred to Miss de Von as a "beautiful artist's model," while the *Washington Post* added that "Cuneo had lavished luxuries on her, and wrote her almost every day while she was in Italy."[10] Both of these newspaper accounts mentioned that Cuneo, a prominent businessman and former banker, was married, that his wife, Joan, was a noted driver of racing automobiles and that they lived in Scarsdale with their children. The ensuing scandal and publicity, which eventually culminated in a public trial, effectively ended the Cuneo marriage, and Joan Cuneo divorced her husband a few months later. The widely reported scandal must have dealt a crushing blow to Joan and her immediate family, not to mention her upstanding Newton relatives.

In 1911, Joan Cuneo gave up trying to re-establish her high-profile racing career and devoted more time to her children and charity work. After she began spending more time at home, Joan must have noticed just how much Andrew Cuneo was away traveling on business in the United States and in Europe. However, it seems she didn't realize just how much her marriage was in jeopardy until she read the *Times* article. Their teenage son must also have realized that there was something wrong at home and, not surprisingly, sided with his mother. By 1911, he had begun to use Newton, his middle name, and his mother's maiden name, rather than Antonio. Antonio Cuneo, of course, was his father's uncle who had started the family fortune and adopted Andrew as his heir. The first time he was referred to as Newton in print ... was in September 1911, during his mother's wild drive to the hospital.[11] Up until this time, he had been referred to Antonio or Sonny.

After the scandal broke, Andrew Cuneo's first impulse was to run away from the mess he had created and his increasingly unpleasant situation at home, He applied for a passport to travel to Japan in February 1915.[12] However, Cuneo changed his mind, upon the advice of his lawyer, and decided to fight the charges. His lawyer had finally found a way to discredit Miss de Von. From the beginning Andrew Cuneo had firmly denied Miss de Von's accusation that he had promised to marry her, although he admitted to everything else. In August, with the help of his lawyer, Cuneo used her testimony to turn the magistrate's opinion in his favor. Zeroing in on the one part of her sworn affidavit that he thought he could successfully refute, Cuneo accused Miss de Von of perjury, saying she had known from the beginning that he was married.[13]

Although de Von's lawyer, John Reilly, sputtered "that this is a base attempt to deprive this orphan of her day in court," his client didn't help her case when she appeared before the magistrate clad in a clinging gray satin gown and picture hat.[14] Reilly then tried another tactic, saying dramatically, "There is a gang of Italian cutthroats in the city who are ready to swear her [de Von's] life away,"[15] intimating that Cuneo had friends in the mob who would have no qualms in lying under oath. Magistrate Corrigan replied that "he was not afraid of cutthroats" and decided to hear Cuneo's case.[16]

The first witness called by Cuneo's lawyer was Edward Rodriguez, the superintendent of the Southern States Alcohol Company and one of Cuneo's business associates in New Orleans. Rodriguez stated that he first met Miss de Von at a luncheon in New Orleans that she attended as Andrew Cuneo's companion. Rodriguez testified that he had pointedly asked his friend about the health of Mrs. Cuneo while they were at the table. Joan Cuneo was well known in New Orleans because of her racing success in 1909. Rodriguez believed that because of the many times he had inquired about Mrs. Cuneo there was no way that Miss de Von could have been unaware that Cuneo was a married man.[17]

Another friend, Eugene Cassaza, stated that when he had first introduced Andrew Cuneo to Miss de Von her first remark upon meeting the banker had been, "Isn't it strange that every nice man I meet is married?"[18] Cassaza, a Brooklyn insurance broker, said that he met the strikingly attractive Miss de Von for the first time at a French Students' Ball in New York and she soon became his constant companion. However, when Cuneo saw Cassaza and de Von dining together at the Astor Hotel he was immediately struck with the young model's beauty and later asked his friend for an introduction. Before he introduced Cuneo to Miss de Von, according to Cassaza, he told the young woman all about the banker, stressing that he was a married man. Cassaza, obviously, didn't want to lose his lady friend to the wealthy Cuneo. Despite Cassaza's attempts to dissuade her, de Von was still eager to meet the dapper and wealthy banker, and Cassaza finally arranged a meeting at the Wall Street subway station. Cuneo then invited de Von to see a play at the Broadway Theater, later that evening. When Reilly inquired what play they had seen, Cassaza responded, *A Fool There Was.* Those attending the trial burst into laughter at his response.[19]

Andrew Cuneo was then called to testify and repeated his denial of any promise to marry Miss de Von. However, he did not deny that they had had an affair, saying that he had "taken her to hotels, rented an apartment for her ... and given her a duplicate of a ring he wore as well as a plain gold band.... He also sent her to Italy to study acting ... but denied he had promised to build her a theater."[20] He also admitted that he had written to her a number of times, although he couldn't recall how often, and had indeed given her $3,000 for a general release, but "only to avoid publicity."[21] Although Cuneo's friends had every reason to support his testimony, it seems very unlikely that they were lying. It is hard to believe that Miss de Von didn't know that the banker was married. Joan Newton Cuneo was a well-known member of New York Society whose activities had been regularly reported in the newspapers at the time she first met Cuneo. She was always referred to as the wife of the wealthy banker Andrew Cuneo.

After hearing the testimony, Magistrate Corrigan surprised John Reilly, Miss de Von's lawyer, by denouncing what he called "shameless, shyster lawyers" who were willing to take any case for a chance of profit. Corrigan said he was not specifically referring to Reilly, who he believed to be an honorable lawyer, or his case. The judge was disgusted with lawyers who thought they could extort hush money by cooking up false evidence to intimidate their victims. Corrigan clearly sympathized with Cuneo, saying "that the courts and the district attorney are strongly opposed to any suit brought against a man, when there was no meritorious cause and the case was based on the belief that he [the victim] would settle rather than face publicity. Any man in the city is liable to find himself a victim."[22] Although denying that he referred to the case before him, Corrigan strongly hinted that he believed Miss de Von had initially hoped to force Cuneo to settle out of court to avoid publicity.

Although neither Andrew Cuneo nor Yvette de Von could be described as admirable characters and both were equally to blame for the mess they were in, after Corrigan's diatribe there was a subtle shift in sympathy away from the model to the banker. The final outcome of this trial provides an excellent example of the powerful male-oriented bias that existed in the court system at the time. In court cases involving married men, they were often portrayed as helpless victims of scheming, gold-digging females who were after their money, rather than equally guilty adulterers.

Reilly, seeing that the case was going against Miss de Von, tried his best to keep his client out of jail, asking the magistrate to dismiss the case, saying, "If you hold her [for trial], she will have been prejudged before the case reaches the jury."[23] However, Cuneo's lawyer, Jonah J. Goldstein, remarked sanctimoniously, "These proceedings would never have been started if she had not tried to try her case in the newspapers."[24] Magistrate Corrigan ignored Reilly's plea to dismiss the case, but he did offer Miss de Von a chance to testify in her own defense. When she declined to take the stand, Corrigan decided to hold her over for trial and Miss de Von burst into tears.[25] Although he won his case, Andrew Cuneo's marriage had been destroyed and he was up to his ears in debt. He moved out of the family home in Scarsdale, leaving Joan Cuneo with custody of 16-year-old Newton and 13-year-old Maddalena. Andrew Cuneo then set to work rebuilding his life and career after a divorce and bankruptcy largely of his own making. While he would eventually succeed in restoring most of his wealth, there were few opportunities for Joan

Cuneo, now a divorcée 38 years old with two teenage children, to maintain her social standing and wealth.

The summer of 1915 found Joan Cuneo in a difficult situation that she had neither foreseen nor created. She had been married for 17 years and had no career to fall back on except her experience as a race-car driver and a successful organizer of charity events. To complicate matters further, she no longer had a wealthy husband who supported her expensive pastime, and her friend and longtime mechanic, Louis Disbrow, had long since embarked on his own racing career. Finally, women of her class were not supposed to work. For several months during the summer, she briefly toyed with the idea of returning to the track, this time not just for fun but to earn prize money! However, this would not be easy, as she couldn't race in any AAA-sanctioned events nor did she have the funds to maintain a stable of expensive race cars.

It is difficult to know just how well off Joan Cuneo was at this point. Andrew Cuneo left her in possession of their house in Scarsdale, and although her marriage dowry went to her husband, she had inherited 15 percent of her father's estate after John Carter Newton died in 1899. As it was not part of her dowry, she held her inheritance, whether cash or property, in her own name. If she wanted to race, Mrs. Cuneo had two options. She could participate in unsanctioned events at local tracks, attempting to set new women's speed records, or she could join a barnstorming group of racers who put on programs of races at county fairs throughout the country. Her age and family responsibilities seemed to indicate that the second option was not a viable choice. Coincidentally, her thoughts of returning to racing coincided with the formation of a race-sanctioning group far different from the AAA and one that has managed to keep up with the times.

The International Motor Car Association (IMCA) is the oldest active automobile-racing sanctioning body in the United States and it is nearing its 100th year of operation. John Alexander Sloan (1880–1937) was one of its founders, a native of Pittsburg, Pennsylvania, who graduated from Ohio Wesleyan University after starring on its football team. The athletic Sloan started out as a sportswriter and then served as editor of the *St. Paul Daily News*. In 1906, Sloan was smitten by the new sport of auto racing and became an authentic speed bug. He initially partnered with Will Pickens, better known as Barney Oldfield's agent, to stage races at the Minneapolis–St. Paul fairground.[26] Pickens and Sloan soon created an unofficial racing circuit, setting up events at fairgrounds all over the country and in Canada. For a time, they were able to attract drivers such as Louis Chevrolet, Ralph De Palma, Barney Oldfield, and Earl Kiser to participate in these non-sanctioned events. However, by 1909, when the AAA had finally established itself as the chief (and only) sanctioning body in charge of auto racing in the United States, promoting unsanctioned races became much more difficult. The AAA dealt harshly with drivers who competed in non-sanctioned events. Its routine punishment was to ban or outlaw the guilty drivers from sanctioned competition for extended periods of time. Barney Oldfield, who would drive anywhere if there was a chance for a profit, was frequently on the wrong side of the AAA.

Consequently, there was still plenty of room for other race-sanctioning organizations, like IMCA, despite the AAA's insistence that all races had to be sanctioned by them. Not all tracks wanted to go through the bother of having their races sanctioned by the AAA. If the three AAA's was in charge, it would force the club or organization to follow its draconian rules, which included controlling the types of events that were held and forbidding female entrants. Automobile racing was extremely popular in the United States, but in many places people wanted to see racing that was more spectacle than sport. Automobiles, like airplanes, were still a novelty to many residents of rural America. They came in large numbers to see races, speed trials and other forms of exhibitions. Besides holding regular races, drivers at non-sanctioned events would attempt to set new (often bogus) speed records and automobiles were pitted against airplanes or horses to draw in even more spectators. Often, the actual races were choreographed so that the most popular driver won most of the time. If these races didn't involve out-and-out cheating, the competing cars were often owned by the same person, who saw to it that the favored driver got the best equipment. What the fans didn't know was that often the drivers did not get the prize money that they had supposedly won but instead were paid a weekly or monthly salary. This process of hipping or hippodroming had been a fact of life during the heyday of bicycle racing. Since many bicycle racers had taken up automobile racing, as their sport declined in popularity they took readily to hippodroming as long as they were well compensated. Obviously, the conservative middle-class leadership of the AAA did not approve of these tactics, and they worked hard to established the credibility of auto racing and make it respectable.

Realizing that auto racing could be profitable if it drew large crowds in small-town America, J. Alex Sloan, along with Ralph Sanderson, Verne Soules and the Friedman brothers, established the International Motor Car Association, or IMCA, in 1915. Although the AAA quit race sanctioning in 1955, IMCA is still going strong, having long outgrown its outlaw status.[27] Because IMCA had no connection with the AAA, it could stage events that were prohibited by AAA rules. Drivers who had been banned by the AAA were also welcomed into the IMCA fold. Although most of the IMCA regulars were not from the top tier of drivers, AAA regulars were allowed to drive in IMCA events during their period of suspension. Barney Oldfield could be found periodically racing at IMCA events.

Sloan, whose IMCA programs were mainly held at fairgrounds and smaller dirt tracks throughout the country, often added special events featuring women drivers disbarred from AAA events. It is rumored that Joan Cuneo and Elfrieda Mais actually held IMCA licenses in 1915. Mais, a daring female thrill seeker, drove at IMCA events for many years, putting on a number of speed exhibitions, and she probably had some kind of IMCA license. However, IMCA headquarters has no record that Mrs. Cuneo was ever licensed by their organization in 1915 or later.[28]

The first IMCA races were held in the Detroit area at the Michigan State Fairgrounds in the summer of 1915. They were followed by a series of other race programs that were held on horse tracks at a number of midwestern state fairs. Joan Cuneo may have contacted IMCA, or perhaps Sloan contacted her. No matter who made the initial contact, it seems that for a while, she was definitely interested in racing again. On August 25, an Iowa newspaper reported that Joan Cuneo was going to appear at the Michigan State Fair. The fair would be holding the first official IMCA race program, and since it welcomed women drivers, this could have been possible. The paper also reported that this was the first time Mrs. Cuneo would race since she set her last speed record on the Long Island Motor Parkway in 1911.[29] However, Mrs. Cuneo's name did not appear in the published results of the IMCA program held at the Michigan State Fair that summer. It is fair to assume that Joan did not race there: if she had, it would have made the news.

Just a week earlier, on August 15, 1915, *Horseless Age* wrote that according to reports from Detroit, Mrs. Cuneo would return to the dirt tracks, racing at Hamlin, Minnesota (the site of the Minnesota State Fair), on September 11, giving a ten-mile exhibition and racing against an airplane. In this article, the author repeated the common belief that Joan Cuneo's success at New Orleans was the reason why women were banished from racing. By this time, even she was convinced she had been banned because of her success in New Orleans and mentioned it in her *Country Life* article in 1914.[30] By 1915, it does seem that many people who followed and wrote about auto racing were convinced that the exclusion of women was all Joan Cuneo's fault, so it is not surprising that a number of recent articles and books have repeated this argument.

The possibility of Joan Cuneo's return to racing was big news and a number of newspapers throughout the Midwest picked up the story. One newspaper had her planning to drive at the Springfield State Fair in Illinois, to be held a week after the Minnesota fair, on September 17 and 18. According to several other newspaper stories, she had been offered a purse of $5,000 if she could break the records that Louis Disbrow, Bob Burman and Barney Oldfield had made at other state fairground dirt tracks.[31] However, none of the newspaper accounts of the races that were actually held at the state fairs in question made any mention of Joan's presence. Because her return to the track would have been major news, especially if she had raced against an airplane, the fact that she was not mentioned indicates she didn't race anything, anywhere.

Why didn't Joan Cuneo return to the track in 1915? She may have briefly considered it, as she still loved racing and fast driving. The large purse offered by the organizers of the Illinois State Fair would also have been tempting; after her divorce from Andrew Cuneo, she had to depend on her own funds. It seems likely that she prudently decided that, as a 39-year-old single parent, it might not be wise to take such chances. Although Joan Cuneo was still confident in her skill as a driver, she was also a realist. She no longer had the funds to purchase the latest-model race car on an impulse. Her Knox Giantess was a fast car, but it was a 1910 model, more than five years old. The cars driven by Disbrow, Burman and Oldfield were newer, faster and more powerful. She knew it would take a miracle for her to be able to equal or surpass their records in a five-year-old car, no matter how good it had been in 1910. If she didn't break any records, she couldn't claim the purse. She would then have the expense of shipping her car to the state fairs and home again with nothing to show for it.

After her divorce, Joan Cuneo and her children spent the summers at her cottage at Lake Raponda, as they had in former years. No doubt she wanted to get away from gossip about the scandal that still dogged her, not only because of Andrew's infidelities but also because she was now a divorced woman. Sixteen-year-old Newton was away at school most of the year, while 14-year-old Dolly lived at home with her mother. In 1917, Mrs. Cuneo rented their home on Heathcote Road in Scarsdale, New York, finally severing her ties with New York, and moved to Vermont.

Her divorce and the ensuing scandal, coupled with her husband's bankruptcy, contributed to Joan Cuneo's moving even farther from New York. Although Vermont was not so far away, Ontonagon, Michigan, where she would move in the 1920s, was still a remote area with few roads, almost another world. Although the scandal and financial reverses were not of her making, they had effectively removed her from the social set in which she had formerly been one of the leaders. By 1920, she would be largely forgotten in New York City, except by her particular friends whom she occasionally visited.

However, before she sailed for Europe on the *Mauretania* in January 1914 Joan Cuneo wrote one last brief article for *Country Life in America*. In it she discussed the 18 cars she had owned to date, the trials and triumphs she had enjoyed as an automobilist, and the great happiness that came to her from her Orphans' Outing charity. In closing, she wondered what changes would come to automobiles in the next ten years: "Living over the trials and tribulations as well as the joys and triumphs of the eighteen automobiles I have owned, I cannot help wondering what the next ten years may bring — for surely it seems that the car of today had reached nearly the top notch of comfort in every respect and we wonder how some of them can be improved upon."[32]

Joan was amazed by all the improvements that had been made in automobile construction by 1914, including electric lights and the electric starter, along with improved braking and handling, more powerful motors and better suspension. In her assessment as to what the automobile would be like in ten years, she was not far off the mark. Major improvements to automobiles would not be available to the motoring public until after World War II, long after her death in 1934. It is interesting to speculate what she might think about the handling, speed and air-conditioned comfort of today's cars, not to mention the opportunity to drive on thousands of miles of paved roads. Surely she would have loved the acceleration, comfort and steering of modern cars, but she might have missed, just a little, the mystery and adventure that waited just around the corner for the lady driver during Joan's automotive heyday.

12

Contemporaries and Rivals: American Women Racers and Tourists, 1900–1920

During the dozen years that Joan Cuneo held the public eye as a "driver of large racing automobiles," she was not the only American woman who found the sport of automobiling exciting and compelling. She was, however, by far the best known. Even after Mrs. Cuneo was banned from racing, her exploits made news across the country for years, while nearly all the others enjoyed brief periods of fame and then faded from view.

For a few months in 1905 and 1906, Mrs. H. Ernest Rogers and Mrs. Clarence C. Cecil Fitler briefly made the sports pages because of their exploits on the track. However, after successful first attempts they lost interest in racing and focused on other interests.[1] In 1909, Mrs. K. R. Otis drove part of the Trans-Continental Relay from Seattle to Philadelphia, setting a new record on her leg of the route. She made the drive from Pittsburg, Pennsylvania, to Upper Sandusky, Ohio, a distance of 220 miles, in 10 hours and 30 minutes.[2] In 1908 Mrs. Otis had won the Cleveland Hill Climb in her 60 hp Stearns, and in 1909 she planned to motor to New York City in hopes of entering more races, "if the management will permit a woman to enter."[3] Of course this never happened; Mrs. Otis fared no better than Mrs. Cuneo in entering sanctioned events in 1909.

Other women enjoyed the touring aspects of motoring that Joan Cuneo also loved. At 22, Alice Huyler Ramsey became a national celebrity as the first woman to drive across the United States, in 1909. Ramsey had already distinguished herself in several endurance runs before she took off on her cross-country expedition. A growing number of women like Mildred Schwalbach, who participated in the 1909 New York to Atlanta Good Roads Tour with Joan Cuneo, saw driving automobiles as a potential means of income. Miss Schwalbach, an athletic but feminine young woman who loved motoring, applied for a permit to drive a taxicab in New York City.[4] She advertised for a part-time position as a chauffeur, explaining that she hoped to earn money to finance her education as a teacher of the Montessori method. She said that her love of motoring took nothing away from her femininity as she enjoyed household tasks such as baking and sewing and loved working with children.[5]

After 1909, a small but determined group of women including Ruth Wightman and Blanche Scott gave up racing fast cars and took up the even more dangerous sport of flying, which, oddly enough, did not ban women. A few others with show business aspi-rations saw driving and posing with late-model automobiles as a way to gain publicity or notoriety. Finally a mixed group of women, some young and relatively poor, others well off, tried racing between 1915 and 1920, either as barnstorming members of IMCA or with other non–AAA-affiliated groups. This brief resurgence of racing in the West had played out by 1920, when AAA racing resumed after World War I. Between 1920 and 1945, only a small number of women raced. Those who did competed in obscure local events on dirt tracks throughout the country. Considering the obstacles they faced, it is surprising that so many women continued to challenge male superiority for decades.

Women automobilists were not fazed by the prevailing male belief, often supported by scientists and clergymen, that women were too nervous or physically feeble to drive a car. Unfortunately, male prejudice did not go away, even after hundreds of women proved they were capable drivers and mechanics. In a 1912 article on its automobile page, the *New York Times* provided a summary of current attitudes on whether or not women should be allowed to race. The *Times* reported that support was growing in Britain for allowing women to compete in races. The newspaper added: "It is contended in certain quarters that as it has been fully demonstrated that women are perfectly capable of driving cars, therefore they should be permitted to pilot racing cars."[6] But the *Times* did not fully sup-port this belief.[7] It felt that in big contests "where there may be trade interests at stake, or other reasons with which only the promoters are concerned, it may be wiser to confine the entries to men," although informal club meetings in the summer months might be opened to women.[8]

The *Times* then reversed itself, saying that women had never been seriously considered as competitive drivers in the United States, even though it conceded that many women, especially Mrs. Joan Cuneo and Miss Blanche Scott, "have shown their ability to drive cars safely at a high rate of speed."[9] That the *New York Times* should have listed Blanche Scott as a racing driver is problematic. By 1912, she was already well known as a pioneer aviatrix, having flown for the first time in 1910. She did, however, have the same kind of nerve and daring possessed by Joan Cuneo, coupled with a relentless drive for self-pro-motion.

The *Times* concluded the problem was that there were very few informal club meet-ings in the United States that provided opportunities for women to race. According to the *Times*, the social side of racing, which allowed informal competition, was not as important in the United States as it was in Britain. In this they were correct, as competition and making a profit were the most important elements of race meetings in the United States. To confuse the issue even further, the *Times* ended its discussion of women racers with yet another opinion recently published in *Motor*.

Motor believed that although informal women's events could be scheduled, women would not be totally satisfied by competing against other women. Like Joan Cuneo, before she and all other women were banned from AAA-organized racing, many women wanted to compete against the best drivers, whether they were male or female. *Motor* rejected the belief that "lady drivers" were "the worst sort of chauffeurs," guilty of "showing off and keeping to the crown of the road too much [driving down the middle of the road and refusing to allow another vehicle room to pass] when meeting other vehicles."[10] The author then listed those he thought were the worst drivers on the road. They fell into several categories, including professional chauffeurs and male drivers "whose lackadaisical heads are often to be seen lolling back in large cars, with one arm hanging carelessly over the side ... with the inevitable cigarette almost dropping from their mouths ... showing how easy the management of a big motor car is to them, and indulging in stunts to impress their female friends."[11] To the author, they were far more dangerous than any female driver. The worst group of drivers, he believed, were those who had started as drivers of horse-drawn vehicles, who hadn't managed to master the rules of driving a mechanized vehicle.[12]

In 1915, most sportswriters and automobile columnists believed that Joan Newton Cuneo was the best female driver of her time. Were there any other American women who excelled in the sport of motoring between 1900 and 1920? Did they received the same treatment as Joan Cuneo? A small group of American women raced their cars during this period, but almost all gave up racing after less than a year. Other women set records in cross-country drives, but these were all individual efforts, sponsored by an automobile manufacturer. After 1909, none was allowed to compete in an AAA-sanctioned race or tour. Instead they competed against other women in so-called powder puff events.

There were two women whose skills equaled Joan Cuneo's but only one who had a similar racing career, and neither raced in the United States. The first was Mademoiselle Camille du Gast (1868–1942), a larger-than-life Belle Époque French beauty and sportswoman, famous for her skills as a road racer in 1902–03. Although she was an excellent driver, Camille du Gast did not have the single-minded love of racing automobiles that characterized Joan Cuneo; she loved danger, which she faced with courage and nerve. When the Automobile Club de France banned women from racing in 1904, she pursued other interests instead.[13]

Dorothy Levitt (1882–1922) was another story. Levitt started racing in 1903 and stopped competing in 1909. She also wrote a book about women and automobiles along with many articles on motoring. During her career, she did very well in competition against male drivers but got few opportunities to drive against men in "real" races.[14]

Levitt broke into the racing scene as a protégé of Selwyn F. Edge, winner of the Gordon Bennett Cup and manager of the Napier Motor Car Company. She would be the first celebrity driver created by an automobile manufacturer (Napier) with real talent as a racer. Edge first noticed the attractive young woman working as a typist in the Napier office. Dorothy Levitt was petite, pretty and vivacious, and Edge quickly decided she could be better employed drawing attention to Napier models in competitions than pounding the keys of a typewriter. According to Jean Francois Bouzanquet, she "had long legs and eyes like pools ... in a bid to promote his cars and no doubt having found other hidden qualities in her, [Edge] decided she should take part in a race."[15] There was one hitch: he first had to teach her how to drive. Luckily for Edge, Levitt had natural ability behind the wheel and was not afraid of speed. After an initial trial, driving Napier-powered motorboats, in which she set a water speed record, he put her behind the wheel of a Napier race car in 1903. The young woman who had come out of nowhere (she was just 21) immediately impressed spectators by her ability.

A few years later, Cecil Byng-Hall created an upper-class backstory for Miss Levitt in the foreword to her book, *The Woman and the Car: A Chatty Little Handbook for All Women Who Motor or Want to Motor.*[16] In it, she was portrayed as the daughter of a well-to-do family who had ridden to hounds and was an excellent shot; "quick of eye and sure of hands, nerves troubled her not."[17] According to Byng-Hall, she had learned to drive in the country, becoming so competent that she attracted Edge's notice.[18] However, no matter what the truth of her origins, she was the first Englishwoman to compete in a public race. Shortly afterwards she won a number of competitions and quickly became famous as a motorista and journalist who wrote about women and automobiles.

In 1904, she had driven an 80 hp Napier in the Brighton Speed Trials so well that the French Mors Motorcar Team tried to recruit her to drive a Mors in the Tourist Trophy Race. When Edge heard about the Mors offer, he refused to let his protégé participate. She was his discovery and he wanted her to drive only for Napier. Levitt was heartbroken but didn't rebel, as she owed quite a bit to Edge, even though she would have been driving the Mors in a real race.[19] In 1906, she set a number of records in hill climbs and time trials, all in Napier equipment. In 1907, Levitt went to France as part of the Napier competition team and won her class in several events. When Brooklands, the premier British auto-racing facility, opened in 1907, Levitt wanted to enter some of the races to be held there. Just as Joan Cuneo had been barred from AAA competitions, Brooklands management rejected her entry despite the support of Selwyn Edge, who was wealthy, influential, and one of the leading British racing drivers of the day. In 1908, as a member of the Napier team, she drove the demanding Herkomer Trial in Germany without fault. The Herkomer was a reliability run that included both speed and time trials, and Levitt received a silver plaque for her efforts.

Only Levitt's origins as related in the *Chatty Little Handbook* are suspect; her comments in the rest of her book bear a striking similarity to Joan Cuneo's. Levitt worked on her own cars wrapped in a voluminous overall and she believed the details of an engine could be easily mastered by a woman if she was willing to apply herself. She did qualify this statement by mentioning that she referred to a single-cylinder automobile, common in 1908, as it was the easiest for a woman to drive and work on alone.[20]

Her book was profusely illustrated with artistic photographs of Levitt, which showed a petite young woman with dark hair, a straight nose and large, expressive eyes. When it was published she was living in a fashionable neighborhood in London's West End in a well-furnished flat, presided over by a housekeeper and maid. Between 1903 and 1909, the apartment was her home base, while she hobnobbed with auto enthusiasts, royalty and bohemian types in British society. She competed in a number of races, all with no

Dorothy Levitt in a glamour shot from the frontispiece of her book, *The Woman and the Car*, published in 1909 and in public domain. It was supposedly her favorite picture of herself.

visible sign of support. Levitt set a ladies land speed record, going 91 mph in a 90 hp six-cylinder Napier racing car at Blackpool in 1906. Like Joan Cuneo, Levitt had at least one narrow escape during a competition. The bonnet (hood) of the Napier she was driving worked loose during a speed trial. If she hadn't noticed it in time and stopped, she might have been beheaded.

Inexplicably, in 1909 she dropped out of racing.[21] By 1912, she no longer made the racing news or the society pages. Levitt died in obscurity less than ten years later at the age of 40. Current interest in female racers has unearthed more details about her life; Levitt was recently the subject of both radio and television programs in Britain. Although there were many other young women who raced at Brooklands between 1908 and 1920, Dorothy Levitt was the only one who had a public career that rivaled Joan Cuneo's in Europe or the United States.

Back in the United States, there were dozens of women besides Rogers and Fitler who did try their luck racing on the beach or the track before women were banned from sanctioned events.[22] In 1907, a young woman gained fame in Chicago, after setting a speed record at the Harlem Track. Alyce Byrd Potter Tetzer was married briefly to John Tetzer but preferred to be called Byrd Potter. She raced for the first time on a Chicago area track in the summer of 1907 and was crowned "ladies' champion of the West."[23] The petite Miss Potter, like Joan Cuneo, came from a wealthy family. Unlike Mrs. Cuneo,

Miss Potter was an eccentric who enjoyed her life as an independent woman. Described as being five feet tall and weighing about one hundred pounds, she had little trouble handling her large Haynes auto. A year after her success on the track, Potter announced that she and three female friends would drive from Chicago to New York City and back. The local Elgin, Illinois, newspaper reported that Potter was well known in the area as a skilled driver and mechanic and her friends believed that she would have no difficulty making the drive. Potter and her three female companions made no attempt to set any speed records en route and enjoyed being hosted by friendly automobile club members along the way. When an Elgin reporter asked if she carried along any weapons of defense, she said, "Only these," lifting up her thin white arms.[24]

In 1909, the *New Orleans Picayune* reported that Miss Alyce (Byrd) Potter had agreed to challenge Mrs. Cuneo to a woman's race during the Mardi Gras meet in February. Although Joan Cuneo eagerly accepted her challenge, Potter never appeared in New Orleans for the match race, although she and Joan Cuneo had met in 1907 and carried on a correspondence. Byrd Potter went on to live a long and busy life in Elgin. Although she enjoyed driving for the rest of her life, she never raced again.[25]

In 1915, at the same time that IMCA promoters tried to lure Joan Cuneo back to the track another young woman received a license to compete in International Motor Car Association events. Although she probably never competed in a "real race," Elfrieda Hellman Mais La Plante (1892–1934) certainly had the requisite amount of courage and daring.[26] She had begun her professional career as a 20-year-old daredevil in 1912, a wing walker, who risked her life in the barnstorming aero exhibitions, which were popular at the time. After she married race-car driver Johnny Mais in 1911, Elfrieda decided to try her luck at auto racing. In 1916, the *Wichita Beacon* reported that Miss Mais and Mrs. Cuneo were the only female drivers to obtain IMCA licenses but that Mrs. Cuneo had quit racing after she had been defeated by Miss Mais! According to the *Beacon*, Mais was now the only licensed "Speed Queen " of the IMCA Circuit, surrounded by more than a hundred "kings."[27] Most of her "races" were speed trials, although once in while she did compete against a local woman in a powder puff event. No matter where she raced, IMCA publicity regularly exaggerated the skills and racing pedigree of their female daredevil.[28] In her long career as a stunt driver, she was consistently billed as the "women's champion" and at least once as a "German lady." The same article proclaimed the reason for her success was her marriage to an Indianapolis multimillionaire who financed the construction of her race cars.[29] In surviving advertisements for IMCA races, Mais was often scheduled to compete against other women for the "women's championship of the United States." For the most part, the other women either never showed up or were not willing to risk their lives on a dirt track. Supposedly, in 1924 she took part in a match race against Louis Disbrow on a dirt track at the Canadian Exhibition Grounds in Toronto and won. Likely this was another of the famous IMCA–scripted finishes, as Disbrow was a particularly talented dirt track racer.[30]

By the end of the 1920s the automobile was no longer a novelty and interest in women's speed trials declined. Spectators wanted to see the best male drivers duel one another behind the wheels of fast cars, not a solitary female attempting to set a new speed record. In the latter years of her lengthy IMCA barnstorming career, Elfrieda Mais became a stunt driver as death-defying feats were incorporated into IMCA race programs. Eventually her luck ran out and on September 26, 1934, she was killed when her car went out of control after she had driven through a fiery board wall at the Alabama State Fair. Her car left the track, crashed through a fence, bounced off a road scraper and smashed through the fairgrounds wall. According to her second husband, Ray La Plante, who witnessed the accident, his wife had already been injured several times when performing this stunt, first in 1928 in Jackson, Mississippi, and the preceding winter in Tampa, Florida.[31] She was 42 years old and had been racing for more than 20 years.

A number of Joan Cuneo's female contemporaries reached celebrity status because of their skill, mechanical ability and endurance as cross-country drivers. The most famous of this group was Alice Huyler Ramsay, who earned the title of the "first woman to drive across the United States." She later wrote about her trip, in the appropriately titled *Veil, Tire Iron and Duster*. Alice Ramsey's skill was first noticed by Carl Kelsey when she drove in a 1908 endurance run.

The 25-year-old Kelsey understood the value of publicity in selling cars. He first brought Maxwell to the notice of the motoring public when he drove one up the steps of the Philadelphia Mercantile Club in 1905. Kelsey was so successful at selling cars that he was hired to be the company's national sales manager in the same year. Kelsey believed in entering Maxwell runabouts in race meets and first sponsored Joan Cuneo, already quite well known, to drive a Maxwell in several events in 1906.[32] Kelsey himself successfully drove a Maxwell in several races and Glidden Tours but was annoyed when the Pierce-Arrow automobiles won the Glidden Trophy several years in a row. Although the Maxwell company challenged Pierce-Arrow to an endurance run, this never came about and Kelsey looked for other ways to promote the sales of his beloved Maxwells.[33]

The best known and most successful of Kelsey's promotions was Maxwell's sponsorship of Alice Huyler Ramsey's (1886–1983) cross-continent drive from New York to San Francisco in 1909. Several similar well-publicized runs had already been made, but not by a woman driver. The trip was known to be doable but difficult, because of the poor quality or nonexistence of roads in the West and the lack of suitable accommodations for gently reared ladies en route. When the Maxwell Company announced that a young woman and three female companions planned to attempt the trip, it attracted nationwide publicity.

Ramsey was married to John Rathbone Ramsey, a well-to-do lawyer from Hackensack, New Jersey, who later became a congressman. Only 22, she had attended Vassar, was the mother of a small son, and had only been driving for a few months. Her doting husband, alarmed at his wife's inability to control a horse and buggy, bought her a bright red Maxwell Junior, although he preferred horses to autos all his life. Like Joan Cuneo, Ramsey loved driving from the start, had considerable mechanical aptitude, joined the

Women's Motoring Club of New York, and had quickly entered a reliability contest. Kelsey was impressed by her skill when he saw her complete a 150-mile endurance run earning a perfect score. He knew then that he had the perfect woman to attempt the drive. Ramsey was taken aback when Kelsey asked her if she was willing to be the first woman to drive across the United State in a Maxwell. She took some convincing, but with her husband's blessing Alice finally agreed to attempt the trip, but only if Maxwell would pay all expenses and provide spare parts if needed at Maxwell dealers across the country.[34]

The intrepid foursome, Alice Ramsey, her sisters-in-law, Nettie Powell and Margaret Atwood, and her young friend Hermine Johns, departed from the Maxwell showroom on Broadway on June 9, 1909, in a downpour. Ramsey's friend and rival, Joan Newton Cuneo, was there to see her off. At Poughkeepsie, New York, the Ramsey party met the automobile editor of the *Boston Herald*, John D. Murphy, who would be their advance agent in charge of news coverage and accommodations as they traveled across the country.[35]

After many adventures, with Alice Ramsey doing all the driving and some of the repairs and tire changing en route, they reached San Francisco August 6, 1909, making the trip in little less than two months. There they were met by cheering throngs of spectators, on foot, and waving from the windows of long lines of automobiles. The residents

Alice Huyler Ramsey sometime after her 1909 record-setting drive across the country. She is dressed for winter motoring in an open car, clad in a large fur-trimmed coat (public domain photograph).

174

of California had been well informed about the progress of Ramsey's party, due to the publicity generated by Murphy and the Maxwell Company while they were en route.[36]

Ramsey never participated in another competition after her historic drive, but she retained her love of automobile touring throughout her life and drove thousands of miles every year. During her long life, she made more than 30 trips across the United States, with her children and grandchildren. Her last challenge was to drive the six passes of the Swiss Alps; she made five before snow closed the sixth for the season. Her doctor forbade her to go back to the Alps because she was now wearing a pacemaker. In 1960, she was named Woman Motorist of the Century by the AAA and First Lady of Automotive Travel by the Automobile Manufacturers Association. She was also the first woman nominated to the Automotive Hall of Fame in Detroit, Michigan. The author feels that Joan Newton Cuneo should have been named the Woman Motorist of the Century for her many and varied accomplishments during the brass age of automobiles. However, Alice Huyler Ramsey was also a worthy recipient. She worked for the Red Cross Motor Corps during World War I. She wrote *Alice's Drive*, a book about her 1909 adventures, in 1961, toured across the United States and, Europe many times, and, unlike Joan, only got one ticket during more than 70 years of driving. Ramsey died in 1983 at the age of 96.[37]

Ramsey's well-documented trip inspired many other women to attempt the drive, including Emily Price Post, who later gained fame as the doyenne of etiquette. Although Post didn't do any of the driving herself (she recruited her son for this chore), she planned the lengthy trip and wrote an account of their adventures that was published in 1916.[38] Post was an acute observer of humanity and noted that western women had more freedom, had broken with convention and took readily to motoring by themselves into open country.[39] This may well help to explain why western women continued to try their luck in powder puff races during the twenties and thirties.[40]

Blanche Stuart Scott's public career is not easy to categorize. Many of the women who learned to fly between 1910 and 1920 tried racing or touring before turning to the air. Scott had a brief brush with fame as an automobilist but had a much longer and better-known career as an aviatrix.

Nine years younger than Joan Cuneo, Blanche Stuart Scott was born on April 8, 1885, in Rochester, New York. Like most female drivers of the day, she came from a well-to-do family. Her parents, Belle and John Scott, were solidly middle-class: John Scott was a successful businessman who manufactured and sold patent medicines. He had enjoyed driving automobiles from the first days of their appearance on the Rochester, New York, streets and allowed his teenaged daughter to drive the family car around the city in 1900. There were no age restrictions or even licenses needed to drive an auto yet, but many of the local residents did not appreciate having a young girl driving around the streets of their city. Realizing that they had allowed their daughter to turn into a tomboy, Blanche's parents sent her to several finishing schools to learn proper deportment, but it was too late. Like Joan Cuneo, Blanche Scott attended several schools, including the Misses School for Girls in Rochester, Howard Seminary in Massachusetts and Fort Edward

College in New York.[41] Evidently the finishing schools had little effect on Blanche Scott's impulsive and free-spirited character, as she would have a strong interest in automobiles and mechanics for the rest of her life.

In a 1910 interview, before the start of her drive across the United States, Scott contradicted the account of when she had learned to drive recounted in her obituary. She said that she had taken up motoring only five years earlier. This would have made her 20 when she started driving. Rather than her being a robust, outdoor-loving tomboy as implied in her obituary, Scott said she took up motoring because she was in poor health and her father bought her a small car in hopes that spending time outdoors would improve her physical condition. The automobile changed her life almost overnight, as, she said, "I immediately became tremendously enthusiastic in the pure enjoyment of the sport with its wide range of possibilities in the quest of pleasure, travel and experience."[42] However another reporter described her as "a short, aggressive woman with a big ego, and a relentless self promoter so it is a toss-up as to which account is true."[43]

Scott, like Joan Cuneo, loved driving and owned several high-powered cars. She also became adept at working on them and changing tires when needed. However, her exploration of the possibilities of automobiling did not extend to racing on a track or the beach, although she was already an experienced driver years before women were banned by the AAA. Blanche Scott's niche in automobile history resulted from her determination to drive across the continent in 1910, acting as her own mechanic, with only a woman friend as companion. Even though she would not be the first (Alice Huyler Ramsey already had this distinction and many other women had already traveled cross-country as passengers), Scott's proposed trip again caught the public's attention.

Scott left on her well-publicized trip on May 16, 1910, with Gertrude Buffington-Phillips, a reporter from New York City. They took roughly 60 days to get to San Francisco, arriving on July 23, 1910 about the same time as Alice Ramsey. Scott drove an Overland, appropriately named Lady Overland, as her trip was sponsored by the Willys-Overland Company. Scott and Buffington-Phillips traveled over mostly unpaved roads, with Scott doing the driving and making necessary repairs and Buffington-Phillips reporting on their adventures. Overland promoted Scott's feat as the "first cross-country drive by a female," although it obviously wasn't, and she actively encouraged this view. Not only was her car much more luxurious than Ramsey's, but the three women stayed at the best hotels available along the way.[44]

Her epic trip inadvertently piqued Scott's interest in flying and ended her career as a motorista. One of her stops on the way west was Dayton, Ohio, where she took time to visit the Wright Flying School. Newspaper stories about her trip caught the notice of aviation pioneer Glenn Curtiss. Because he liked what he read, he agreed to give her flying lessons when she showed up at his Hammondsport, New York hanger at the end of that summer. Before she gave up driving, Scott and her companions made a side trip to see the new Indianapolis Motor Speedway. There she supposedly met Barney Oldfield, who let her drive his Peerless Green Dragon. According to Scott, when she drove on the Speedway track "I couldn't get it [the Green Dragon] above eighty miles an hour, though not all the horses were going for me," and then added, "Speed beyond that was too much for me. I wasn't strong enough to hold the wheel on the oblong track."[45]

A number of adventure-seeking, risk-taking young women of the time took up flying after 1909. It is probably a coincidence that the first American woman got a flying license the year after women were excluded from automobile competitions. Although she loved flying, Blanche Scott also wanted to expand opportunities for women in the new field of aviation. No doubt the early women pilots loved to fly, but few had Joan Cuneo's desire to race against the best. This trait emerged in the second generation of female fliers during the twenties and thirties.

Scott's first flight was the result of an accident. The fact that she survived it and many others is a testament to her skill, but it seems she also shared some of Joan Cuneo's luck. During one of Scott's introductory lessons, Glenn Curtiss set the controls of her plane so that she would only be able to taxi around the field, which was derisively called grass cutting at the time. However, a sudden gust of wind lifted the biplane into the air, and before she knew it Scott's plane was 40 feet above the ground. She was able to land without incident and that was the end of her grass-cutting practice sessions. As she later said, "In those days they didn't take you up into the air to teach you. They gave you a bit of preliminary ground training. Told you this and that. You got in. They kissed you good-by and trusted to luck you'd get back."[46] For her first biplane flight, Miss Scott sat, without a seat belt, in what she called "an undertaker's chair, in front of a motor that sounded like a whirling bolt in a dish pan."[47] Because of her accidental takeoff and landing, the Early Birds of Aviation list Scott as the first American woman to make a solo flight in an airplane.[48]

Flying soon became her occupation as well as an addiction for Blanche Scott. She joined the Curtiss exhibition team as a professional pilot for the first time at an air show in Fort Wayne, Indiana, and was the first woman to fly in a public event in America. Because of her daring as an exhibition flyer, she was called the Tomboy of the Air. In one of her stunts, she flew upside down; in another, called the death dive, she climbed to four thousand feet, pointed the plane towards the earth and pulled up only two hundred feet from the ground. She later said she hoped her achievements would stimulate more opportunities for women. Scott was well paid for her aerobatics, sometimes making as much as $5,000 a week.[49]

Just as competing troupes of auto racers barnstormed the country, so did groups of pioneer pilots. Both tried to make their shows as exciting as possible, and women pilots were now as much of a curiosity as women auto racers had been. Blanche Scott's daring stunts were such a crowd favorite that Lincoln Beachy, a famous stunt pilot of the day, tried to cash in on her fame. He announced that he had found another female pilot as talented as Scott. Donning a flaxen wig and long skirts, Beachy took off from a field in Los Angeles and performed a number of thrilling stunts until he was unmasked after he lost his wig and skirts![50] In reality there were few American women capable of performing

Blanche Stuart Scott seated at the controls of an airplane similar to the one in which she took her first, accidental flight (public domain photograph).

the dangerous stunts of Blanche Scott, just as there were few women who had Joan Cuneo's talent behind the wheel.

Hoping to cash in on the popularity of auto racing, a race between four leading women aviators, Matilde Moisant, Harriett Quimby, Blanche Scott and Suzanne Dutrieu, was proposed at Nassau, New York, in the fall of 1911.[51] The competition was well publicized, but the race never took place. Although air racing gained in popularity through the years, it never became as popular as auto racing because of the dangers involved and the difficulty of watching an air race from the ground.

Scott retired from barnstorming in 1916 because she was disappointed that the aviation industry kept women from working as mechanics or engineers and also because of the public's ghoulish interest in crashes. Despite a varied career and three marriages, she always remained interested in flying and was the first American woman to fly in a jet, a TF-80C with Chuck Yeager at the controls. Irrepressible to the end, she said, "God in his infinite wisdom gave me three husbands but no children. If I had a son, he'd probably be a delinquent."[52]

Promoting their show business careers was another reason why young women drove race cars before World War I. Florence Webber, an Indiana native, came to Atlanta in 1910 as the leading lady of the Climax Theater Troupe. While starring in a play at the Orpheum Theater, she was encouraged to try out the Atlanta Motordrome track as the guest of Asa Candler Jr. and other members of the Atlanta Motor Club. The athletic Miss Webber was invited to spend the morning playing golf at the Atlanta Athletic Club course and participate in a private speed exhibition hosted by club members in the afternoon. According to the *Constitution*, she was granted this opportunity not because of her "histrionic ability" alone but also because she was reputed to be a skilled driver. Happy to oblige the young sportsmen, Webber got a chance to drive a number of speedy racers owned by Atlanta club members. They included two of Candler's cars, a powerful 60 hp Fiat and a Renault, as well as the E-M-F Bullet, a speedy Buick, a Pope-Hartford and several others.[53]

The impromptu meet was a huge success. Miss Webber got to drive all the members' cars, which, according to the *Constitution*, she handled with style, and a good time was had by all. The young men got to flirt and compete against a pretty young actress, not quite respectable but fun, while generating sorely needed publicity for the Atlanta speedway as well as the Climax Theater Troupe. Both hoped to sell more tickets for their upcoming events. As no times were mentioned, Florence Webber, although skilled, would not have been a match for Mrs. Cuneo on the track; however, she was not the first and would not be the last actress to use an automobile for publicity purposes.[54] Actresses driving fast autos did make the news, and silent film star Bebe Daniels used it to advantage in 1921. She was arrested for speeding in Tustin, California, after she was caught driving her Marmon sports car through the streets at 56 mph, more than 20 miles over the speed limit. Daniels served ten days in jail, although she didn't have to wear an orange jumpsuit, and was serenaded by a local band during her incarceration. The resulting publicity got her at least three movie roles, and a song was written about the event.[55] This was exactly the type of publicity more conservative auto manufacturers hated.

The last hurrah for women's racing before its 50-year hiatus occurred in 1918 in Southern California. A group of wealthy women, calling themselves the Speederettes, who loved fast driving, wanted to try doing it legally, on a track. They decided to put together an all-female race program at Ascot Park near Los Angeles. Because the AAA had discontinued sanctioned racing during World War I, they did not have to face the disapproval of the AAA. California was a logical place to hold the races because the state already had a well-developed hot rod and racing culture and car ownership in California was widespread. Many of the best male drivers from the East regularly traveled cross-country to compete there.

What made the Ascot Park event unusual was that not only did women drive in the races, but women worked in the pits as well. The officiating was also done by women, and Mrs. Barney Oldfield acted as starter for the races. The cars the women drove were a mixed lot of secondhand race cars including a Marmon and a Stutz, a variety of stock cars stripped for racing, and a few cycle cars (small lightweight vehicles, a cross between an auto and a motorcycle). Although the cycle cars had their own class, the stock and race cars were combined in several races. Not surprisingly, Mrs. C. H. Wolfeld, who drove the Stutz, won the five-mile championship race, bettering the women's record set by Mrs. Cuneo in 1909 by 20 seconds.[56] Miss Ruth Wightman, a fearless 18-year-old, won the cycle-car race, closely followed by Nina Vitagliano, another speed-mad young woman. Although Wightman went on to become a pioneering aviatrix, Vitagliano's racing career would end abruptly only a month later.

Born into wealthy Italian nobility, Nina Vitagliano (1890–1918) had emigrated to California with her family; they hoped that Vitagliano Sr.'s health would improve in sunny California. In Italy, Nina had enjoyed driving fast automobiles. Although she was now 28 years old and married to Stephen Torre, a shipping executive, she still loved fast driving and was determined to race with the Speederettes. After her heady experience at Ascot Park, she wanted to race again, against her parents' wishes, although her husband, Stephen Torre, seemed willing to indulge his fearless wife.

Although the *Los Angeles Times* had initially referred to the February races at Ascot disparagingly as "Sunday's Big Girlie Show," the event drew ten thousand people to the mile concrete oval. Those who came to scoff or out of curiosity were impressed by the determination of the Speederettes.[57] This positive reaction to the women's race caught the attention of Omar Toft, a middle-rank racer who had turned to promoting races instead of driving in them. Toft, sensing a chance to make some money, organized another women's race program that would be held at the Stockton Fairgrounds, a mile dirt track, a few weeks later.

Most of the women who had competed in the first event at Ascot were eager to race again, especially Ruth Wightman and Nina Vitagliano. The impetuous Wightman challenged Vitagliano to race against her, which she would later regret, and the equally impetuous Vitagliano quickly accepted. The ante had been upped in the second set of races as Toft had rented "real" race cars from their owner-drivers for the March races. He had also hired experienced mechanics to ride with the female drivers, instead of the women friends who filled this role a month before. Toft had a hunch that some of the relatively inexperienced women would have trouble driving these powerful cars, and he did everything he could to ensure the safety of the competition. He added a pre-race meeting to go over AAA rules and safety precautions even though the event would not be sanctioned by the AAA. Toft stressed over and over that it was much too dangerous when driving these cars to pass on the turn, probably staring at Vitagliano as he spoke.[58]

Nina Vitagliano had been assigned the number 8 Stutz, a locally famous race car that had been driven by male professionals in the past. Toft paired her with "Bud" Currie, an experienced mechanic and driver who was familiar with the Stutz. When the Italian community of Stockton learned that their countrywoman was going to compete again at Stockton, they paid for a silver trophy cup to be awarded to Nina Vitagliano after her victory.[59] Vitagliano, behind the wheel of the powerful Stutz, narrowly defeated Wightman in the first race, a one-lap sprint. With a number of Italians in the stands cheering her on, Vitagliano started the five-lap second race slightly behind Ruth Wightman. Determined to get around her, Vitagliano ignored Toft's advice about not passing on a turn and stepped on the gas. The inexperienced young woman lost control of number 8 and it hit a pine tree. The Stutz lost its front wheels and axle, hurtled down the berm, and crashed through the track fence, hitting three spectators. It finally turned over, a mangled heap of metal.[60] Vitagliano was killed instantly, suffering massive head and neck injuries.[61] Bud Currie also suffered head trauma and died the next day in the hospital. There has been much discussion by racing historians over the cause of Vitagliano's fatal crash, but whatever the cause, the combination of a powerful car and inexperienced driver is never a good one. Although a few of the women withdrew from the competition after Vitagliano was killed, the majority finished the rest of the races with heavy hearts, although they must have been keenly aware of the danger.

Although there was public concern about the deaths of Vitagliano, Currie and a young spectator, there was no great outcry over the death of a female racer. However, the Stockton newspaper did comment that "Miss Nina Vitagliano forfeited her life at the Stockton race track yesterday while attempting to prove that auto racing is a woman's sport," implying exactly the opposite. The death of a spirited young member of their group disheartened the Speederettes, and the Stockton meeting was their last attempt at racing.

After the disbanding of the ill-fated Speederettes, there were literally no opportunities for women to race in "real" competition until after World War II. However, a number of informal and often scripted races for women were staged during this period. For example, in 1923 the *Chicago Daily Tribune* reported that a number of "Fair Speed Demons" would race at the North Shore Polo Grounds, a half-mile dirt track, in a ten-mile race. According to the *Tribune*, Miss Elfrieda Mais, the holder of the women's mile record, would be there along with seven others, including Miss Simone Soudan. Soudan and Mrs. Oliver G. Temme were pictured on the front page looking sporty in the leather racing helmets of the day with their goggles pushed up. Mrs. Temme evidently did not wish to try the ten-mile scramble and was to attempt an exhibition race instead. The winner would earn the right to "challenge any woman driver in America for the ladies' championship and race against the winner of the men's 25 mile race."[62] Of course, every time women raced during this period, it was for the "women's championship of the world." Mais may have driven in the Chicago races, but it is also possible that none of the women showed up to race.

Although the *Tribune* prominently advertised the meet, it did not bother to print the results; this was common for local, amateur events of this kind. Evidently the accomplishments of women racers were no longer "news" as they had been a decade ago. Most had accepted the fact that women could be killed or maimed in an auto accident, and since thousands of women now drove autos, it had become a relatively common occurrence. Nevertheless, middle-class women were still excluded from pursuing other activities and occupations that were considered masculine, such as serving in the military and police and fire departments. Women who wanted to race were restricted to semi-serious competition until prejudice against women racers was gradually overcome by determined, talented and experienced women drivers 50 years later. One result of these long years of exclusion is that as yet no women have won many races, much less a championship, at the highest levels of track or road racing.[63] Less than 10 percent of the thousands of males who currently race have the combination of attributes that make up a champion racer; since the number of females who race at any level is much smaller, the lack of female champions is not surprising.

Finally, rumors exist that some daring young women disguised themselves as men to enter races during the period in which they were banned from the track. One " Masked Marvel" legend that is supported by fact comes from the Walker family. The Walkers are Californians who have been involved in auto racing for several generations. According to family lore, 23-year-old Dorothy Walker disguised herself as a man to enter a Memorial Day race at an Overland Park, Colorado, one-mile dirt track in 1926, driving her husband's "big car." A "big car" was a 1920s version of the open-wheel race car of today. Built for racing, the big car was stripped of all the niceties of a stock car and had room for one or two people in narrow bucket seats. Although Walker was able to make a satisfactory qualifying run, she made a critical error on the second lap of the five-mile race. Her car skidded into the fence on the first turn and swerved wildly; Walker was thrown out of the car and died almost instantly.[64] It is possible that other female masked marvels also competed, disguised as males, during the twenties and thirties, but there is not much evidence one way or another to prove that they did. Walker had the dubious honor of being the first woman killed in an open-wheel race, although Nina Vitagliano's life also ended at the controls of an open-wheel car.

Those who believed that women should not be allowed to drive in races nodded sagely after they heard of the accidents that caused the deaths of Vitagliano and Walker, sure that they had made the right decision. However, the discrimination against women drivers that started in 1909 may have actually caused more accidents than it prevented. Right or wrong, the AAA's decision to ban women from racing in 1909 had far-reaching consequences. Even though automobile racing is now a sport where physical strength is not a priority and, at least in theory, men and women compete on a level playing field, the majority of race-car drivers today are still overwhelmingly male.

Epilogue

In 1917, after leasing her Scarsdale home, Joan Cuneo and her daughter, Dolly, moved permanently to Vermont.[1] Joan's ties with Holyoke were long gone, and since her divorce there were no compelling reasons to stay in the New York City area. Her sisters, Harriet (Mrs. Walter Draper) and Mary Elizabeth (Mrs. Harry Cushing), were now established in their own homes, and the sister Joan had been closest to, Eveleen (Mrs. William Packard), had tragically died at the age of 30 in 1908.[2] However, Mrs. Cuneo had a number of friends in Vermont and her sisters and their families also came up to the cozy resort area near Wilmington to stay in their summer cottages. In 1915, Joan had bought a number of lots at Lake Raponda, 8 with lake frontage and 18 across the road from the lake. She may have invested some of her funds from her divorce settlement in Vermont real estate hoping to develop them later on; however, in 1922 she transferred them to her son, Newton Cuneo, shortly after they moved to Ontonagon, Michigan.[3]

While Dolly lived at home with her mother, Newton Cuneo attended the Taft School in Watertown, Connecticut. However, in January 1918, in a burst of patriotism, Newton, along with three schoolmates, enlisted in the Navy. Young Cuneo served on the U.S. Navy ship *Leviathan* until he was honorably discharged in July 1919. In 1922, Newton Cuneo moved to the Upper Peninsula of Michigan to take an entry-level job at the Ontonagon Fiber Company, which resulted from the rekindling of an old friendship. Joan Newton and James Francis Sickman had been childhood sweethearts in Holyoke, but each married someone else. After her divorce, Joan Cuneo, by chance, renewed her friendship with Sickman, and when he took a job as manager of the Ontonagon Fiber Company in 1921 he offered a job to Joan's son. Newton eventually worked his way up through the ranks, remaining with the company until he retired as its manager in 1969. By that time the company had changed ownership four times.[4] Newton Cuneo married Elizabeth Reardon of Ashland, Wisconsin, in 1928. Unfortunately, Newton and Elizabeth's first two children died shortly after they were born in 1929 and 1930. As Elizabeth couldn't have any more children, the couple adopted a son, John, in 1931 and a daughter, Joan, in 1939.[5] Newton Cuneo made Ontonagon his home, and he lived there for the rest of his life.[6]

Coincidentally, when Newton Cuneo traveled there to take up his new job, Ontonagon, Michigan, resembled Wilmington, Vermont when it was initially developed by the Newton brothers; it was a remote small town largely populated by loggers and miners, It is ironic that John Carter Newton's grandson took a job in the same industry that his grandfather had been instrumental in developing in Massachusetts and Vermont. While

Newton Cuneo, wearing dress blues, is standing with his proud mother, Joan Cuneo. The picture was taken circa 1918–19, during his hitch in the U.S. Navy (courtesy of Harriet Newton Draper).

she lived in Vermont, Joan Cuneo continued her work with local charities. She and her daughter joined a local church and even contributed recipes to a cookbook compiled by the ladies' church group.[7] Their acceptance by Vermont society was relatively easy, because Joan Cuneo had both friends and family in the Wilmington area where they stayed every summer. When they moved to Ontonagon, she would have to start the process all over again.

Joan Cuneo and her daughter, Dolly, moved to Ontonagon, Michigan, in 1922, when Newton moved there to take up his new job. As manager of the company that was the town's major employer, James Francis Sickman held an important position in Ontonagon, helping the Cuneos' acceptance by the local community. The Ontonagon Fiber Company, which produced corrugated boxes, employed most of the town's population. It was a small town with a population that never exceeded twenty-five hundred, either before or after the depression years.[8] In some ways Michigan's upper peninsula resembled the Vermont countryside and small towns the Cuneos had left behind, as it was covered with forested rolling hills interspersed with bare patches that had been shorn of their blanket of white pine. However, it fronted awesome Lake Superior, rather than the tiny, by comparison, Lake Raponda. The main difference was that in Vermont Joan was not far from the extensive Newton clan and numerous friends; when she and Dolly moved to Ontonagon, at first they knew only Newton.

Main Street, Ontonagon, Michigan, in 1940 (courtesy of Jack Deo, Superior View Photos).

It did not take the Cuneos very long to find their place in the community. Dolly met and married an Ontonagon man, Lloyd Heard. They had one son, Gilbert, who was born in 1929 and died a well-respected member of the community in 1992. Dolly and Lloyd eventually divorced when Gilbert was still a child. She had never been happy in Ontonagon and, leaving her son behind, returned to New York City, where she went to work for Paramount Pictures as a film splicer. She later married William Scholes, whom she met at Paramount and who was also totally deaf. Her second marriage was a good one. The couple lived happily in a small apartment in Greenwich Village, New York, until her death. Dolly never returned to Ontonagon to live.[9]

Joan Cuneo eventually remarried in Ontonagon. James Francis Sickman had married Catherine McDonald, but she died after they had been together only briefly. Joan Cuneo and James Sickman rekindled their friendship before either of them moved to the Upper Peninsula. They eventually married there on November 16, 1929.[10]

During the decade she lived in the Upper Peninsula, Joan Newton Cuneo Sickman left her past life of celebrity and wealth behind; however, she and her son, Newton, were among the first to own cars in Ontonagon. She plunged energetically into the life of the small community she now called home. Besides her involvement with social groups such as the bridge club and other ladies' organizations, she worked tirelessly to improve the Ontonagon community as the president of the Civic League. Continuing her concern for the children of the area, she worked with both Boy and Girl Scouts and was responsible for the creation of a scout camp in the area.[11] Joan and her second husband shared the same interest in community improvement and she worked for the establishment of a land-ing strip in Ontonagon as well as the first golf club. Her friend Henry Ford visited her in the Upper Peninsula, where he had built an auto plant and a home.[12]

Unfortunately, the strong, healthy and energetic woman who never visited a doctor did not live to reach the age of 60. On March 24, 1934, she died suddenly at home, after a week's illness; she was only 58. The *Herald* reported that "the news of her death was an unexpected shock to the whole

This studio portrait of Joan was taken after she moved to Ontonagan, probably close to the time of her marriage to James Francis Sickman, circa 1928–29. She would have been in her early fifties (courtesy of Joan Cuneo Zbacnik).

community."[13] After funeral services were held in the Sickman home, her daughter-in-law, Elizabeth, accompanied Joan's body home to Holyoke, with her son following shortly afterwards. Joan Newton Cuneo Sickman was buried in the Newton family plot along with her parents and other family members.

Andrew Cuneo also spent the rest of life out of the spotlight but outlived his first wife by 23 years, well into his eighties. By 1930, he also had remarried and he and his second wife, Edna, were living in Franklin, New Jersey. Although his wife was more than 20 years younger, they had no children.[14] Andrew and Edna Cuneo remained in touch with Newton and Dolly; Newton visited him in New York City every year, and as Andrew aged Newton took care of his finances.[15] By the end of World War II, Andrew Cuneo had managed to recoup some of his losses, and until his death in August 1957 he and his wife enjoyed a comfortable life, living in a large apartment on Port Washington Street in New York City. Evidently Andrew Cuneo had managed to retain some of his property in the Mulberry Street area that today is the heart of New York's Chinatown. His granddaughter, Joan, met him for the first time in 1957, four months before he died. She recalled that, in his eighties, he was a small, dapper man with a goatee who carried a gold cane.[16]

Louis Disbrow retired from the track in 1929, after a successful racing career that lasted 24 years. Despite his slight build (he weighed only 140 pounds), he, like Joan, showed amazing strength in handling the balky, difficult-to-handle old-time racing cars. Over the years, he competed in the Indy 500 and Vanderbilt Cup races, and at Jacksonville Beach and IMCA dirt tracks all over the country and in Canada. In 1916, he tried his hand at manufacturing a sports car but lost money at it. He also worked for several companies that manufactured auto products but always came back to racing. After he retired he served as a racetrack official, promoted midget-car races and even worked at a morgue on a WPA project.[17] Disbrow raced until his fifties, outlasting all his friends and rivals from the first decades of racing, who had either retired or been killed. In 1929, he had a narrow escape when he was pronounced dead after a bad accident. Disbrow woke up in the morgue suffering from shock and two broken legs."[18] He retired from racing shortly afterwards.

Disbrow was married three times but had no children. He died at his West Philadelphia home of a heart attack after an illness that lasted ten days, on July 9, 1939, at the age of 62, and was survived by his wife, Mrs. Mary Meighan Disbrow.[19]

Joan Cuneo's death went unnoticed in the *New York Times*, unlike that of her longtime friend and racing mechanic, Louis Disbrow. In all fairness, it had been nearly 20 years since she had competed and she was now known as Mrs. Sickman, not Mrs. Cuneo. It is sad that a woman who had such an important role in early racing history died in obscurity and is largely forgotten today. Hopefully this book will help to restore Joan Cuneo to her proper place in history.

Only the *Brooklyn Daily Eagle,* which had interviewed her often in the past, noticed the news item from Ontonagon and gave her passing two brief paragraphs. Although the

Eagle erroneously reported that she had been a leading contender in the Vanderbilt Cup races, they did get one thing right. According to the *Eagle*, "her passion for speeding led her into many clashes with the police, particularly when her zest for speeding took her through New York streets at 42 miles per hour."[20] What better epitaph for a woman who loved to race!

Appendix I:
Joan Newton Cuneo's Cars
(by Elsa Nystrom)

1. 1902 Locomobile — 10 hp at most, probably less
2. 1903 White steam car — 10 hp
3. 1904 model — nameless gasoline touring car; Cuneo sold it because the whole tonneau had to be lifted off to get at the engine, making it impractical to work on

Joan Newton Cuneo at the wheel of her brand-new Renault American Special. She picked up the car from the Renault dealership in September 1910 and promptly put it through a grueling test on the mountain roads of Vermont. Renault printed her glowing endorsement of their car along with this photograph in a full-page ad later that year. It was the car she used to take her injured son to the hospital in North Adams, Massachusetts (courtesy of Harriet Newton Draper).

Renault with fancy European coachwork owned and modified by Joan Cuneo circa 1910; note sidelight near passenger door (courtesy of Harriet Newton Draper).

4. 1905 White steam car — 15 hp
5. 1906 nameless model — said to be the first side-entrance seven-passenger touring car sold in New York area
6. 1906 White steam car — chassis only used for racing, 18 hp
7. 1906 Maxwell Speedster — 18 hp
8. 1907 model Rainier touring car — 30–35 hp
9. 1908 model Rainier touring car — 40–50 hp
10. 1909 model Knox Giant — 50 hp
11. 1910 model Knox Giantess — 50 hp
12. 1910 model Renault American Special Touring Car — 45–50 hp
13. Renault c. 1910 enclosed body
14. 1911 model electric brougham, make unknown
15. 1914 Ford, model unknown — Joan Cuneo listed as the licensed owner in New York

In an article she wrote for *Country Life Magazine*, published in 1914, Joan Cuneo said she had owned 18 automobiles when the article was written in late 1913. We have only been able to identify 15, and several of those are nameless. She probably owned a few more before her death in 1934. Her son, A. Newton Cuneo, was said to have one of the first cars in Ontonagon, Michigan.

Appendix II: Racing the Knox
(by Dick Newton)

Researching the story of Cousin Joan has been a fascinating and rewarding journey of continuing discovery, but through it all there has been a missing element. For me, as a former race-car builder and driver, it was understanding the mechanical aspects of the cars that she drove and what it felt like for her compared to my own experiences, that held the most appeal.

The performance and mechanical metrics that we know today did not exist in the early 1900s, and as far as I have been able to determine, there is only one Knox race car that still exists, and it was with Knox that Joan achieved her most notable successes. I will, however, try to create the environment that Joan was in when she was racing; this will be based on Knox 1909 product literature and discussions with John Hess and his own experience driving Knox cars of that era. Also, the race cars of that era were basically production cars "stripped down" to reduce weight but operationally very close to their original production specifications.

1909 Knox Race Car

In her 1909 Knox race car, Joan was completely exposed to the elements. She sat very high in a single bucket-style seat with the high steering wheel close and at face level. There was no windshield or small windscreen to deflect the air away from her face; she did wear goggles in some pictures. She did not have a special driver's (fireproof) suit or special shoes or gloves and wore a flower-covered hat, as crash helmets did not exist. Some drivers did wear airplane pilots' leather helmets, but these offered no crash protection. She most likely had no earplugs or sound protection from the loud engine. There was no rollover bar or seat/shoulder belts; gas tank(s) were directly in back of her seat and were not leak proof. Steering was very heavy, as there was no "power steering" and the very narrow tires were prone to get caught in ruts, requiring strength to keep the car on its intended course. There were two pedals — one for the clutch and the other for the gas. To her right were two levers — one for the rear-wheel brakes and the other for shifting the three-speed transmission. The transmission did not have "synchromesh," which made shifting easier by synchronizing the speeds of the gears as they were shifted

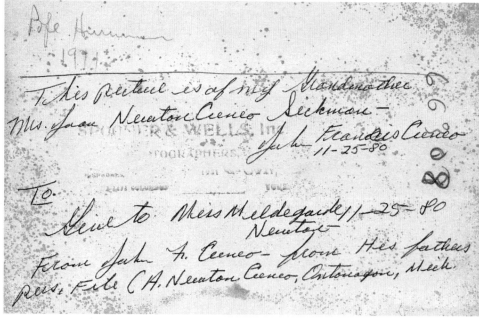

Top and above: Newton family photograph of Joan in her Knox racer, incribed on the back to Miss Hildegarde Newton, from John Francis Cuneo, son of A. Newton Cuneo (courtesy Dick Newton).

up (1-to-2) or down (2-to-1), and required "double-clutching" (engaging the clutch in neutral as the transmission is shifted up or down). The brakes required a sensitive touch, as locking up the rear-wheel brakes could easily result in the back of the car skidding into a slide. Frequent shifting was required, as the big engine did not have a wide rpm (revolutions per minute) range. To her immediate right at hip level was the open and unprotected chain that drove the car, which would be spattering her with lubricant at speed. Ultimately the car would reach 72 miles per hour and required constant attention to steering, shifting, and braking, all of which had no power assistance. Joan had to have incredible endurance and strength to drive at race speeds for hours. Today I marvel at her strength, her stamina, her ability to be competitive and win races, and that she never was hurt badly in a crash. The drivers of that era were heroic, facing danger with no safety protection, driving mechanically unreliable cars with tires that frequently wore out or exploded, tracks that deteriorated, and no immediate medical services in the event of a crash and injury. Though Joan's 1909 Knox was a state-of-the-art race car, requiring special skills to race it, today any compact economy car with the most unskilled driver could beat it in acceleration, top speed, cornering speeds, braking, and driver protection.

Chapter Notes

Foreword

1. The rumor about getting rid of the trophies definitely was not true, as Joan Cuneo's children and their children still have most of her trophies.

Introduction

1. Jean-François Bouzanquet, *Fast Ladies: Female Racing Drivers 1888—1970* (Dorchester, UK: Veloce, 2009), preface.

2. Ancestrylibrary.com/cgi-bin/sse.dll?db=1900us-fedcen%2c&rank=0&gsfn=joa, accessed 9/21/2009.

3. From http://search.Ancestrylibrary.com/cgi-bin/sse.dll?db=1910USCenIndes%2c&rank=0&gsfn, accessed 9/21/2009.

4. Robert Sloss, "What a Woman Can Do with an Auto," *Outing Magazine* 56 (1910): 64. See also Richard Duffy, "Out-door Women: Their Sports and What They Have Done for Them," *Good Housekeeping* 1, no. 6, whole no. 380.

5. In a 1905 interview with the *New York Times*, Joan Cuneo was quoted as saying she was an experienced driver and had been driving for five years. However, this is probably an error, because in several other interviews she says that she learned to drive in 1902.

6. Joan Newton Cuneo, "A Woman's Automobile Racing Record," *Country Life in America* 25 (15 November 1910): 127. In this interview, Joan Cuneo discusses the progression of her success in racing competition.

7. "Woman Stops Blazing Auto," *New York Times*, 3 October 1906.

8. Cuneo, "A Woman's Automobile Racing Record," 127.

9. Duffy, "Out-door Women," 684. She was approximately five feet, two inches tall and weighed from 110 to 130 pounds but must have been amazingly strong to keep the rough-handling heavy race cars she later drove on the track with no power steering or power brakes.

Chapter 1

1. Andrew Cuneo's father was listed as Louis De Martini and his mother as Carlotta Casazza. "Massachusetts Marriages, 1695–1910," Free Family History and Genealogy Records, page 1, https://www.family

search.org/s/recordDetails/show?uri+http%3A2F%2F pilot.family search, accessed 1/8/2011.

2. The Newton-Cuneo wedding is described in detail in "Newton-Cuneo, a Brilliant Home Wedding in Ward Six — the Decorations and Guests," *Holyoke Daily Transcript*, 17 February 1898.

3. Ibid.

4. See 24 March 1898 and http://TheGreat OceanLiners.com/Normandiei.html., accessed 2/14/ 2012. These ships were among the fastest of their day but much smaller than the *Titanic*. *La Normadie* had two hundred first-class cabins but could carry up to one thousand immigrants in steerage.

5. Ibid.

6. Money was indeed the most important element the early female racers had in common, as all the women who toured or drove competitively came from families of means.

7. "Money and Careers," *Boston Globe*, 6 November 2011, section G.

8. Mary Howe, Joan's great-grandmother and mother of James Newton, was a descendant of Stephen Hopkins, Jr., a passenger on the *Mayflower*.

9. Dick Newton to Elsa Nystrom, e-mail, 25 January 2011. Dick Newton added that this was long before the hymn was popularized by Judy Collins/ Willie Nelson, although the family was unsure of the exact relationship.

10. Brian A. Donelson, *The Coming of the Train, the Hoosac Tunnel and Wilmington and Deerfield River Railroads and the Industries They Served*, vol. 1: *1870–1910* (Rowe MA: NJD, 2008), iii–2. Donelson provides a brief history of the Newton brothers in this volume, including their impact on western Massachusetts and southern Vermont. iii–2.

11. Ibid.

12. Ibid., iii–3.

13. Ibid., iii–4.

14. Ibid., iii–5.

15. Ibid., iii–9.

16. "Directory of Descendants of James and Esther Hale Newton," compiled for the Newton Family Reunion, June 16–18, 1988, xiv, unpublished document furnished by Richard Newton.

17. As the youngest of the family, John Newton may just have been slow to mature and reach his potential.

18. The term "normal" when applied to a school in the nineteenth century meant its purpose was the education of teachers.

19. For information on Newton's business career, see "John C. Newton," *History of the Connecticut Valley in Massachusetts, 1879,* at http://www.holyokemass.com/hcv_1879/jcn.html, accessed 4/13/2010, and also Donelson, *The Coming of the Train.*

20. John Carter Newton died unexpectedly on September 30, 1899, at his home in Wilmington after an operation for appendicitis. Donelson, *The Coming of the Train,* xii–2.

21. John C. Newton obituary, *Holyoke Daily Transcript,* 2 October 1899.

22. Page 164, Census Record for Holyoke, Hampden Country, Massachusetts, enumerated on the fifth day of August 1870 by Amos Andrews.

23. "Glidden Tour Trophy Winner May Be Queen," *New York Evening World,* 23 March 1908.

24. From brief biography of Joan Newton Cuneo published in *The Motor Cyclopedia Yearbook,* 9th ed. (1909), page 159, accessed on Google Books 10/21/2011.

25. Oneida County Historical Society, the Utica Free Academy, http://www.oneidacountyhistory.org/Landmarks/UFA/UFA asp, accessed 1/19/2012.

26. Dr. Moses Bagg, who helped organize the Female Seminary that became Mrs. Piatt's school was both member and Sunday School teacher at the Utica First Presbyterian Church. http://www.uticaod.com/guest/x742403886/Guest-view:Family had a starring role in Utica's history — Utica NY, accessed 1/19/2012.

27. Ibid.

28. "The Catherine Aiken School, Stamford Connecticut, 1855–1913," http://www.stamfordhistory.org/rg3.htm, accessed 1/21/2012.

29. Ibid. One of the Catherine Aiken School's most illustrious teachers was the dashing 27-year-old Georges Clemenceau, who taught French and horseback riding there in 1867. Clemenceau fascinated both teachers and students but soon fell in love with a student, married her and returned to France.

30. See John I. White, *It's About Time: A Presbyterian Minister Helped Set a Standard for Our Clockwatching* (Atlanta, GA: Presbyterian Pub. House, House of the Presbyterian Church, U.S.A., 1985).

31. "Glidden Tour Trophy Winner May be Queen."

32. "Cuneo's Rise to Wealth," *New York Times,* 24 June 1896.

33. 1900 Census: Census Place: Richmond Ward 3, Richmond, New York; Roll: 1154; Page: 8A; Enumeration District: 600; FHL microfilm: 1241154. The 1900 census lists Maddalena Cuneo as emigrating from Italy in 1855 when she was 15.

34. "General City Notes," 6 December 1861.

35. Census of 1870.

36. Antonio Cuneo's lawyer, M. Anderson, was a witness at the ceremony. See record C 500, U.S. District Court, New York, NY.

37. "To Make a Test Case," *New York Times,* 21 April 1885.

38. Ibid.

39. http://the selvedgeyard.wordpress.com/2011/02/26/bandits-roost-nyc-and-to-think-that-I-saw-it-on-mulberry-street, accessed 12/02/2012.

40. "Italian Catholic Church Suits," *New York Times,* 26 October 1894.

41. "Funeral of Antonio Cuneo," *New York Times,* 6 September 1896.

42. "Cuneo's Rise to Wealth," *New York Times,* 24 June 1896.

43. Ancestry.com, New York City Directories, 1882, 1888, 1891.

44. Of course, Antonio Cuneo may also have benefited from a connection to the Italian Mafia in New York, but even so, his achievements were outstanding.

45. "Cuneo's Rise to Wealth." According to the article, Antonio Cuneo had a brother living in San Francisco at this time, but it was his brother-in-law Louis De Martini and Antonio's nephew, Andrew De Martini Cuneo, who took over Antonio's business after his death.

46. "Banana King in Hospital," *New York Times,* 24 June 1896.

47. Ibid.

48. *San Francisco Chronicle,* Tuesday Morning, 30 June 1896.

49. "Funeral of Antonio Cuneo," *New York Times,* 6 September 1896.

50. Ibid. The *New York Times* description of Antonio Cuneo's funeral bears a striking resemblance to a Mafia Don's, and it is very likely that Cuneo, a Sicilian, had some connections to the 1896 version of this organization. However, it is not the sort of information that would have been reported in the *Times.* However, it would explain why Cuneo knew the Wall Street men but was not one of them and would also explain why the Newtons did not hold a big church wedding for young Joan, who was her father's favorite daughter.

51. New York Supreme Court, Ref. # GA — 977, Cuneo, Maddalena, Plaintiff.

52. "Guide to the News," *New Orleans Picayune,* 16 September 1906, page 4.

53. Ibid.

54. *New Orleans Picayune,* 24 April 1908.

Chapter 2

1. *Holyoke Daily Transcript,* 17 February 1898.

2. Year 1900; Census Place: Richmond Ward 3, Richmond, New York; Roll 1154; Page 8A, Enumeration District 600: Federal Census (database on-line) Provo, UT, USA: Ancestry.com Operations Inc. 2004.

3. http://en.wikipedia.org/wiki/Port_Richmond_Staten_Island, accessed 3/3/2012.

4. "Joan Zbacnik to Elsa Nystrom, "Have a couple of questions," email, 17 September 2012.

5. According to census records, in 1900, Andrew and Joan Cuneo were living with Andrew's aunt Maddalena on Staten Island; Louis de Martini was also living with them at that time, U.S. Census 1910 Place: Richmond, New York: Roll T623_1154; Page:8A; Enumeration District:600.

6. Robert Sloss, What a Woman Can Do With an Auto," *Outing Magazine,* 64.

7. Ibid.

8. "Autos Interest Women," *Brooklyn Daily Eagle,* 10 November 1900.

9. "Miss Mudge Shows the Superiority of the Auto Over the Horse and Yacht," *Brooklyn Daily Eagle* 10 November 1900. Genevra Delphine Mudge (Genevra Delphine was her stage name; her birth name was Eva) was a young vaudeville actress who would enjoy some popularity as a comedienne in the New York music halls in the next decade. She was also credited by a secondary source as being the first woman to drive in a auto race in 1902. She may well have done so but I haven't been able to find any print record in the newspapers of the time. Mudge was 19 in 1900, having moved from her birthplace in Michigan to further her career. See 1900 Census; Census Place: Manhattan, New York, New York Roll T623_1103; Page 7B; Enumeration District 477.

10. *New York Times,* 27 April 1902.

11. Mrs. Andrew Cuneo, *"Why are there so few women automobilists?" Country Life,* Vol. 13, March 1908. In the same year, Dorothy Levitt, her British counterpart, would recommend a single cylinder gas engine car.

12. Foxhall Keene and his father were noted for the quality of their stables and young Keene was an excellent rider, polo player and sportsman. He was one of the many who "crossed over" from horse racing to auto racing.

13. This story may be just a myth but it is worth repeating. According to Sydney Davis, who knew Du Gast, there was talk of the value of parachutes for balloon pilots as early as 1895. Camille du Gast, intrigued by this idea decided to test it and equipped herself with a rudimentary parachute that would horrify a modern pilot. She then ascended to a height of 2000 meters (over 6500 ft.)in a balloon with the famous aeronaut Louis Capazza, founder of the Belgian Aeronautical Club, also equipped with a parachute. They then ripped open the balloon and jumped from the basket. Du Gast's luck held, the parachutes opened and they made a hard but safe landing with nothing but a bruise or two. See Sydney Charles Houghton Davis, *Atalanta: women as racing drivers* (London: G. T. Foulis, 1955) 25–26.

14. For information on Camille du Gast, see Jean-Francois Bouzanquet, *Fast Ladies: Female Racing Drivers 1888–1970,* (Dorchester, England: Veloce Publishing, 2009) 13–14, "Camille du Gast," Historic Racing, 10 March 2011, http://www.historicracing.com/driversFemale.cfm?fullText=3048 and Sydney Charles Houghton Davis, *Atalanta: women as racing drivers* (London: G.T. Foulis, 1955)

15. *Mme Du Gast Fine Chauffeur, Says She is Surprised That American Women Don't Enter Races,* special cable—1903, *Atlanta Constitution,* 30 May 1903.

16. In one interview, Joan Cuneo said she learned to drive in 1901, see Richard Duffy, *Outdoor Women , their Sports and what they done for them," Good Housekeeping Magazine,* Vol. 1, #6, Whole No. 380, June 1910, 686. This seems unlikely as her daughter was born in 1901 and she probably wouldn't have taken up driving while pregnant.

17. http://www.whitesteamcar.com/White_Steam_Car_Registry/Models.htmln. In 1903 Locomobile would switch to building gasoline engine cars. Their gas engine cars were just as well built and sturdy as the steam cars were flimsy.

18. Many early cars were built by bicycle manufacturers and high wheels were preferred because of the deep ruts in the dirt highways of the day.

19. "Glidden Tour Trophy Winner may be Queen," *The (New York) Evening World,* 23 March 1908.

20. http://centralparkhistory.com/timeline/timeline_1880_iron.html

21. For an account of her first driving lesson, see Robert Sloss, "*What a woman can do with an auto," The Outing Magazine,* 64 and "Glidden Trophy Winner may be Queen," (New York) *Evening World,* 15 March 1908.

22. The dealer probably didn't mention that the boiler only ran 20 miles or so on one fill-up or water or that it took a long time to develop a head of steam and sometimes burned up in the process. http://www.google.com/search?sourceid=navclient&aq=0h&oq=&ie=UTF-8&rlz=1T4DMUS_enUS392US392&q=locomobile+the+best+built+car+in+america

23. *Country Life,* January 1914, 49.

24. 1900; Census Place: Queens Ward 4, Queens, New York: T623_1149; Page 15!; Enumeration District: 677, accessed on Ancestry.com 1900 United States Federal Census online database, 1/7/2011.

25. "Disbrow May Be On the Sea," *New York Times,* 15 June 1902.

26. cetus@mindspring.com to enystrom @Kennesaw.edu, 19 February 2011.

27. "Drowned During Trip in an Boat at Night," *New York Times,* 15 June 1902.

28. Ibid.

29. Ibid.

30. Ibid.

31. Ibid.

32. Ibid.

33. Ibid.

34. "Drowning Tragedy's New Developments," *New York Times,* 16 June 1902.

35. "Drowned During Trip on Boat at Night," *New York Times,* 15 June 1902.

36. Ibid.

37. Ibid.

38. Ibid.

39. "Disbrow May Be On the Sea," *New York Times,* 15 June 1902.

40. New York Marriages, 1686—1980, Record M00552, New York, ODM—1503718.

41. "Louis Disbrow Indicted," *New York Times,* 26 September 1902

42. "Four Jurors Chosen to Try Louis Disbrow," *New York World,* 12 January 1903. The more flamboyant *World,* called Disbrow handsome, with blue eyes and dark hair and about 5'7" tall.

43. "Louis Disbrow Indicted."

44. "Disbrow Witness Gone," *New York Times*, 14 January 1903.

45. "Prosecution Set-Back At The Disbrow Trial," *New York Times*, 14 January 1903.

46. "Death of J. S. Lawrence," *New York Times*, 2 April 1903.

47. "Louis Foster's Body Found," *New York Times*, 3 February 1903.

48. *Long Island Boroughs and Counties*, Borough of Queens, Long Island Biographical, 1925, 36–37. This was very close to where Joan Cuneo ran into a horse drawn cart and was sued for $2500 in damages.

49. "Famous Woman Automobile Driver Arrives for Fair Grounds Races," *New Orleans Picayune*, 12 February 1909.

50. *Country Life*, January 1914, 49.

51. There are many photos of Joan Cuneo in her 1905 White because this is the car she used for her first competitive ventures; and I recently found a picture of Joan and her family and friends in the 1903 White.

52. Information on the White Steam car models comes from the White Steam car registry, http://www.whitesteamcar.com/White_Steam_Car_Registry/Models.html, accessed March 10, 1011.

53. The White Steam Car Registry doesn't list the horsepower or wheelbase of the 1903 model; the largest auto White produced was the 1910 Model M, with a 122" wheelbase and 40 hp.

54. *The Horseless Age*, Vol. 10, 26 November 1902.

55. Mrs. A. Sherman Hitchcock, "A woman's viewpoint of motoring," *Motor*, April 1904, 19

56. "What the motor girl is wearing," *Motor*, November 1902, 30.

57. *Motor*, 30.

58. Mrs. F. P. Avery, "Touring in Horseless Carriages, a few suggestions," *The Automobile*, January 1901, 5.

59. Carl E. Ballenas, Richmond Hill historian, email, 10 March 2011.

60. *(New York) Evening World*, 23 March 1908.

61. City and Borough Register of the Residential Districts of the Borough of Queens, Trow Directory Printing and Bookbinding Co., Manhattan, 1899, 1901, 1904.

62. There has been much speculation about the nature of the relationship between Joan Cuneo and Louis Disbrow. They were the same age, Disbrow was handsome, slight but strong, with blue eyes and dark hair. Joan though not a beauty, was an attractive and accomplished woman, and they spent much time together traveling to automobile factories, races and on tour. However, I have not found a hint of gossip intimating that they were having an affair which is surprising since they quickly became public figures. Joan Cuneo's exploits were national news as late as 1912. On the other hand, Andrew had a roving eye, which when combined with his disinterest in automobiles, might well have driven Joan Cuneo to find a friend who shared her interests. Curiously Andrew Cuneo also seems to have considered Louis Disbrow as a friend;

perhaps he was only too happy to have someone who could help his car mad wife. Andrew Cuneo, like Jean Crespin, was supportive of his wife's love of autos and racing; she never lacked the means to buy a new model car while she was competing.

63. John Bentley, *Great American Automobiles: A Dramatic Account of Their Achievements in Competition* (New York: Prentice-Hall, 1957) 124–127.

64. Distances are approximate, as the highways of the time had minimal signage and no mile markers.

65. Bentley, 162–63.

66. The original Glidden trophy is now displayed in the AAA Headquarters in Florida.

67. Bentley, 127.

68. Although many women participated in the Glidden Tours as passengers, Joan Cuneo was the only woman who was the driver of an entered vehicle until the 1908 tour.

Chapter 3

1. *Long Island Biographical, Dictionary, Boroughs of Brooklyn and Queens* (1925), 35, 36. Undoubtedly, the White Steamer was bought from the Disbrow agency, before the Disbrows would change to Chalmers and Rainer autos, slightly more upscale than the Fords and Whites they had started handling in 1903. This was not uncommon at a time when hundreds of automobile makers flooded the market with a variety of machines.

2. Joan Newton Cuneo, "America's Most Famous Woman Motorist," *Country Life in America*, January 1914, 49.

3. Joan Cuneo had joined the AAA early in 1905.

4. Mrs. Glidden never publicly expressed a desire to learn to drive and seemed content with her role as passenger.

5. "Glidden Tour Plans and Conditions," *The Automobile*, 6 July 1905, 13–14.

6. The White company would abandon steam power for the gasoline engine the following year and would ultimately become an important American manufacturer of trucks for many years.

7. "Chicago to St. Paul Tour," *The Automobile*, 6 July 1905, 16.

8. Cutler would suffer a painful injury on the second half of the trip when his Knox collided with a wagonload of lumber on the way back to Worcester. His foot was severely pinched under the generator as the Knox ran into the back end of the lumber wagon as its driver swerved into their path. *The Automobile*, 27 July 1905, 101.

9. http://www.allbusiness.com/marketing-advertising/marketing-techniques-sponsorship/6170222–1.html, accessed 5/10/2011. Today the trophy is on permanent display in the atrium of the AAA national office in Heathrow, Florida. "Nation's largest Annual Antique Auto Tour Sept 24–28 in Northern Michigan AAA says," Allbusiness.com/marketing. advertising/marketing.

10. *New York Times*, Sunday, 12 June 1905, 7.

11. This is probably a reference to Glidden's round-the-world trip in a Napier in 1903. See "Mr. Glidden Girdling the Earth with an Automobile," *New York Times*, Sunday, 18 June 1905, 7.

12. John Bentley, *Great American Automobiles, a Dramatic Account of Their Achievements in Competition* (New York: Prentice-Hall, 1957), 130.

13. "Glidden Tour Information," *The Automobile*, 6 July 1905, 13, 14.

14. A number of secondary sources when describing her experiences in the 1905 Glidden Tour referred to her as a well-known automobile driver of the day, but this was not yet true. See Bentley, *Great American Automobiles*, 132.

15. "Glidden Tour Is a Great Success," *The Automobile*, 20 July 1905, 82.

16. "Mrs. Cuneo's Car Goes into ditch," *Boston Globe*, 12 July 1905, and *New York Evening Telegram*, 11 July 1905.

17. "The 1905 Glidden Tour," *Automobile Quarterly* 30, issue 3 (1992): 18 – 27. She would not be the only one to drive her car off a bridge during the tour and was only one of a large group who were later ticketed in a speed trap.

18. *New York Tribune*, Wednesday, 12 July 1905, 1.

19. "Thrown from Her Auto," *New York Times*, 14 July 1905.

20. "Glidden Tour Is a Great Success," 82.

21. Ibid., 78.

22. Ibid., 72.

23. "That evening there was a banquet for the gentlemen which 150 Hartford motorists attended. Mrs. Cuneo, on the other hand, was shunted off to a separate banquet where she was 'entertained by a special committee of Hartford ladies,' in a private dining room of their own. "1905 Glidden Tour," 18–27. This was taken from Bentley, *Great American Automobiles*.

24. Bentley, *Great American Automobiles*, 83. "The menu included cocktails and clams, soft shell crabs and sauterne, broiled squab, chicken and champagne and punch, coffee and cigars and more than 100 guests sat down at the table." The number alone would indicate that all were invited, as only 33 cars were entered and most carried only two passengers.

25. Ibid., 136. This obviously came from a newspaper account, but I haven't located it yet and Bentley did not include his sources.

26. The first car to arrive was George T. Tyrell's White at 12:19 P.M. *The Automobile*, 20 July 1905, 80.

27. Ibid., 82.

28. Ibid.

29. Ibid.

30. Ibid.

31. Ibid.

32. Ibid., 86.

33. "Autoists in Danger, Collision on Mount Washington and One Car on Brink of precipice," *New York Times*, 17 July 1905.

34. "Plucky New York Woman, Mrs. Cuneo Will Drive Her Auto up Mount Washington Next Year," *New York Times*, 20 July 1905.

35. *Pittsburg Press*, 23 July 1905.

36. As I have learned more about Joan Newton Cuneo, I realize just how many secondary sources took the information about her participation in the 1905 Glidden Tour from the detailed accounts published in *The Automobile* on July 20 and 27 1905. They all missed the fact that she was refused permission to compete in a speed contest for the first time in 1905, although it would not be until 1909 until all women were banished from AAA-sanctioned events.

37. Bentley, *Great American Automobiles*,156; *The Automobile*, 27 July 1905, 101.

38. *The Automobile*, 27 July 1905, 98.

39. "1905 Glidden Tour," *Manchester* (NH) *Union* editorial accessed at http://www.vmcca.Org/bh/1905. html.

40. Ibid.

41. "Mrs. Andrew Cuneo, Only Woman in the Glidden Auto Tour, Says She Is Ready To-Day for Another Race of the Same Sort," *New York Evening World*, 25 July 1907.

42. "Echoes of the Glidden Tour," *New York Times*, 29 July 1905.

43. "Glidden Cup Autoists End Tour with Parade," *New York Times*, 23 July 1905.

44. One was withdrawn because of a passenger's illness and another quit because the party wanted to stay in Massachusetts for more touring. The 50 hp French-built Panhard also failed due to mechanical problems. Ibid.

45. "Glidden Cup Autoists End Tour with Parade," *New York Times*, 23 July 1905.

46. Augustus Post, a contemporary of the Wright brothers, was, along with Glidden and several other members of the Automobile Club, a co-founder of the Aero Club of America in 1905. See "About NAA," http://naa.aero/html/about Naa/index.cfn?cmsid=136, accessed 3/20/2012.

47. Ibid.

48. Percy Pierce was the president of the company that built the Pierce-Arrow.

49. "Auto Touring Events in Popular Favor," *New York Times*, 23 October 1905.

Chapter 4

1. Allan E. Brown, *The History of America's Speedways Past and Present*, 3rd ed. (Comstock Park, MI: self-published, 2003), 460. Brown says there was a half-mile track on the beach at Cape May from September 4, 1905, to April 28, 1906. If Brown's dates are correct, the racing the *New York Times* reported on August 26, 1905, was held on the beach as part of a lengthy race program featuring several well-known drivers, including Chevrolet and Cedrino. It seems to have been a mile straightaway on which Mrs. Fitler set her records.

2. "Woman Auto Driver Scores Two Victories," *New York Times*, 27 August 1905.

3. Jacob Schaad Jr., "'Automobilists' Once Raced the Beaches of Cape May," Wednesday, 7 March 2012.

4. "A Woman's Automobile Racing Record," *The Automobile*, 127.

5. Ibid.

6. "Atlantic City," *Oahu* (HA) *Evening Bulletin*, 25 September 1905.

7. Ibid.

8. Brown, *The History of America's Speedways*, 458.

9. "Auto Races a Failure," *New York Times*, 5 September 1905.

10. "A Woman's Automobile Racing Record."

11. Ibid.

12. Robert Sloss, "What a Woman Can Do with an Auto," *Outing Magazine* 56 (April 1910): 99.

13. "Rival Chauffeurs Were Eagerly Awarded Right of Way," *New York Evening World*, 9 March 1906.

14. "Thrilling Auto Races at Driving Park Terminate County Fair," *Poughkeepsie* (NY) *Unity Eagle*, 30 September 1905.

15. Ibid.

16. "A Woman's Automobile Racing Record," 127.

17. Emanuel Cedrino, a champion racer in Italy, came to the United States, to compete at Briarcliff and in other races but was killed in May 1908 when his car hit a fence and he broke his neck.

18. "Thrilling Auto Races."

19. Ibid.

20. "Autos Driven Fast," *New York Times*, 29 September 1905.

21. "A Woman's Automobile Racing Record," 127. This would be one of many speeding tickets she collected.

22. Ibid.

23. Ibid.

24. "Only One Make Autos in Empire City Run," *New York Times*, 8 November 1905.

25. "Oldsmobile Owners Celebrate Fifth Year of Machine's Advent, NEW RECORD FOR MRS. CUNEO," *New York Times*, 8 November 1905.

26. "News and Trade Miscellany," *The Automobile*, 29 March 1906, 588.

27. "Final Results," *New York Evening World*, 26 April 1906.

28. "Cup Car Meets Defeat," *New York Daily Tribune*, 27 April 1906.

29. "Final Results."

30. "A Woman's Automobile Racing Record."

31. "Auto Selling Races in Atlantic City Meet; Winning Car Must Be Sold to the Highest Bidder," *New York Times*, 20 March 1906.

32. The selling race had some similarity to the claiming race long popular with race horse owners.

33. "Automobile Notes of Interest," *New York Times*, 8 May 1906.

34. "Atlantic City Crowds," *New York Daily Tribune*, 15 April 1906.

35. Anthony J. Yanik, *Maxwell Motors and the Making of Chrysler Corporation* 40.

36. "Mrs. Cuneo as a Gliddenite," *Trenton Evening Times*, 15 July 1908.

37. "A Woman's Automobile Racing Record," 127.

38. Ibid.

39. "Women Drive Autos Fast," *New York Times*, 10 September 1905.

40. No mention was made of the maker of the automobile in the article.

41. "Woman Stops Blazing Auto, Mrs. Cuno [*sic*], Though Burned, Shuts Off Power and Gasoline Before Jumping," *New York Times*, 3 October 1906.

42. Ibid.

43. "Ten in the Big Event. Benning Track in Good Condition for Auto Races. MRS. CUNEO ARRIVES IN CITY," *Washington (DC) Herald*, 30 May 1907.

44. Brown, *America's Speedways*, 189. It was located east of the Anacostia River and is now the site of the Mayfair Mansions Housing Development.

45. See "Lost Washington, the Arlington Hotel." The Arlington was a favorite of foreign notables as well as wealthy and distinguished Americans. http://greaterwashington.org/post/6836/lost-washington-the-arlington-hotel/, accessed 04/11/2012.

46. "Big Preparation for Meet," *Washington Post*, 28 May 1907.

47. "Ten in the Big Event."

48. Ibid. This was the first and only time I found any information that indicated Joan Cuneo had raced on the beach at Ormond, but that doesn't mean more information isn't out there somewhere.

49. Ibid.

50. Ibid.

51. "Autos to Race at Benning," *Washington Post*, 30 May 1906.

52. "Breaks Auto Record," *Washington Post*, 31 May 1907.

53. Ibid. There doesn't seem to be any information available about the United States Motor Racing Association; evidently it didn't have a very long life.

54. John Bentley, *Great American Automobiles, a Dramatic Account of Their Achievements in Competition* (New York: Prentice-Hall, 1957), 162.

55. Daniel I. Vieyra, *Fill 'Er Up: An Architectural History of America's Gas Stations* (New York and London: Collier, 1979), 111.

56. Ibid., 111–113.

Chapter 5

1. Interestingly, the Pierce Great Arrow automobile, driven by Percy Pierce, the company's owner, still had its speed regulated by a hand throttle rather than the familiar gas pedal of today.

2. "Army of Autoists Ready for Tour" and "Severe Rules Imposed," *New York Times*, 7 July 1907.

3. Ibid.

4. Ibid.

5. Ibid.

6. Included were long-forgotten makes such as the Apperson, the Dragon, the Shoemaker, the Welch, the Autocar, the Pungs-Finch, the Acme, the Aerocar, the Royal Tourist, the Meteor, the Gaeth, the Mitchell,

the Premier, the Berliet, and the Lozier, as well as slightly more familiar ones such as the Maxwell, the White, the Pierce, the Packard, the Stoddard-Dayton, and the Reo. Only the Berliet had four-wheel brakes!

7. Joan Newton Cuneo, *A Woman's Experience in the Glidden Tour 1907* (New York: Rainier Motor Car, 1907). I only located two copies of her booklet; the one I read is in the Benson Ford Library Archives in Deerfield, Michigan.

8. Ibid.

9. "First Day of Glidden Tour," *New York Times,* 11 July 1907.

10. Cuneo, *A Woman's Experience.*

11. Ibid.

12. "Women Are Out of Contest," *Chicago Record Herald,* 13 July 1907.

13. Ibid. This is just one of many examples of erroneous reporting of proposed races during the early years. If Joan Cuneo had actually driven in either of the reported events, it would have been featured in many newspapers all over the country; however, neither she nor Disbrow took part.

14. Cuneo, *A Woman's Experience.*

15. "Mrs. Cuneo Hits Tree," *New York Times,* 23 July 1907.

16. Ibid.

17. Cuneo, *A Woman's Experience.*

18. Ibid.

19. "Mrs. Andrew Cuneo, Only Woman in the Glidden Auto Tour, Says She Is Ready To-Day for Another Race of the Same Sort," *New York Evening World,* 25 July 1907.

20. Ibid.

21. Ibid.

22. Ibid.

23. Ibid.

24. Ibid.

25. Ibid.

26. Ibid. In this interview, she again says that her first car was a Locomobile. Perhaps she didn't consider the electric used for trips to the station a real car.

27. "Broadway Parade of Dusty Autos," *New York Times,* 25 July 1907.

28. Ibid.

29. M. Worth Colwell, "The Worst Roads in America, Discovered by the Motorists Who Were Contestants in the Recent Fourth Annual Tour of the AAA," *Outing Magazine,* November 1907, 246 — 24.8.

30. Ibid.

31. Ibid.

32. Ibid.

33. Ibid.

34. Ibid.

35. That doesn't mean it wasn't in the paper, but I have not been able to find any mention of it as yet.

36. Edith M. Peters, Respondent v. Joan N. Cuneo, Appellant, Supreme Court of New York, Appellate Division, Second Department 123 A.D. 740; 108 N.Y.S. 264;1908 N.Y. App. Lexis 179, Decided 17 January 1908.

37. Ibid.

38. Ibid.

39. "Crowd at Auto Show," *New York Daily Tribune,* 6 November 1907.

40. "Some Gossip for Auto Fiends," 12 July 1908.

41. Ad, circa 1909, courtesy of the private collection of Carl Ballenas, Richmond Hill historian.

42. "Auto Track Races May Be Stopped," *New York Times,* 20 September 1907.

43. "Women Autoists Skillful Drivers," *New York Times,* 29 September 1907.

Chapter 6

1. "Woman Driver in New Year's Endurance Run," *Los Angeles Herald,* 29 December 1907.

2. "Mrs. Cuneo Wants to Race, Makes Trip over Briarcliff Course and Says It's a Good One," *New York Times,* 12 January 1908.

3. "Do Not Want Woman in Big Auto Race, Briarcliff Cup Committee Rejects the Entry of Mrs. John Cuneo," *New York Times,* 15 January 1908.

4. "Woman Auto Driver Applies for Entry in 300-Mile Race," *Washington Post,* 12 January 1908.

5. Ibid.

6. Homer George, "Shaking Dice with Death," *Collier's,* 1909, 15.

7. "Joan Cuneo Nominated for Queen of Auto Carnival," *New York Evening World,* 6 March 1908.

8. Cedrino would be killed a month later at Pimlico. Of course Joan also knew Barney Oldfield well by this time.

9. "Thousands to See Briarcliff Race, *New York Times,* 24 April 1908.

10. "No Auto Race for Mrs. Cuneo," *Atlanta Constitution,* 12 February 1908.

11. "Woman Is Refused Permit to Compete, Mrs. Newton Cuneo Will Not Drive Car," *Los Angeles Herald,* 31 May 1908.

12. Ibid.

13. Indy auto museum archivist Donald Davidson concurs that the 1908 Contest Board minutes do not mention this issue, while the AAA archives from 1907 to 1908 are either lost or packed away but, in any case, not available.

14. To read the entire article, see Mrs. Andrew Cuneo, "Why Are There So Few Women Automobilists?" *Country Life Magazine,* March 1908, 515–516.

15. Ibid.

16. Ibid.

17. Ibid.

18. There was a period of at least ten years, starting in the early 1900s, when there was much conflict between the supporters of the horse and proponents of automobile travel. As we know, the horse would lose this contest, but not without bad feelings on both sides. Automobile "haters" often scattered nails, tacks, glass and even trip wires on the roads.

19. "Glidden Tour Trophy Winner May Be Queen," *New York Evening World,* 23 March 1908.

20. Ibid.

21. "King Leonard and Queen Joan Are to Rule over the Auto Carnival," *New York Evening World*, 4 April 1908.

22. I have no idea why this make was chosen for the Queen's carriage; perhaps the dealer offered it.

23. *Holyoke Transcript*, 7 April 1908.

24. "Half a Million See Auto Parade," *New York Times*, 8 April 1908.

25. *Motor World Wholesale* 79–18 Jan–Jun, 47–48, HathiTrust Digital Library, http://babel.hathitrust.org/cgi/pt?id=mdp.39015080109088;seq=491.

26. Ibid.

27. "Half a Million See Auto Parade."

28. "Elwood Haynes Arrested," *New York Times*, 8 April 1908.

29. "Half a Million See Auto Parade."

30. "Half a Million See Auto Parade."

31. "Autos in Night Parade Along a Glittering Way," *New York Evening World*, 7 April 1908.

32. Ibid.

33. John Bentley, *Great American Automobiles, a Dramatic Account of Their Achievements in Competition* (New York: Prentice-Hall, 1957), 162–63.

34. M. Worth Colwell, "The Glidden Tour," *Motor*, August 1908, 34.

35. Ibid. For some reason Colwell didn't mention Mrs. Shirley in his narrative.

36. "Glidden Tourists Ready to Start," *New York Times*, 9 July 1908.

37. "Automobile Gossip," *San Antonio Light*, 19 July 1808.

38. "Paper Served on Mrs. Cuneo," *The Horseless Age* 22 (July 19, 1908), 70.

39. Ibid. This may or may not have been an attempt to extract money from a wealthy woman.

40. "Leaders Still Tied, Hard Day for Drifters," *New York Daily Tribune*, 12 June 1908.

41. "Mrs. Cuneo as a Gliddenite," *Trenton Evening Times*, 15 July 1908.

42. "Mrs. Cuneo Barely Misses Express," *New York Times*, 17 July 1908.

43. M. Worth Colwell, "The Tour Day by Day," *Motor*, August 1908, 38.

44. Ibid.

45. Ibid., 39.

46. Ibid.

47. Ibid.

48. "Mrs. Cuneo's Motor Record," *Hamilton (OH) Daily Republican News*, 5 December 1908.

49. "Sparkplug and Speedometer," *New York Daily Tribune*, 28 July 1908.

50. "Mrs. Cuneo's Motor Record."

51. Ibid.

52. "Some Auto Gossip for Auto Fiends," *New York Times*, 9 August 1908.

53. Rainier Display Ad, *New York Times*, 20 September 1908.

54. "Some Gossip for the Auto Fiends," *Atlanta Constitution*, 16 August 1908. The lady driver was Alyce Byrd Potter, whom Joan Cuneo had met in Chicago at the Harlem Track.

55. "Business News," *New Orleans Picayune*, 24 April 1908.

56. "Business News," *New Orleans Picayune*, 20 August 1908.

57. See "Women Start Long Auto Run Today," *New York Times*, 11 January 1909; "Mrs. Cuneo Leads Women Autoists," *New York Times*, 12 January 1909; and "Women's New York–Philadelphia Run," *Motor*, February 1909, 89, 90.

58. Ibid.

59. "Mrs. John [*sic*] Cuneo First in New York," *Trenton Evening Times*, 13 January 1909.

Chapter 7

1. http://www.fairgroundsracecourse.com/about-track/history, accessed 7/13/2011.

2. "Track Being Hardened with Preparation Instead of Oil," *New Orleans Picayune*, 10 January 1909.

3. It obviously didn't work, as there was discussion about oiling the track for the February 1909 races in an article about the 1910 races. See "Automobile Races Will Find Track Here Fast," *New Orleans Picayune*, 10 November 1909.

4. "Track Being Hardened" and "Automobile Races." "The Fair Grounds track is now in fine shape for auto racing, because of the great quantity of oil put on it last February."

5. It was more likely the 30 hp Haynes that Alyce Potter drove on her trip to New York and back. "Women to Drive Racing Autos in Coming Fair Ground Meet," *New Orleans Picayune*, 10 January 1909. See also "Auto News," *New York Daily Tribune*, Sunday, July 28, 1908, and "Ladies Touring in Auto," *Salt Lake City Truth*, 8 August 1908.

6. According to Linda Rock, Alice Potter, or Byrdie as she was called, married John Tetzer in 1895. She had been born in Elgin, Illinois, in 1875. Her father was a wealthy Elgin businessman and Potter was a year older than Joan Cuneo. Potter and her husband had no children and divorced amicably in 1908. Byrdie had many interests and was a talented musician and composer as well as the first woman car salesperson in northern Illinois. She sold Haynes automobiles. Linda Rock, phone interview by Elsa Nystrom, 23 July 2011. See also Amber Hart, "Lady Driver Brazenly Proves Need for Speed Went Soft," http://www.examiner.com/history-in-Chicago/lady-driver-brazenly-proves-need-for-speed, accessed 7/19/2011.

7. "Homer George's Summer," *New Orleans Picayune*, 14 April 1909.

8. "Auto Advertisers," *New Orleans Picayune*, 18 January 1909. Unfortunately, no copies of the brochure seem to have survived.

9. Ibid. The advertising campaign was undoubtedly bankrolled by Campbell and George, as they were the only club officers mentioned in the article and they had the most interest in bringing automobile tourists and race fans to New Orleans.

10. At the Harlem Track, the other two female competitors chickened out and Ms. Potter set her record by herself. See also "Chicago Clubman in Mardi Gras Automobile Amateur Race. Arthur Grenier to Bring Big Party Here and Was Means of Securing Woman Entry. Mrs. Cuneo and Miss Potter [sic] to Drive," *New Orleans Picayune*, 3 February 1909.

11. "Speed Instead of Endurance Racing," *New Orleans Picayune*, 4 February 1909.

12. Ibid. Obviously no one was concerned about ground pollution in 1909.

13. "Robertson, Cup Winner in Carnival Auto Meet," *New Orleans Picayune*, 7 February 1909.

14. "Women Auto Racers," *New Orleans Picayune*, 8 February 1909.

15. Ibid.

16. Of course, Joan Cuneo did not do very well in the Bennings race, but the *Picayune* readers didn't know this.

17. Ibid.

18. "Women Cannot Race," *New Orleans Picayune*, 11 February 1909.

19. E-mail from WMSH Library archives received 19 August 2011. Ironically, professional auto racer Wilfrid Bourque and his mechanic Harry Holcombe would be killed when their Knox Giant crashed into a fence during the Prest-O-Lite trophy race at the then new Indianapolis Motor Speedway. *New York Times*, 20 August 1909, 4.

20. "Famous Woman Automobile Driver Arrives for Fair Grounds Races, Little New York Woman, with Fine Record in Motor Racing World, Comes with Seven-year-old Son," *New Orleans Picayune*, 12 February 1909.

21. Ibid.

22. The Grunewald was at that time the best and most expensive hotel in New Orleans; it still exists and has recently been totally renovated as the Roosevelt.

23. "Autoists at New Orleans," *New York Times*, 13 February 1909. The *El Paso* was owned by the Southern Pacific Railroad and sailed between New York and New Orleans on a regular basis.

24. "Auto Carnival Here Will Be a Great Event, Bringing Together Leading Drivers of Three Lands to Compete for World Honors," *New Orleans Picayune*, 14 February 1909.

25. I checked to see if the Auto Carnival took place while Barney was suspended by the AAA and barred from competition, but this was not the case.

26. Frederic J. Hoskin, "The American Chauffeur," *New Orleans Picayune*, 12 February 1909.

27. *New Orleans Picayune*, 16 February 1909. Of these, Chevrolet and Potter were no-shows.

28. "Strang and De Palma, Famous Drivers, Here," *New Orleans Picayune*, 17 February 1909.

29. "Ninety Miles an Hour, Woman at the Wheel," *New Orleans Picayune*, 19 February 1909.

30. Ibid.

31. Ibid.

32. Ibid.

33. "De Palma Smashes 10 Mile Record at Fair Grounds Auto Races," *New Orleans Picayune*, 21 February 1909.

34. Ibid. There is no way of knowing if Joan Cuneo's time was accurate, but she was not afraid to mix it up.

35. According to the *Picayune*, Ryall made a slight misjudgment in a turn in the second mile and sent his Matheson skidding towards the rail and he was thrown out of the car. The hospital staff hurried to the scene, but there was no caution and the race continued. While rumors circulated that Ryall was badly injured, this was not the case. After he was treated in his rooms at the Grunewald, he and his young wife returned to watch the last day of racing on the twenty-second. *New Orleans Picayune*, 22 February 1909.

36. Ibid.

37. In recent years, the Rex Parade has been held on Shrove Tuesday afternoon, before Lent begins on Ash Wednesday; however, the *Picayune* article says that Rex was getting ready to parade on Monday.

38. Ibid.

39. "Auto Carnival's Close: De Palma's Greater Triumphs," *New Orleans Picayune*, 23 February 1909.

40. Ibid.

41. "Auto Heroes Night," *New Orleans Picayune*, 25 February 1909.

42. "Mardi Gras Automobile Races at the Fair Grounds Today," *New Orleans Picayune*, 20 February 1909.

43. "Attitude of Local Agents Regretted," *New Orleans Picayune*, 24 February 1909.

44. Joan Newton Cuneo to Knox Automobile Co., "The Exhaust," Knox Motor Car Club of America, December 2011.

45. "De Palma's Fiat in Auto Carnival," *New Orleans Picayune,* 24 January 1909, and "Attitude of Local Agents Regretted."

46. Ibid.

47. Mrs. Cuneo Lingers," *New Orleans Picayune*, 7 March 1909.

Chapter 8

1. Joan Newton Cuneo, "America's Most Famous Woman Automobilist," *Country Life in America* 25, January 1914.

2. Richard Newton, interview of Alice Newton Childs Smith, Holyoke, Massachusetts, 27 December 2011.

3. "Among the Automobilists," *New York Sun*, 27 April 1909.

4. "Benz Car Wins Fort George Hill Climb," *New York Times*, 27 April 1909.

5. "Among the Automobilists."

6. "Benz Car Wins."

7. Ibid.

8. Ibid.

9. "Among the Automobilists"; "Benz Car Makes Record for Mile," *New York Times*, 28 April 1909.

10. Ibid.

11. "Only Woman Pilot in Racing Event," *Washington Times*, 12 February 1911. Joan Cuneo actually did make these runs, as Lazarnick took a picture of her roaring up the hill at Giant's Despair at Wilkes-Barre.

12. The Manufacturer's Contest Association was made up of members from the four groups associated with the manufacture and sales of automobiles in the United States: the North American Automobile Manufacturers, the Association of Licensed Automobile Manufacturers, the American Motor Car Manufacturers Association and the Importers' Salon. The Importers' Salon was a group of American businessmen who imported and sold European makes like Mercedes, Fiat and Benz. Renault, Fiat and Benz entered their cars in many races at this time. See "May Bar Women from Glidden Tour," *New York Times*, 14 March 1909.

13. Many women got to race at county fairs as, judging by newspaper accounts, they were less rule oriented.

14. "Auto Track Races to Be Restricted," *New York Times*, 31 October 1907. At this time 27 of the 33 member auto clubs who voted on the track-racing issue voted against issuing any track-racing sanctions, three voted for limited sanctioned racing and three for unrestricted track racing.

15. "Auto Makers Side with AAA Board," *New York Times*, 31 May 1908. Also see "AAA Strengthens Auto Racing Control," *New York Times*, 11 February 1909.

16. Ibid.

17. "Auto Makers Side with AAA Board."

18. "Auto Race Control Plan Progressing," *New York Times*, 5 February 1909.

19. "Auto Situation Stirred Up Again," *New York Times*, 13 February 1909.

20. Ibid.

21. *Motor*, July 1909, as referenced in Claude Milot, "Racing & Motor: The Early Years," *Motor*, March 2003, 33. For these reasons, auto manufacturers would continue to support racing for decades.

22. "Launch Auto Race Governing Body," *New York Times*, 22 January 1909.

23. "M.C.A. Drafts Race Classifications," *New York Times*, 10 April 1909.

24. "Auto Race Control Plan Progressing," *New York Times*, 5 February 1909.

25. "Auto Situation Stirred Up Again, Suggestion Made That AAA May Not Agree to Proposed Cooperation of Makers," *New York Times*, 13 February 1909.

26. "Auto Body Accepts Makers' Proposal," *New York Times*, 16 February 1909.

27. "Auto Combination Ratified by the AAA," *New York Times*, 25 February 1909.

28. Ibid.

29. Joan Cuneo did travel to Britain at least once after 1909, and although I have found no records of this visit, it is easy to imagine that she might have visited Brooklands and driven a hot lap or two.

30. "Ignores AAA Men," *New York Times*, 5 March 1909.

31. See https://imca.com/about-imca/. IMCA was founded in 1915 and had a somewhat checkered reputation for a while.

32. "Social Gossip," *Washington Post*, 14 January 1908.

33. Ibid.

34. M. Worth Colwell, "Glidden Tour," *Motor*, 1908.

35. "Woman Makes Hard Auto Run," *New York Times*, 31 January 1909.

36. "May Bar Women from Glidden Tour," *New York Times*, 14 March 1909. The MCA consisted of delegates from the North American Automobile Manufacturer's Association, the American League of Auto Manufacturers, the American Motor Car Manufacturers Association and the Importers' Salon.

37. Ibid.

38. "Prominent Entrants and Two Trophies for Famous Glidden Tour," *New York Times*, 15 October 1911.

39. Ms. Potter was actually married at this time, but she and her husband were amicably separated. She disliked her first name and was known throughout her long life as Byrd Potter.

40. " Women Drivers in Arms Against Men; Scream Aloud Because of Being Barred," *Los Angeles Herald*, 18 April 1909.

41. Information on early Trip Tix sent to me by Michael Britt, expert on late Glidden and Good Roads Tours in Georgia.

42. "Women as Auto Drivers Are Safer than Men," *Atlanta Constitution*, 7 November 1909. The following year, Willys would hire Blanche Scott to drive an Overland cross-country.

43. "Autoists to Entertain Orphans Wednesday," *New York Times*, 6 June 1909.

44. "Mrs. Cuneo Caught Speeding," *New York Times*, 17 July 1909. The *Richmond Hill* (NY) *Record* has a slightly different account. "Mrs. Cuneo Arrested," *Richmond Hill* (NY) *Record*, 24 July 1909.

45. "Mrs. Cuneo's Knox Giantess," *New England Automobile Journal*, September 1909, 67. Perhaps this permission had been granted because of Barney Oldfield's influence, but the document no longer exists today.

46. Ibid.

47. "Sports on Jamaica Track," *New York Times*, 6 July 1909.

48. "Mrs. Cuneo Breaks Auto Record," *New York Times*, 6 October 1909. Immediately following her record the paper recorded that August Belmont's Japanese dogs had been winners in the dog show. "Mrs. Cuneo Makes New Auto Records," *New York Times*, 10 October 1909.

Chapter 9

1. The Good Roads Committee also recruited Ty Cobb, at the height of his fame as a baseball player, to attract his fans, and many did come out to get a glimpse of the great man driving his blue Chalmers-

Detroit. See "Automobile Notes," *Washington Post*, 28 November 1909.

2. *The Weed*, Weed Chain Tire Grip Company, 1909.

3. Ibid., 17.

4. For more information on the Candlers, see http://en.wikipedia.org/wiki/Asa_Griggs_Candler, accessed 10/14/2011, and Kathryn W. Kemp, *God's Capitalist: Asa Candler of Coca-Cola* (Macon, GA: Mercer University Press, 2002.).

5. The Indianapolis Motor Speedway holds the record for the most racing-related fatalities in the United States. A total of 66 people have been killed at the track, including drivers, mechanics, track workers and spectators. See http://indymotorspeedway.com/500fatal.htm.

6. "Great Atlanta Two-Mile Speedway; Origin and History of the Automobile Track — the Two Men Who Made It," *Atlanta Constitution*, 7 November 1909. This article provides a comprehensive account of the building of the speedway.

7. Because of the similarity of their names, the newspapers of the day often credited Candler Sr. with the founding of the track, but Candler Jr. was a racing enthusiast and it was he who pushed the construction of the track.

8. Ibid. In 1909 a successful accountant might earn $2,000 a year and a mechanical engineer $5,000.

9. For more information on the Good Roads Movement, see W. C. Hiles, "The Good Roads Movement in the United States: 1880–1916," master's thesis, Duke University, 1958, and Christopher W. Wells, "The Changing Nature of Country Roads: Farmers, Reformers and the Shifting Uses of Rural Space, 1880–1905," *Agricultural History* 80 (Spring 2006): 143–166.

10. "Three Drivers Coming Here," *Atlanta Constitution*, 10 October 1909.

11. "Crowds Pour Out to Track," *Atlanta Constitution*, 4 October 1909.

12. "In the Automobile World," *Washington Post*, 28 October 1909.

13. "A Race, a Run and a Trophy Won," Rainier Motor Car Company, New York, 1909. This publicity piece published by Rainier provides an excellent account of Joan Cuneo's exploits on the tour.

14. "Mrs. Cuneo Breaks Auto Record," *New York Times*, 6 October 1909, and "Mrs. Cuneo Makes New Auto Records," *New York Times*, 10 October 1909. The first account reported the faster time for the mile.

15. "Good Roads Tourists," *New York Times*, 24 October 1909.

16. Ibid.

17. Fairmount Park maintained its road course from 1908 to 1911, and it was reported that four hundred thousand people attended a race there in 1910. See Allan E. Brown, *America's Speedways Past and Present*, 3rd ed. (Comstock Park, MI: self-published, 2003), 608.

18. "A Race, a Run and a Trophy Won."

19. Ibid.

20. Ibid.

21. Ibid.

22. Ibid.

23. "Mrs. Joan Cuneo Makes Fast Time," *Atlanta Constitution*, 5 November 1909.

24. "Only Woman Pilot in Racing Event," *Washington Times*, 11 February 1911.

25. "A Race, a Run and a Trophy Won."

26. "Mrs. Cuneo Makes Fast Time."

27. "First Speed Trials to Be Made Today," *Atlanta Constitution*, 23 October 1909.

28. "Seven World's Records Broken at the Speedway," *Atlanta Constitution*, 10 November 1909; "Chevrolet Wins Big Event in Atlanta's Auto Races," *Atlanta Journal*, 10 November 1909.

29. Several accounts mention that the trophy was made of gold; if so, it would certainly have been worth $10,000.

30. "Winners in Atlanta Motordrome Automobile Races," *New York Times*, Sunday, 14 November 1909.

31. "Classified Ad 7 — No Title," *Atlanta Constitution*, 8 November 1909.

32. "A Race, a Run and a Trophy Won."

33. "Gossip of the Automobilists and Notes of the Trade," *New York Times*, 16 January 1910.

34. "Favors Eastern Tours," *New York Times*, 20 February 1910.

35. Ibid.

Chapter 10

1. Mrs. A. Sherman Hitchcock, "Women in the Motor World," *New England Automobile Journal*, 26 February 1910, 52.

2. Ibid., 56.

3. Ibid.

4. Ibid., 58.

5. Ibid.

6. Ibid.

7. Robert Sloss, "What a Woman Can Do with an Auto," *Outing Magazine* 56 (April 1910).

8. Ibid., 68.

9. Ibid.

10. Ibid.

11. Richard Duffy, "Out-door Women, Their Sports and What They Have Done for Them," *Good Housekeeping* 1, no. 6, whole no. 380 (June 1910): 684.

12. Ibid.

13. Ibid.

14. Ibid., 684.

15. Ibid., 685.

16. Ibid.

17. Phone interview, Joan Zbacnik, by Elsa Nystrom, 26 September 2012.

18. Duffy, "Out-door Women," 686.

19. Ibid., 686.

20. Ibid. My interpretation of this statement is that Joan Cuneo believed women should not adopt a masculine or outlandish style of dress for driving.

21. "Fred Wagner Gets Cup from Drivers," *New York Times*, 11 January 1911.

22. *New York Times*, 1 May 1911.
23. "Disbrow Breaks Hill-Climb Record," *New York Times*, 19 June 1911.
24. "Port Jefferson Climb," *New York Times*, 24 June 1911.
25. "Sporting News in Brief," *New York Times*, 18 June 1910.
26. Claudette Hollenbeck, *Lake Raponda, Wilmington, Vermont: A Brief History, 1751–1961* (NP, ND).
27. "Automobile Trade Gossip," *New York Times*, 23 October 1910.
28. "Speed Carnival on Pablo Beach," *Atlanta Constitution*, 29 March 1911.
29. Allan E. Brown, *The History of America's Speedways Past and Present* (Comstock Park, MI: self-published, 203), 206. According to Allan Brown, the Pablo Beach 5.0 mile beach oval at Jacksonville Beach was in operation from March 28 to November 31, 1911.
30. "Automobile Trade Gossip" and Palm Beach Historical Society, visited May 2011.
31. "Mrs. Cuneo Pilots Auto at Fast Clip," *Atlanta Constitution*, 18 April 1911.
32. *Washington Times*, 18 April 1911, and *Suffolk County* (New York) *News*, 18 April 1911.
33. "Mrs. Joan Cuneo Is Arrested for Fast Driving," *New York Evening Telegram*, 5 May 1911.
34. Ibid.
35. "Pleaded by Telephone," *New York Evening Telegram*, 7 May 1911.
36. See "Banker's Wife Agrees to Eat One Squab a Day on Bet," *Lowell Sun*, 24 January 1911; "Bets Wife Can Eat Squab a Day for Thirty Days," *New Brunswick* (NJ) *Times*, 25 January 1911; and "Will East Squab Thirty Days," *Oakland* (CA) *Tribune*, 9 February 1911.
37. "De Palma Wins Race; Auto Driver Defeats Chevrolet and Disbrow at Spaghetti Eating," *New York Times*, 12 April 1911.
38. "Mrs. Cuneo's Night Ride," *Brattleboro* (VT) *Phoenix*, 15 September 1911. Several accounts of Newton's accident were published in New England papers, but the most accurate came from the *Phoenix*, a relatively local paper.
39. Around this time, Antonio decided to use his middle name, Newton, instead of Antonio. For the rest of his life, he would be known as A. Newton Cuneo.
40. "Mrs. Cuneo's Night Ride." Mike Eldred, the editor of the *Deerfield Valley News*, said that he had driven over that road several times and it is still a dangerous drive today.
41. "Raced with Death," *Lowell* (MA) *Sun*, 8 September 1911. Another source also contains an account of her participation in the squab-eating contest. "Women Who Love the Bright Face of Danger," *Richmond Times-Dispatch*, 16 June 1912.
42. I have not been able to determine the make of this car and Mrs. Cuneo never mentioned it in anywhere else. She may have been asked to try it out for an advertisement by the dealer, since she never claimed to own an electric car.

43. Evidently Mrs. Cuneo employed a new chauffeur, as Disbrow was now traveling the racing circuit.
44. "Mrs. Cuneo, Noted Automobilist, Hits Boy with New Car," *New York World*, 10 May 1912; "Mrs. Cuneo Runs Down Boy," *New York Tribune*, 11 May 1912; and "Mrs. Joan Cuneo," *Mansfield* (OH) *News*, 13 May 1012.
45. "Grieves over Accident," *Washington Herald*, 13 May 1912.
46. "For Women Motorists," 22 February 1912.
47. "Auto News of the Day," *New York Tribune*, 22 February 1912.
48. "Mrs. Cuneo on Highway Improvement," *New York Times*, 11 March 1912.
49. "Thousand Women at Victory Feast with Mrs. Wilson," *Washington Times*, 21 December 1910.
50. "File: Louis Disbrow in Jay-Eye-See, 1912," wikipedia.org.?wiki/File: Louis_Disbrow_in_Jay-Eye-See_1912.jpeg#filehistory, accessed 8/5/2012.
51. "Mrs. Cuneo Drives Fast Mile," *New York Times*, 11 January 1913.
52. "Test of Quick Stops," *New York Times*, 16 January 1913.

Chapter 11

1. "Cuneo Stops Run on His Bank," *New York Sun*, 20 February 1914.
2. Joan Newton Cuneo, "America's Most Famous Woman Motorist," *Country Life in America* 25 (January 1914): 49. I have included a list I put together of the cars she owned in the appendix.
3. Ibid.
4. "Business Troubles," *New York Times*, 26 August 1914.
5. "Bankruptcy Notices (2)," *New York Times*, 17 November 1914.
6. "Business Troubles," *New York Times*, 19 December 1914.
7. "War Aids Bankrupt Banker," *New York Times*, 19 December 1914.
8. "Society News," *Toronto Star*, 19 June 1914.
9. "Ex-Model Sues for $53,000," *New York Times*, 26 January 1915.
10. "Paid $3000 for 1,000 Love Notes He Wrote, Girl Says," *New York Evening Telegram*, 26 January 1915; "Paid for 1,000 Letters," *Washington Post*, 27 January 1915.
11. "Mrs. Cuneo's Night Ride," *Vermont Phoenix*, 15 September 1911.
12. Passport Application of Andrew Cuneo, New York, 1915, http://search.ancestrylibrary.com/iexec/Default.aspx?htx=5542&dbid=1174&iid, accessed 6/22/2010.
13. "Miss de Von Put on Trial," *New York Times*, 21 August 1915.
14. Ibid.
15. Ibid.
16. Ibid.
17. Ibid.

18. "Swears Actress Knew Banker Had Wife," *New York Evening World*, 23 August 1915.
19. Ibid.
20. "Trickish Lawyers Denounced in Court," *New York Times*, 24 August 1915.
21. Ibid.
22. Ibid.
23. Ibid.
24. Ibid.
25. Ibid.
26. Sprint Car Hall of Fame, sprintcarhof.com/Filebrelaspit?ID=242, accessed 8/5/2012.
27. National Sprint Car Hall of Fame and Museum, sprintcarhof.com/FileGetaspct?ID=242; also see IMCA.com, accessed 8/4/2012.
28. Mais, slightly younger than Joan Cuneo, was supposed to have defeated her in a 1915 race, but there is no evidence that the two women ever met.
29. "Famous Woman Auto Racer to Appear at Michigan State Fair," *Marshall* (IA) *News Statesman*, 25 August 1915.
30. "Contest Briefs," *The Horseless Age*, 15 August 1915.
31. "A Fast Woman," *Fort Wayne* (IN) *Daily News*, 15 September 1915.
32. Cuneo, "America's Most Famous Woman Motorist," 48–49.

Chapter 12

1. See Chapter 6, "Woman Auto Driver Scores Two Victories," *New York Times*, 26 August 1905, and "Atlantic City," *Honolulu Evening Bulletin*, 25 September 1905. Mrs. Fitler was described as a society woman who challenged the "reckless Mrs. Joan Newton Cuneo who burned up the roads during the White Mountains Tour." Fitler had already defeated male contestants in three events and won three silver trophies.
2. An average of 22 mph may seem slow today, but given the state of the roads in 1909, it was an amazing time.
3. "Gossip of the Automobilists," *New York Times*, 17 October 1909; "Mrs. Otis Heads East Again," *New York Times*, 14 February 1909; "Leading Women Automobilists," *New York Times*, 31 October 1909.
4. "Miss Schwalbach Wants a Chance to Drive Auto as a Public Chauffeur," *Brooklyn Daily Eagle*, 1 July 1917.
5. Ibid.
6. "Women to Drive at Race Meetings," *New York Times*, 20 October 1912.
7. Ibid.
8. Ibid.
9. Ibid. When I read this article, my first thought was who in the world was Blanche Scott, as she never raced an automobile to my knowledge. However, she said in an interview that she had driven Barney Oldfield's Green Dragon at the Indianapolis Motor Speedway in 1910.

10. Ibid.
11. Ibid.
12. Ibid.
13. "Mme. Du Gast Fine Chauffeur," *New York Times*, 30 March 1903.
14. Recent scholars have found that Dorothy Levitt was the daughter of a respectable Jewish family who lived in the London area, not a debutante who enjoyed horseback riding and other country sports. Ann Kramer, e-mail to Elsa Nystrom, 27 August 2012; www.annkramer.co.uk. Ms. Kramer is a British scholar who has written about Dorothy Levitt.
15. Jean-François Bouzanquet, *Fast Ladies: Female Racing Drivers 1888–1970* (Dorchester, UK: Veloce, 2009).
16. Dorothy Levitt, *The Woman and the Car: A Chatty Little Handbook for All Women Who Motor or Want to Motor*, foreword by Cecil Bying-Hall (London: Jon Lane, New York: Bodley Head, 1909).
17. Ibid.
18. Ibid., 5. Much later details of her true background emerged. Levitt was actually born Dorothy Levi. Her father, a tea agent, changed his name to Levitt. As a working girl, she would have had neither the time nor the money to ride to hounds. See Tredelyn.blogspot.com/2007/10/dorothy.levitt.html and http://en.wikipedia.org/wiki/Dorothy_Levitt.
19. Some racing historians, including Bouzanquet, believe that Edge set Levitt up as his mistress, paying for her apartment and stylish clothes and creating an upper-class background for her.
20. Ibid., 32.
21. One source has Levitt attempting to qualify as a pilot.
22. "Women Autoists Skillful Drivers," *New York Times*, 29 September 1907. This article mentions Rogers and Fitler and other noted women drivers of the time.
23. "Women Auto Drivers in Endurance Run," *New York Times*, 31 October 1909.
24. "Byrd Potter, Woman Driver," http://gailborden:infor/freedom/ElginA Women's History.pdf. 49. See also "Obituary for Alice Birdie Potter Tetzer," *Elgin Courier News*, 23 August 1955. See also Chapter 7.
25. "Obituary." She died at the age of 80, after a lifelong involvement with music and charitable works.
26. She definitely had a license but did not compete in many "real" races.
27. "Famous Woman Auto Racer to Drive in Wichita Races," *Wichita* (KS) *Beacon*, 1 July 1916. Bob Lawrence, a sprint-car authority, has copies of the IMCA drivers' lists for 1915 and 1916. Although MAIS was listed as a driver both years, he is sure that she would not have been allowed to drive in anything other than an exhibition at that time. Bob Lawrence to Elsa Nystrom, 21 August 2012.
28. For more background on the early years of IMCA, see Buzz Rose, *Show-Biz Auto Racing*.
29. "Auto Races," *Des Moines* (IA) *News*, 31 August 1916.

30. Norris McDonald, "Speeding Through Toronto, a Tradition," Wheels Canada, http://www.wheels.ca/article%20Category/article/754047, accessed 4/7/2010.

31. "Stunt Woman at Owatonna Races Killed," *Albert Lea Minnesota Evening Tribune*, 27 September 1934.

32. Joan Cuneo drove Kelsey's Maxwell's at Atlantic City, where she defeated Mrs. H. Ernest Rogers in another Maxwell runabout. See "Atlantic City Race Meet," *Cycle and Automobile Trade Journal*, June 1906, 89.

33. Anthony J. Yanik, *Maxwell Motors and the Making of the Chrysler Corporation* (Detroit: Wayne State Press, 2009), 38–39, 40–46.

34. Ibid., 59–60.

35. Ibid., 61.

36. Ibid., 62.

37. "Following Alice Ramsey 100 Years Later," ice-ramsey.wordpress.com/about/, accessed 11/19/2011; "A Century of Women at the Wheel," *Los Angeles Times*, 7 June 2009; Cheryl Jensen, "Blazing a Coast to Coast Trail, She Helped Put a Nation on the Road," *New York Times*, 6 June 1999.

38. See Emily Price Post, *By Motor to the Golden Gate* (New York: Appleton, 1916).

39. Ibid.

40. For at least the first half of the twentieth century, the West began in the Old Northwest Territory.

41. "Blanche Stuart Scott, 84, Dies, Made First Solo Flight in 1910," *New York Times*, 13 January 1970. There are several dates given for her birth; the *Times* said she was 84 when she died, but the census states she was born in 1885.

42. "Woman to Drive Auto to Frisco," *New York Times*, 15 May 1910.

43. Todd McCarthy, *Fast Women: The Legendary Ladies of Racing* (New York: Hyperion, 2007), 64.

44. Ibid.

45. Ibid. This may or may not be true. I haven't found the original source for this quotation, and I can't imagine Barney letting an untried female drive his Green Dragon at Indy, although Oldfield raced there in 1910.

46. Ibid., 64.

47. Ibid.

48. http://www.earlyaviators.com/eblanche.htm.

49. Ibid.

50. "Beachy Flies as a Woman," *New York Times*, 28 January 1912.

51. Scott Obituary, *New York Times*.

52. "Blanche Stuart Scott."

53. "Miss Webber Will Race on Speedway," *Atlanta Constitution*, 30 September 1910.

54. "Webber Auto Race Meet Was a Decided Success," *Atlanta Constitution*, 2 October 1910.

55. "Fifty Most Notorious Crimes in Orange County History" and "A Hollywood Star goes to jail," http://50cases.freedom blogging.com/2009/11/04/day-three-ocs-most-notorious-cases/43/, accessed 8/24/2010.

56. The accuracy of any of the records set during this era is open to doubt.

57. Patricia L. Yongue, "Nina Vitagliano and the Speederettes," *Veloce Today*, 14 December 2005, http://velocetoday.com/people/people_39.php, accessed 3/27/2012. Also see Sonja Harris, "Roaring into the Twenties: The Story of the Speederettes, Female Automobile Racers of the 1910s and 1920s," written for Dr. Caroline Cox, Pacific College, Fall 2003.

58. Yongue, "Nina Vitagliano."

59. "Nina Vitagliano Is Killed in Auto Races on Local Track," *Stockton* (CA) *Record*, 4 March 1918.

60. Ibid. The *Record* provided a gruesome account of her injuries. Evidently her head had been driven into her chest by the impact, her neck broken in several places, many of her ribs broken, and she had been scalped from the eyebrows back!

61. Ibid.

62. "Fair Speed Demons in Auto Race," *Chicago Daily Tribune*, 30 September 1923, Sports Section.

63. Ironically, women have been much more successful in drag racing, much different from track or road racing though equally dangerous.

64. "The Masked Marvel Dorothy Walker's Success on Track Could Not Be Disguised," *Los Angeles Daily News*, 5 August 2000. See also "Woman Killed," *Joplin* (MO) *Globe*, 1 June 1926, and *Oakland California Tribune*, 1 June 1926. Walker's accident made the front page of many newspapers but had no ripple effect.

Epilogue

1. When she was little, Maddalena was called Dolly, and she retained that nickname in her later life.

2. Obituary clipped from unknown newspaper dated 1908.

3. "Town Clerk's Office," e-mail from Mike Eldred to Elsa Nystrom, 20 August 2012.

4. "A. Newton Cuneo Dies March 9," *Ontonagon Herald*, 11 March 1976.

5. Joan Cuneo Zbacnik, phone interview by Elsa Nystrom, 26 September 2012.

6. Ibid.

7. "Wilmington," *North Adams* (MA) *Evening Transcript*, 20 January 1919.

8. http://hunts-upguide.com/ontonagon.html, accessed 8/24/2012. Today Ontonagon, never large, is in decline with a lack of industry. Its remote location in the Porcupine Mountains of Michigan's Upper Peninsula limits tourism to the more determined travelers.

9. "Check Our Deerfield Valley News," e-mail from Joan Zbacnik to Elsa Nystrom, 5 April 2011.

10. "Funeral Services Held for Mrs. James F. Sickman," *Ontonagon Herald*, 31 March 1934.

11. Ibid.

12. Zbacnik interview.

13. Ibid.

14. 1930 Census: Census Place: Franklin, Somerset, New Jersey; Roll: 1983; Page: 8A; Enumeration Dis-

trict: 18; Image 761.0, Federal Census (database online), Provo, Utah, Ancestry.com, accessed 9/28/2010.

15. Zbacnik interview.

16. Joan Zbacnik e-mail, 17 September 2012.

17. "Louis Disbrow, 62, Ex-Auto Racer," *New York Times*, 11 July 1939.

18. Ibid.

19. Ibid.

20. "Mrs. Joan Sickman, Motor Racer, Dies," *Brooklyn Daily Eagle*, 27 March 1934.

Bibliography

Newspapers

Atlanta Constitution
Atlanta Journal
Chicago Tribune
Detroit Free Press
Indianapolis News
Indianapolis Star
New Orleans Picayune
New York Times
Washington Post

Magazines

Autocar
The Automobile
Automobile Age
Country Life in America
Horseless Age, The
Motor
Motor Trend
Outing Magazine
Scientific American

Unpublished Papers

Harris, Sonja. "Roaring into the Twenties: The Story of the Speederettes, Female Automobile Racers of the 1910s and 1920s." Written for Dr. Caroline Cox, Pacific College, Fall 2003.

Smith, Elizabeth M. "Racing for Fans: Communications Technology, the Total Experience and the Rise of NASCAR." Master's Thesis, James Madison University, 1995.

Books

Banner, Lois W. *Women in Modern America: A Brief History*, 2nd ed. New York: Harcourt Brace Jovanovich, 1984.

Benson, Michael. *Women in Racing*. Philadelphia: Chelsea House, 1997.

Bentley, John. *Great American Automobiles, a Dramatic Account of Their Achievements in Competition.* New York: Prentice-Hall, 1957.

Berger, Michael L. *The Devil Wagon in God's Country: The Automobile and Social Change in Rural America, 1893–1929.* Hamden, CT: Archon, 1979.

Binford, Tom. *A Checkered Past: My 20 Years as Indy 500 Chief Steward.* Carmel, IN: Cornerstone Press, 1993.

Bird, Anthony. *The Motor Car, 1765—1914.* London: B. T. Batsford, 1960.

Bloemker, Al. *500 Miles to Go: The History of the Indianapolis Speedway.* New York: Coward McCann, 1961.

Blue Ribbon of the Air: The Gordon Bennett Races. Washington, DC: Smithsonian Institution Press, 1987.

Boddy, W. *The Story of Brooklands, the World's First Motor Course*, in three volumes. London: Grenville, 1948, 1949, 1950.

Borgeson, Griffith. *The Golden Age of the American Racing Car.* New York: W. W. Norton, 1966.

Bouzanquet, Jean-François. *Fast Ladies: Female Racing Drivers 1888–1970.* Dorchester, GB: Veloce, 2009.

Brown, Allan E. *The History of America's Speedways; Past and Present*, 3rd ed. Comstock Park, Michigan: self-published, 2003.

Bruce, Scott D. *INDY: Racing Before the 500.* Batesville: Indiana Reflections, 2006.

Bullock, John. *Fast Women: The Drivers Who Changed the Face of Motor Racing.* London: Robson, 2002.

Burlingame, Roger. *Machines That Built America.* New York: Harcourt Brace, 1953.

Burns, John M. *Thunder at Sunrise: A History of the Vanderbilt Cup, the Grand Prize and the Indianapolis 500, 1904–1916.* Jefferson, NC: McFarland, 2006.

Clarsen, Georgine. *Eat My Dust: Early Women Motorists.* Baltimore: Johns Hopkins, 2008.

Cuneo, Joan Newton. *A Woman's Experience in the Glidden Tour 1907.* New York: Rainier Motor Car, 1907.

Davis, Sidney Charles Houghton. *Casques' Sketch Book: Motor Car Racing in a Lighter Vein.* Iliffe and Sons, 1932.

Davis, S. C. H. *Atlanta: Women as Racing Drivers.* London: G. T. Foulis, 1955.

De Paolo, Peter. *Wall Smacker: The Saga of the Speedway.* Pittsburgh, PA: De Paolo Press, 4th printing, 1936.

Dick, Robert. *Mercedes and Auto Racing in the Belle Époque, 1895–1915.* Jefferson, NC: McFarland, 2005.

Dulher. *La Grande et Meurtriere Course, Paris–Madrid, 1903.* Paris: Clermont-Ferrand, 1963.

Edge, S. F. *My Motoring Reminiscences.* London: n.p., n.d.

Firestone, Harvey S., and Samuel Crowther. *Men and Rubber.* Garden City, NY: Doubleday, Page, 1926.

Fisher, Jane Watts. *Fabulous Hoosier: A Story of American Achievement.* New York: R. M. McBride, 1947.

Fisher, Jerry M. *The Pacesetter: The Untold Story of Carl Graham Fisher.* Fort Bragg, CA: Lost Coast Press, 1998.

Flink, James J. *The Car Culture.* Cambridge, MA: MIT Press, 1973.

Foster, Mark S. *Castles in the Sand: The Life and Times of Carl Graham Fisher.* Gainesville: University of Florida Press, 2000.

Frostick, Michael. *Pit and Paddock, a Background to Motor Racing, 1894–1978.* Osbourne, Derbyshire: Moorland, 1980.

Golomb-Dettelbach, Cynthia. *In the Driver's Seat: The Automobile in American Culture.* Westport, CT: Greenwood Press, 1976.

Grinnell, John A. *Race Car Flashback, a Celebration of America's Affair with Auto Racing from 1900–1980s.* Iola, WI: Krause, 1994.

Heitmann, John. *The Automobile and American Life.* Jefferson, NC: McFarland, 2009.

Hess, John Y. *The Knox Automobile Company, Images of America.* Charleston, SC: Arcadia, 2000.

Homberger, Eric. *Mrs. Astor's New York: Money and Social Power in the Gilded Age.* New Haven, CT: Yale University Press, 2002.

Hough, Richard, Alexander Frostick and Michael Frostick. *A History of the World's Racing Cars.* New York: Harper and Row, 1965.

Howard, Fred. *Wilbur and Orville, a Biography of the Wright Brothers.* New York: Alfred A. Knopf, 1987.

Jarrott, Charles. *Ten Years of Motors and Motor Racing.* London: Grant Richards, 1912.

Jewell, Derek. *Man & Motor, the 20th Century Love Affair.* New York: Walker, 1967.

Karslake, Kent. *A History of the French Grand Prix.* London: Abingdon, 1949.

_____. *Racing Voiturettes.* London: Abingdon, 1950.

Kimes, Beverly Rae. *The Star and the Laurel, the Centennial History of Daimler, Mercedes and Benz, 1886–1986.* Montvale, NJ: Mercedes-Benz of North America, 1986.

Kroplick, Howard, and Al Velocci. *The Long Island Motor Parkway (NY).* Images of America. Charleston, SC: Arcadia, 2008.

Leerhsen, Charles. *Blood and Smoke: A True Tale of Mystery, Mayhem, and the Birth of the Indy 500.* New York: Simon & Schuster, 2011.

Levitt, Dorothy. *The Woman and the Car: A Chatty Little Handbook for All Women Who Motor or Want to Motor.* Foreword by Cecil Byng-Hall. London: John Lane, New York: Bodley Head, 1909.

Lewis, David Lanier, and Laurence Goldstein, eds. *The Automobile and American Culture.* Ann Arbor: University of Michigan Press, 1980, 1983.

Lewis, Tom. *Divided Highways: Building the Interstate Highways; Transforming American Life.* New York: Viking Penguin, 1999.

Loeper, John J. *Galloping Gertie, by Motorcar in 1908.* New York: Athenaeum, 1980.

Lurani Cemuschi, Giovanni. *A History of Motor Racing.* Verona, Italy: Arnoldo Mondadori Editore, 1972.

_____. *History of the Racing Car: Man and Machine.* New York: Thomas Y. Crowell, 1972.

Maxim, Hiram Percy. *Horseless Carriage Days.* New York: Harper and Brothers, 1936, 1937.

McCarthy, Todd. *Fast Women: The Legendary Ladies of Racing.* New York: Hyperion, 2007.

McConnell, Curt. *A Reliable Car and a Woman Who Knows It: The First Coast-to-Coast Automobile Trips by Women, 1899–1916.* Jefferson, NC: McFarland, 2000.

Monkswell, Mary Josephine Hardcaste Collier, baroness. *A Victorian Diaress: Extracts from the Journals of Mary Lady Monkswell,* 1st ed., 1895–1909. London: John Murray, 1946.

Mull, Evelyn. *Women in Sports Car Competition.* New York: Sports Car Press, 1958.

Nauen, Elinor, ed. *Ladies, Start Your Engines; Women Writers on Cars and the Road.* Boston and London: Faber and Faber, 1996.

Nevins, Allan. *Ford, the Times, the Man, the Company.* New York: Scribner's, 1954.

Nicholson, T. R. *Racing Cars and Record Breakers, 1898–1921.* New York: Macmillan, 1971.

North, Louise Ann. *Bonneville Salt Flats.* Osceola WI: MBI, 1999.

Osmer, Harold. *Auto Racing Venues in Southern*

California 1900–2000. Chatsworth, CA: Harold L. Osmer, 2002.

Pactolus, William. *The Great American Toy, Automobiles in American Culture.* New York: Herder & Herder, 1970.

Post, Emily Price. *By Motor to the Golden Gate.* New York: Appleton, 1916. Reprinted, ed. by Jane Lancaster. Jefferson, NC: McFarland, 2004.

Post, Mary D. *A Woman's Summer in a Motorcar.* New York: n.p., 1908.

Postman, Neil. *Technoply: The Surrender of Culture to Technology.* New York: Vintage Books, Random House, 1993.

Preston, Howard Lawrence. *Accessibility and Modernization in the South, 1885–1935.* Knoxville: University of Tennessee Press, 1991.

Punnett, Dick. *Racing on the Rim: A History of the Annual Automobile Racing Tournaments Held on the Sands of the Ormond-Daytona Beach, Florida, 1903–1910.* Ormond Beach: Tomoka Press, 1997.

Punnett, Dick, and Yvonne Punnett. *Thrills, Chills and Spills, a Photographic History of Early Aviation on the World's Most Bizarre Airport— the Beach at Daytona Beach, Florida 1906–1929.* New Smyrna Beach, FL: Luthers, 1990.

Racing Cars, Seventy Years of Record Breaking. New York: Golden Press, Western, 1972.

Radbusch, Don. *Dirt Track Auto Racing, 1919–1941, a Pictorial History.* Jefferson, NC: McFarland, 2004.

Rae, John. *The American Automobile Industry.* New York: Twayne, 1984.

Ramsey, Alice Huyler. *Alice's Drive: Republishing Veil Duster and Tire Iron.* Tucson: Patrice Press, 2004.

_____. *Veil Duster and Tire Iron.* Pasadena, CA: Castle Press, 1961.

Redford, Polly. *Billion Dollar Sandbar: A Biography of Miami Beach.* New York: E. P. Dutton, 1970.

Richardson, Angelique, ed. *The New Woman in Fiction and Fact: Fin de Siècle Feminism.* New York: Palgrave, 2001

Roberts, Randy, and James Olson. *Winning Is the Only Thing; Sports in America Since 1945.* Baltimore: Johns Hopkins University Press, 1989.

Rose, Buzz. *Show-Biz Auto Racing.*

Rose, Gerald. *A Record of Motor Racing.* London: n.p., 1909. Abingdon, 1949.

Rothman, Sheila M. *Woman's Proper Place: A History of Changing Ideals and Practices, 1870 to the Present.* New York: Basic Books, 1978.

Scharff, Virginia Joy. *Taking the Wheel: Women and the Coming of the Motor Age.* New York: Free Press, 1991.

Sheldon, Bob. *Speedway Photos; Early Auto Racing in Chicago and the Midwest.* Marshall, IN: Witness Productions, 2000.

Sinsabaugh, Christopher George. *Who, Me? Forty Years of Automobile History.* Detroit: Arnold Powers, 1940.

Smith, Philip Hillyer. *Wheels Within Wheels: A Short History of American Motor Car Manufacturing,* 2nd ed., revised. New York: Funk and Wagnall's, 1969, 1970.

Varderman, Don. *The Great Air Races.* Garden City, NY: Doubleday, 1969.

Vieyra, Daniel I. *Fill 'Er Up: An Architectural History of America's Gas Stations.* New York and London: Collier, 1979.

Ward, Hilda. *The Girl and the Motor.* Cincinnati: Gas Publishing, 1908.

White, Gordon Eliot. *Ab and Marvin Jenkins, the Studebaker Connection and the Mormon Meteors.* Hudson, WI: Iconograpfix, 2006.

_____. *Lost Race Tracks: Treasures of Automobile Racing.* Hudson, WI: Iconograpfix, 2002.

Williamson, Harold F. *American Petroleum Industry, 1899–1959, the Age of Energy.* Evanston, IL: Northwestern University Press, 1963.

Yanik, Anthony J. *Maxwell Motors and the Making of the Chrysler Corporation.* Detroit: Wayne State Press, 2009.

Yates, Brock W. *Racers and Drivers: The Fastest Men and Cars from Barney Oldfield to Craig Breedlove.* Indianapolis and New York: Bobbs-Merrill, 1968.

Articles

"The Automobile in Newport." *Town and Country* 27 (September 1902).

Avery, Mrs. F. P. "Touring in Horseless Carriages, a Few Suggestions." *Automobile,* January 1901.

Buist, H. Massac. "A Gossip About the Grand Prix Race." *Autocar,* July 11, 1914.

Cuneo, Joan Newton. "America's Most Famous Woman Motorist." *Country Life in America* 25, January 1914.

Cuneo, Mrs. Andrew. "Why Are There So Few Women Automobilists?" *Country Life Magazine,* March 1908.

Duffy, Richard. "Out-door Women: Their Sports and What They Have Done for Them." *Good Housekeeping* 1, no. 6, whole no. 380 (June 1910).

Hitchcock, Mrs. A. Sherman. "A Woman's Viewpoint of Motoring." *Motor,* April 1904.

_____. " For Women Who Hold the Wheel." *Automobile,* May 26, 1910.

_____. "Women in the Motoring World." *New England Automobile Journal,* June 1910.

Innes, Sherrie A. "On the Road and in the Air: Gender and Technology in Girls' Automobile and Airplane Serials, 1909–1932." *Journal of Popular Culture* 30(2) (1996).

Lehman, Milton. "The First Woman Driver." *Life*, September 8, 1952.

Maxim, Hiram Percy. "Learning to Drive a Motor Carriage." *The Horseless Age*, April 1898.

Milot, Claude. "Racing & Motor: The Early Years." *Motor*, March 2003.

"Now the Motor Woman." *The Horseless Age*, June 1897.

Romalov, Nancy Tillman. "Mobile Heroines: Early Twentieth-Century Girls' Automobile Series." 28(4) (1995).

Sloss, Robert. "What a Woman Can Do with an Auto." *Outing Magazine* 56 (April 1910).

Ward, Hilda. "The Automobile in the Suburbs from a Woman's Point of View. *Suburban Life*, November 1907.

Index

217